ANCIENT JUDAISM
Debates and Disputes

Fourth Series

SOUTH FLORIDA STUDIES IN THE HISTORY OF JUDAISM

Edited by
Jacob Neusner
William Scott Green, James Strange
Darrell J. Fasching, Sara Mandell

Number 132
Ancient Judaism
Debates and Disputes

Fourth Series

by
Jacob Neusner

ANCIENT JUDAISM
Debates and Disputes

Fourth Series

Historical, Theological, Scholarly, and Contemporary
Religious Arguments

by

Jacob Neusner

Scholars Press
Atlanta, Georgia

ANCIENT JUDAISM
Debates and Disputes

Fourth Series

Publication of this book was made possible by a grant from the Tisch Family Foundation, New York City. The University of South Florida acknowledges with thanks this important support for its scholarly projects.

Library of Congress Cataloging in Publication Data
Neusner, Jacob, 1932–
    Ancient Judaism : debates and disputes : fourth series / by Jacob Neusner.
        p.   cm. — (South Florida studies in the history of Judaism ; no. 132)
    "Historical, theological, scholarly and contemporary religious arguments."
    Includes bibliographical references.
    ISBN 0-7885-0215-8 (cloth : alk. paper)
    1. Judaism—History—Talmudic period, 10–425. 2. Ecomonics—Religious aspects—Judaism. 3. Judaism—Doctrines. 4. Judaism—History—Book reviews. 5. Judaism—20th century. I. Title. II. Series.
BM177.N464   1996
296'.09—dc20   95-51825
                                                        CIP

Printed in the United States of America
on acid-free paper

TABLE OF CONTENTS

PREFACE

Through debate learning makes its way, and through dispute scholarship renews itself. When issues are clearly drawn and systematically set forth, then the stakes emerge, and the choices — and the bases for making them — come to the fore. Debates and disputes mark the vitality of a field of study — all the more so of a field at which religious beliefs, convictions concerning transcendent questions of eternal meaning come under learned inquiry. This collection of papers, fourth in its series,[1] offers strongly-held propositions concerning questions of importance for the study and practice of Judaism — the study of Judaism in its formative age, the practice of Judaism today.

One paper takes up the history of Judaism, with special reference to the Judaic doctrine of economics set forth in the classical documents, from the Mishnah through the Bavli.[2] Since the Judaism of the dual Torah sets forth a coherent account of the social order of holy Israel, the economic component of that account requires attention in its own terms. These direct attention to two matters, first, why that Judaism to begin with invoked economics as a medium for the statement of its religious system, and, second, how that statement itself underwent remarkable revision, as economics came to be transformed into something quite other than the conventional subject concerning the rational disposition of scarce resources.

The next four papers address theological questions, two in a descriptive, two in a constructive framework; the former fall into the category of historical scholarship on religion, specifically, the description of the theology of a religious system, the latter into a statement of prescriptive and normative matters. The first question, one that has engaged my attention for nearly a decade, concerns the correct medium for the description of the theology of Rabbinic Judaism. I have struggled with that question in a variety of books and have not come to a final

---

[1] *Ancient Judaism. Debates and Disputes.* Chico, 1984: Scholars Press for Brown Judaic Studies; *Ancient Judaism. Debates and Disputes. Second Series.* Atlanta, 1990: Scholars Press for South Florida Studies in the History of Judaism; *Ancient Judaism. Debates and Disputes. Third Series. Essays on the Formation of Judaism, Dating Sayings, Method in the History of Judaism, the Historical Jesus, Publishing Too Much, and Other Current Issues.* Atlanta, 1993: Scholars Press for South Florida Studies in the History of Judaism.
[2] Here I treat in a single statement the principal results of two books: *The Economics of the Mishnah.* Chicago, 1989: The University of Chicago Press, and *The Transformation of Judaism. From Philosophy to Religion.* Champaign, 1992: University of Illinois Press.

solution for the problem of theological description.[3] What concerns me is to define a method that contains its own correctives, that will tell me not only when I am right but also when I am wrong, and that will nurture the formulation of null hypotheses subject to testing within the pertinent data of theological knowledge. The second paper in this volume portrays matters as best I can, and the third turns from theological knowledge to theological examination of religious experience: the encounter with God in the Torah that Rabbinic Judaism uniquely affords and identifies as its métier. The fourth paper addresses a problem that, on the surface, remains narrowly historical — what do the authoritative writings say about a given subject — but that is, in fact, profoundly contemporary and acutely theological in a constructive framework. For formulating a feminist theology of Judaism within the framework of the Judaism of the dual Torah, a concern of mine from the 1970s, continues to challenge those of us who wish to think philosophically about religion and thereby compose theology.[4] The fifth paper sets forth a different kind of theology, that is, apologetics; here I address the theological challenge to Judaism

---

[3] The main work is these two books: *Judaism States its Theology: The Talmudic Re-Presentation.* Atlanta, 1993: Scholars Press for South Florida Studies in the History of Judaism and *Judaism's Theological Voice: The Melody of the Talmud.* Chicago, 1995: The University of Chicago Press. But, in addition, I have pursued the matter in the following, among other books: *The Initial Phases of the Talmud's Judaism.* Atlanta, 1995: Scholars Press for South Florida Studies in the History of Judaism. IV. *Theology; From Description to Conviction. Essays on the History and Theology of Judaism.* Atlanta, 1987: Scholars Press for Brown Judaic Studies; *From Literature to Theology in Formative Judaism. Three Preliminary Studies.* Atlanta, 1989: Scholars Press for Brown Judaic Studies; *Symbol and Theology in Early Judaism.* Minneapolis, 1991: Fortress Press; *The Foundations of the Theology of Judaism. An Anthology.* I. *God.* Northvale, 1990: Jason Aronson, Inc. A main selection of the Jewish Book Club. *The Foundations of the Theology of Judaism. An Anthology.* II. *Torah* Atlanta, 1992: Scholars Press for South Florida Studies in the History of Judaism; *The Foundations of the Theology of Judaism. An Anthology.* III. *Israel.* Atlanta, 1992: Scholars Press for South Florida Studies in the History of Judaism; *Judaism Transcends Catastrophe: God, Torah, and Israel beyond the Holocaust.* Macon, GA, 1994: Mercer University Press. I. *Faith Renewed: The Judaic Affirmation beyond the Holocaust; Judaism Transcends Catastrophe: God, Torah, and Israel beyond the Holocaust.* Macon, GA, 1995: Mercer University Press. II. *God Commands; Judaism Transcends Catastrophe: God, Torah, and Israel beyond the Holocaust.* Macon, GA, 1996: Mercer University Press. III. *The Torah Teaches; Judaism Transcends Catastrophe: God, Torah, and Israel beyond the Holocaust.* Macon, GA, 1997: Mercer University Press. IV.. *Eternal Israel Endures; Judaism Transcends Catastrophe: God, Torah, and Israel beyond the Holocaust.* Macon, GA, 1998: Mercer University Press. V. *Faith Seeking Understanding: The Tasks of Theology in Twenty-First Century Judaism.*

[4] My scholarly contribution to the solution of the theological problem is set forth in *Androgynous Judaism. Masculine and Feminine in the Dual Torah.* Macon, 1993: Mercer University Press.

coming from faithful Christianity and take seriously, and in its own terms, the Christian défi. For while Judaism can be Judaism without Christianity, Christianity can never become autonomous of Judaism, so history has shown; in every form it addresses the task of explaining what it is not, in tandem with accounting for what it is. Apologetics within the Judaic theological framework begins at that intersection, always, always turning back to the parting of the ways.[5]

Debates with other scholars carry forward my long-term project of reading and responding to every important work of scholarship in the field of my own specialization, and, truth be told, many outside that field as well. I deal with critics of my work, as is only reasonable, and criticize the work of others as well. Four of the five debates concern issues of historicism in Judaism, that is to say, the appeal to historical fact in the court of theological debate.[6] Of the four, Cohn-Sherbok's constructive theology, while intellectually lightweight, illustrates the method that predominates in all reformist Judaisms, the appeal to historical narrative in the exposition of a theological position and system. But Baron and Schorsch contribute to Judaic religious life through historical research, and Schorsch says so in so many words. So reviews of their writings (Schorsch) or career and oeuvre (Baron) fall well within the theological framework.

The debate with Goldberg and Schäfer[7] takes place here because when I sent the chapter to Schäfer for his comment, he returned it to me unopened. That

---

[5] These books amplify the Judaic apologetics I mean to set forth: *A Rabbi Talks with Jesus. An Intermillennial, Interfaith Exchange.* N.Y., 1993: Doubleday; *Children of the Flesh, Children of the Promise. An Argument with Paul about Judaism as an Ethnic Religion.* Cleveland, 1995: Pilgrim Press. I have found in Christian theological circles, both Catholic and Protestant, considerably greater interest in issues of theological apologetics than I have encountered in Judaic ones. I have the impression that rabbis and other exponents of (a) Judaism do not grasp the challenge that Christian belief presents to those Jews who also seek a religion and want to know whether the Judaism that forms their heritage offers that religion that they seek. But the issue transcends politics and sociology (for example, matters of demography, which so vex Jewish secular organizations). The unique relationship between Judaism and Christianity allows for intriguing dialogue, since sharing a common Scripture and differing about a single agendum of issues (Messiah-ism for instance, the role of the Torah in salvation, for another) make possible a kind of interfaith dialogue, on the one side, and apologetics, on the other, that no other religions can contemplate (or would want to). The more I find my way in Christian theological circles, the more interesting I discover the intellectual challenge to be.

[6] My main statement of issues of historicism in Judaism is in *The Presence of the Past, the Pastness of the Present. History, Time, and Paradigm in Rabbinic Judaism.* Bethesda, 1995: CDL Press.

[7] See also *The Documentary Foundation of Rabbinic Culture. Mopping Up after Debates with Gerald L. Bruns, S. J. D. Cohen, Arnold Maria Goldberg, Susan Handelman, Christine Hayes, James Kugel, Peter Schaefer, Eliezer Segal, E. P. Sanders, and Lawrence H. Schiffman.* Atlanta, 1995: Scholars Press for South Florida Studies in the History of Judaism.

unwillingness to deal with people critical of his ideas does not for one moment suppress free debate or change its outcome, but it does require a different venue. None of us has the power either plausibly to review our own books or effectively to define the conditions for the debate of our ideas. All of us bear the responsibility of dealing in a constructive manner with our critics, and those who do not carry out that responsibility will in the end cease to play a consequential role in the future course of scholarship, even though, for some ephemeral moment or two, matters appear otherwise. For my part, I have taken pleasure in systematic debates with my critics, weighty and otherwise.[8]

As is my way, I comment on the contemporary life of Judaism, the religion, and in the eleventh and twelfth chapters I pursue this line of inquiry. Both chapters derive from public addresses, the eleventh at Calvin College, Grand Rapids, Michigan, and the twelfth at Temple Beth Israel, Longboat Key, Florida. I express thanks to both for the cordial hospitality I enjoyed during my visits. The thirteenth chapter goes over reflections on the diversity of the forms of antipathy to Jews and Judaism that we must sort out. When it was published, it created a remarkable furore in New Zealand, to which I make reference, and in the fourteenth chapter I review some of the reactions. Here again, I was saddened to note how people imagine they have refuted a proposition when they have maligned the one who advances it. Would that we could invent our own reality! But, when we do, the world forms its own judgments. Shading over into an interest in wisdom and morality, which, after all, form the sustaining heart of the Torah (that is, Judaism), I conclude with a reflection on the moral conduct of a career. That marks my sixty-third birthday.

No one in the academic world enjoys more favorable circumstances for scholarship than I do here in Florida. I did most of the project of which this work is part at the University of South Florida as Distinguished Research Professor in the Florida State University System. I express my thanks for not only the advantage of a Distinguished Research Professorship in the Florida state university system, which for a scholar must be the best job in the world, but also of a substantial research expense fund, ample research time, and stimulating, straight-forward, and cordial colleagues, many of whom also are cherished friends.

---

[8] In addition to the item in the foregoing footnote, the following exemplify a much larger enterprise in systematic, public debate with critics: *Judaic Law from Jesus to the Mishnah. A Systematic Reply to Professor E. P. Sanders.* Atlanta, 1993: Scholars Press for South Florida Studies in the History of Judaism; *Are There Really Tannaitic Parallels to the Gospels? A Refutation of Morton Smith.* Atlanta, 1993: Scholars Press for South Florida Studies in the History of Judaism; *Why There Never Was a "Talmud of Caesarea." Saul Lieberman's Mistakes.* Atlanta, 1994: Scholars Press for South Florida Studies in the History of Judaism.

In the time in which this work was done, I served also as Visiting Professor of Religion at Bard College, which awarded me a further research grant. My visits to Bard proved intellectually stimulating and rewarding, and I express thanks for the College's supererogatory support of my work.

JACOB NEUSNER
DISTINGUISHED RESEARCH PROFESSOR OF RELIGIOUS STUDIES
UNIVERSITY OF SOUTH FLORIDA
TAMPA, FLORIDA 33620-5550 U.S.A.
AND
VISITING PROFESSOR OF RELIGION
BARD COLLEGE
ANNANDALE-ON-HUDSON, NEW YORK 12504 U.S.A.

JULY 28TH, 1995
MY SIXTY-THIRD BIRTHDAY

PART ONE

DEBATES ON HISTORY

I

Defining Scarce Resources:
Real Estate or Intellect
and the Transformation of Judaism

I. HOW THE TALMUDS TRANSFORMED THE MISHNAH'S ECONOMICS

Professor Elzinga's fine paper on my *Economics of the Mishnah* leaves room for discussing only one question: what happened then? The answer takes two forms, literary and theological. The Mishnah, which reached closure in ca. A.D. 200, provoked systematic analysis, on the one side, and further collection of traditions of the character of those included in the Mishnah but omitted from that compilation. This labor of exegesis and augmentation produced systematic exegesis of some of the tractates of the Mishnah, thirty-nine of the sixty-three in the Talmud of the Land of Israel, ca. A.D. 400, and thirty-seven in the Talmud of Babylonia, ca. A.D. 600. The Talmuds differ on the Mishnah-divisions that require attention, the Talmud of the Land of Israel addressing the first four of the six, that of Babylonia, the second through the fifth; both ignore the sixth division, on Purities.

The framers of the compositions and composites that found their way into the two Talmuds and the compilers of those Talmuds did two things. First, they faithfully amplified the views of the Mishnah. But, second, they also formed their own program of thought, taking up the same categories of the social order — way of life, world view, theory of the social entity that realizes the way of life and world view — and forming counterpart categories, which answered the same questions in a different manner.[1] How, precisely, did the category, "way of life," defined in terms of economics, fare in the successor-writings and in the documents that compiled those writings? The heirs of the initial, philosophical Judaism received a system in which the subject of economics — the rational disposition of scarce resources — was utilized in order to set forth a systemic statement of fundamental importance. While making every effort to affirm the details of that statement and apply them, the successors in no way contributed to the theoretical work that the economics of the Mishnah can, and should, have precipitated. Consequently, their system repeated the given but made no significant use of what had been received. Instead, as we shall see later on, the heirs of the Mishnah invented what we must call a counterpart-category, that is to say, a category that dealt with problems of the rational utilization of scarce resources, but not with those same scarce resources defined by the philosophical system of the Mishnah. The systemic category for the aborning religious system was not an economics, but corresponded, in the new system, to the position and role of economics in the old.

So far as a well-crafted theory of a social entity knows how and why scarce resources are assigned to, or end up in the hands of, one person or institution or class or other social organization, rather than some other, that system, in designing the social order, has worked out an economics for itself. The Mishnah's system — alone among all of the Judaic (and Christian) systems of late antiquity[2] — set forth as part of its systemic composition a fully-articulated economics, entirely congruent with the philosophical economics of Aristotle, answering questions concerning the definition of wealth, property, production and the means of production, ownership and control of the means of production, the determination of price and value and the like. And that fact signifies that the Judaic system to which the Mishnah attests is philosophical not only in method and message but in its very systemic composition. The principal components of its theory of the social order, its account of the way of life of its Israel and its picture of the conduct of the public policy of its social entity, — all of these in detail correspond in their basic definitions and indicative traits with the economics and the politics of Graeco-Roman philosophy in the Aristotelian tradition. Specifically, the Mishnah's economics, in general in the theory of the rational disposition of scarce resources and of the management and increase thereof, and specifically in its definitions of wealth and ownership, production and consumption, point by point, corresponds to that of Aristotle.

---

[1] In this paper I epitomize the relevant chapters of my *The Transformation of Judaism. From Philosophy to Religion.* Champaign, 1992: University of Illinois Press. My systematic introductions to Rabbinic literature and to the history of Rabbinic Judaism are *Introduction to Rabbinic Literature.* N.Y., 1994: Doubleday. The Doubleday Anchor Reference Library and *Rabbinic Judaism. The Documentary History of the Formative Age.* Bethesda, 1994: CDL Press.

[2] For instance, history defined an important, systemically critical, category for Augustine, economics did not.

The general point in common between Aristotle's and the Mishnah's economics comes first: for both systems economics formed a chapter in a larger theory of the social order. The power of economics as framed by Aristotle, the only economic theorist of antiquity worthy of the name, was to develop the relationship between the economy to society as a whole.[3] And the framers of the Mishnah did precisely that when they incorporated issues of economics at a profound theoretical level into the system of society as a whole that they proposed to construct . That is why (to paraphrase Polanyi's judgment of Aristotle) the authorship of the Mishnah will be seen as attacking the problem of man's livelihood within a system of sanctification of a holy people with a radicalism of which no later religious thinkers about utopias were capable. None has ever penetrated deeper into the material organization of man's life under the aspect of God's rule. In effect, they posed, in all its breadth, the question of the critical, indeed definitive place occupied by the economy in society under God's rule.

There was a common social foundation for the economic theory of both systems. Both Aristotle and the Mishnah's framers deemed the fundamental unit of production to be the household, and the larger social unit, the village, composed of households, marked the limits of the social entity. The Mishnah's economic tractates, such as the Baba Qamma, Baba Mesia, and Baba Batra, on civil law, as well as those that deal with economic issues inhering in agricultural taboos, invariably refer to the householder, making him the subject of most predicates; where issues other than economics are in play, e.g., in the political tractates such as Sanhedrin, the householder scarcely appears as a social actor. Not only so, but both Aristotle and the authorship of the Mishnah formed the conception of "true value," which maintained that something — an object, a piece of land — possessed a value extrinsic to the market and intrinsic to itself, such that, if a transaction varied from that imputed true value by (in the case of the Mishnah) 18%, the exchange was null. Not only so, but the sole definition of wealth for both Aristotle's and the Mishnah's economics was real estate, only land however small. Since land does not contract or expand, of course, the conception of an increase in value through other than a steady-state exchange of real value, "true value,"[4] between parties to a transaction lay outside of the theory of economics. Therefore all profit, classified as usury, was illegitimate and must be prevented. The definition of value identified real estate as wealth.

---

[3] Polanyi, "Aristotle Discovers the Economy," in Polanyi, Karl , Conrad M. Arensberg, and Harry W. Pearson, *Trade and Market in the Early Empires. Economies in History and Theory* (Glencoe, 1957: Free Press), p. 79.

[4] I do not claim to grasp the meaning of "true value." But it certainly cannot be represented as a market-category, contrary to some critics of my *The Economics of the Mishnah.* Chicago, 1989: The University of Chicago Press.

On that matter, the Mishnah's framers concurred. But the authorship of the Mishnah made its own points. The single most striking, already noted, is that the Mishnah's system severely limited its economics — and therefore the social vision and pertinence of the realm of the system as a whole! — to [1] Israelite householders, meaning, [2] landowners, and among these, only the ones who [3] lived on real estate held to fall within the Land of Israel (the borders being difficult to define, to be sure). The economics of the Mishnah eliminated from its conception of the economy [1] gentiles in the Land of Israel, [2] Israelites outside of the Land of Israel, and [3] Israelites in the Land of Israel who did not own land — which is to say, nearly everybody in the world. So the definition of "scarce resources" proved so particular as to call into question the viability of the economics as such and to recast economics into a (merely) systemic component. For when, in the Mishnah, we speak of the economic person, the one who owns "land," it is only land that produces a crop liable to the requirements of the sacerdotal taxes..

Wealth therefore is ownership of *land of Israel* in two senses, both of them contained within the italicized words. It is ownership of land located in the land *of Israel.* It is ownership of land located in the land of Israel that is *of Israel,* belonging to an Israelite. "Israel" then forms the key to the meaning of wealth, because it modifies persons and land alike: only an Israel[ite] can possess the domain that signifies wealth; only a domain within the land called by the name of "Israel" can constitute wealth. It is in the enchanted intersection of the two Israels, (ownership of) the land, (ownership by) the people, that wealth in the system of the Mishnah finds realization. Like Aristotle's selective delimitation of the economy, the Mishnah's economics describes a tiny part of the actual economic life of the time and place and community.

II. THE TALMUD'S TREATMENT OF THE MISHNAH'S ECONOMICS: AMPLIFICATION, EXTENSION, APPLICATION

How was the philosophical economics of the Mishnah received? To begin with, the heirs of the system of the Mishnah read that document not whole and complete but phrase by phrase and sentence by sentence, breaking up its large units of discourse into discrete parts. Consequently, as a matter of hermeneutics, they received not the system, but only its constituent pieces. To those they devoted sustained efforts at clarification. But their exegetical method precluded a perceptive assessment of the document as a whole, focusing as it did on details. That explains why, as we shall see, the economics of the Mishnah defined not a category for exploration, expansion, revision, renovation, and reformation, but only a topic for discussion.

When we fully grasp the fate of philosophical economics in the successor-documents, we shall understand the full dimensions of the achievement of the authorships of the fourth and fifth century in building, essentially new and fresh, a system of their own, while at the same time receiving and preserving the words of the ancients. A consideration of how the philosophical economics was received will allow us to grasp the traits of intellect of the system-builders whose work is realized by the successor-documents. Rather than begin with generalizations on the method of the new authorships, let us turn directly to the concrete case at hand. What we shall see in detail will prepare us to interpret the entire work of the fourth- and fifth-century authorships in its own terms.

Nearly every discourse — perhaps 90% of the whole — of the Talmud of the Land of Israel, on which we focus here, which also is called the Yerushalmi, addresses one main point: the meaning of the Mishnah, read sentence by sentence. That fact gives us the impression, which is false, that for the Yerushalmi, the life of Israel reaches the level of analysis within the integument of the Mishnah. We may say, the Mishnah is about life, while the Yerushalmi is about the Mishnah. So a literary analysis will suggest. Only when we realize that, right alongside its reading of the Mishnah, the authorship of the Yerushalmi and companion-documents are bringing to expression a system of their own, one that is not at all continuous in its categories with the system of the Mishnah, shall we grasp the full subtlety, the polemical power, of the Yerushalmi's character as what appears to be a mere commentary. That commentary-form wishes to lead us to the conclusion that the traits of the Mishnah have defined the problematic, of both intellect and politics, confronting the heirs of the Mishnah, the faithful disciples of the final generation of the Mishnah's redaction and formulation onward. But as a matter of fact, in the invention of a categorical system entirely their own, these same people make a statement of their own, even while purporting to focus upon statements of others, prior to themselves.

The Yerushalmi's authorship invariably does to the Mishnah one of these four things: (1) text criticism; (2) exegesis of the meaning of the Mishnah-sentence or paragraph under discussion, including glosses and amplifications; (3) addition of scriptural proof texts of the Mishnah's central propositions; and (4) harmonization of one Mishnah passage with another such passage or with a statement of Tosefta.[5] The first two of these four procedures remain wholly within the narrow frame of the Mishnah passage subject to discussion. The second pair take an essentially independent stance vis-a-vis the Mishnah pericope at hand.

How in detail, then, does the Yerushalmi deal with the principal components of the economics of the Mishnah, such as the definitions of money, true value, wealth, and like indicators of the presence of a sophisticated system of economics? It amplifies, refines, complements, but it does not revise, innovate, or

---

[5] These four taxa encompass all the Yerushalmi's units of discourse that relate to the Mishnah at all, 90% of the whole of the Yerushalmi tractates surveyed in my *Talmud of the Land of Israel. A Preliminary Translation and Explanation.* Volume Thirty-Five.. *Introduction: Taxonomy.*

even renovate them. For example, in the discussion, critical to an understanding of the philosophical economics of the Mishnah, of the rule, "Silver acquires gold, but gold does not acquire silver, copper acquires silver, but silver does not acquire copper," the Yerushalmi's anonymous voice states as its opener: "This is the summary principle of the matter: Whatever is of lesser value than its fellow effects acquisition of its fellow [when it is drawn or lifted up]" (Y. Baba Mesia 4:1.I.A). The supplied language, of course, is mine, justified by the fact that, to the authorship of the Mishnah — and also therefore to the voice of the Yerushalmi — silver and gold are commodities, pure and simple, and all trade is *au fond* solely barter.

The principal point of expansion, however, concerns not the conception of gold and silver as commodities for barter, but, rather, a quite different issue, hardly prominent in the Mishnah-paragraph though admittedly entirely present there. It has to do with the rules of acquisition, the point, in a transaction, at which one party has fully attained ownership of the object from the other. That is where we are given a variety of cases and expansions of the received rule. And that is not surprising, since, for administrators of the law, the issues of legal theory concerning abstract problems of economics do not impinge, while the concrete cases of who owns property or a person at a given instant require decisions everyday. All of these cases, of course, derive from the basic principle that transfer of funds does not complete a transaction; money is a commodity; only when the object itself has been handed over by the seller and received by the buyer is the transaction done. Up to that point, either party may still retract, and that is so even though money has changed hands.

So the facts of the law of the Mishnah govern, but the category of economics is essentially untouched. When the authorship of the Yerushalmi learns "silver acquires gold, but gold does not acquire silver," they wish to spell out rules of acquisition, — but not principles of commodity barter as against the abstract conception of money, such as Aristotle had set forth and the Mishnah's sages instantiated in the case of gold and silver. And, it goes without saying, the rest of Mishnah-tractate Baba Qamma Chapter Four is treated within that same focus of interest, on the concrete and immediate and not on the theoretical and the abstract; so what is made concrete is the Mishnah's conception of money, not the principle money let alone the category of economics so far as it has to do with principles of the steady-state and self-sufficient economic entity, the household and the village made up of households.

What about the fundamental (if to us mysterious) conception of true, as distinct from market, value? Here too we find neither revision nor renovation, but only restatement; we do not understand the conception better after we have studied what the Yerushalmi's authorship has to say than we did before we heard. There is no effort to explain, only to apply to concrete cases or to harmonize with other principles of law the conception that objects have an intrinsic worth, not dictated by the market, to which the market must conform. For example, at Mishnah-tractate Baba Mesia 4:3A, we are given a definition of fraud: "Fraud is an overcharge of four pieces of silver out of twenty-four pieces of silver to the sela, one-sixth of the purchase price." The given conception, true value or inherent worth independent of the market, to be given by the purchaser and received by the seller of the object ("fraud applies to the buyer and the seller alike"), is restated, but the focus is on the application.

A brief account of the Talmud's treatment of the subject shows the character of the Yerushalmi's reception of the Mishnah's category. We begin with the position that the assessment of fraud at a sixth overcharge is fact; we deem fraud to be an overcharge of a sixth of the true value of an object, so Rab. Yohanan maintains that it would apply to the price paid for the object, not only to the true value of the object. The issue is then addressed of whether or not the transaction is null, or whether the purchaser may return the amount by which he had defrauded the merchant and keep the object. So the issue of retraction is made complicated. Third, we have a discussion of a change in the market value of the object prior to the completion of the transaction: "if one sold an object worth five for six, but did not complete the transaction before the market-price of the object went up to seven, so that the purchaser, who had been subject to fraud, now wishes to complete the purchase, what is the rule? Here again, we see how the Talmud clarifies the received rule, but in no way wishes to expand, or contract, or revise, the category that is realized in detail by the rule.

So far as the Mishnah sets forth the conception of wealth, we find the phenomenon the same: the Yerushalmi receives with respect and restates with precision and accuracy precisely what the Mishnah's authorship has said, without expanding, redesigning, let alone redefining that conception in any material way. The conception of wealth as fixed and unchanging is associated with the prohibition, deriving from Scripture, against what is narrowly translated as interest or increase (Mishnah-tractate Baba Mesia 5:1A), but what is in fact nothing other than profit of more than 18% of the true value of the object, on the one side, or interest on a loan of any kind, on the other. Trading in naked futures, for example, is forbidden; it involves transactions concerning things that are not now in being. The prohibition against profit or interest on loans is extended to gifts in kind or even generous gestures or attitudes. How is the rule worked out in the Yerushalmi? First, may the judges exact usurious interest from one who has received it? The answer is this: "If from this man you exact what he has unlawfully gained, then we shall leave not a thing in the estates of the great nobles of the Land of Israel" (Y. B.M. 5:1.IC). But bonds containing interest-clauses are unenforceable in court.

So far as the issues of economics arise in the Yerushalmi, they invariably are introduced by the requirement of dealing with sentences of the Mishnah, and they are fully spelled out. But is there independent thinking about the same issues? A survey of the tractates of the Yerushalmi fails to yield a *single* important case in which the kinds of writing particular to the Yerushalmi vis à vis the Mishnah produce any thought at all on economic topics. Quite to the contrary, in those other-than-exegetical passages of the Yerushalmi we find ourselves in a world in which no one is thinking about the kinds of scarce resources and their rational utilization, protection, and increase, that economics considers. To state the fact very simply: in the successor-documents, scarce resources, so far as these are of a material order of being, e.g., wealth defined as the Mishnah and Aristotle did, true value understood as philosophy defined it, the matter of profit and increase and market-economics and the rest — all of these simply are systemically neutral in the successor documents. Where wealth, money, trading, and profit enter discourse at all, they are not part of a system that expresses its basic structure through the category of economics. They are trivialized and made to exemplify categories of a different system altogether.

III. THE TALMUD'S OWN RE-PRESENTATION OF SCARCE RESOURCES: FROM REAL ESTATE TO TORAH

Then what takes the place of those scarce resources that form the critical interest of philosophical economics? The answer derives not only from the Talmud of the Land of Israel but also from the associated Midrash-compilations, which provide for Scripture what the Talmud gives to the Mishnah: a reprise but also a new reading. A clear statement of the answer is as follows, which shows explicitly that utterly new rationality as to the definition of value and wealth that would emerge in the successor-system; the passage comes to us in Leviticus Rabbah, dated ca. A.D. 450, a document produced in the same circles that set forth the Talmud of the Land of Israel:

Leviticus Rabbah XXXIV:XVI

1. B.   R. Tarfon gave to R. Aqiba[6] six silver centenarii, saying to him, "Go, buy us a piece of land, so we can get a living from it and labor in the study of Torah together."

   C.   He took the money and handed it over to scribes, Mishnah-teachers, and those who study Torah.

   D.   After some time R. Tarfon met him and said to him, "Did you buy the land that I mentioned to you?"

   E.   He said to him, "Yes."

   F.   He said to him, "Is it any good?"

   G.   He said to him, "Yes."

   H.   He said to him, "And do you not want to show it to me?"

---

[6] The attributions to first century authorities such as Tarfon and Aqiba by a fifth century document such as Leviticus Rabbah need not detain us, since there is no way of validating them. I claim to portray views held or endorsed in the fifth century. It goes without saying that the opinion at hand is not represented by a document that reached closure prior to the one at hand, so if Tarfon and Aqiba really said what is assigned to them, no prior compilers

I. He took him and showed him the scribes, Mishnah teachers, and people who were studying Torah, and the Torah that they had acquired.

J. He said to him, "Is there anyone who works for nothing? Where is the deed covering the field?"

K. He said to him, "It is with King David, concerning whom it is written, 'He has scattered, he has given to the poor, his righteousness endures forever' (Ps. 112:9)."

It would be difficult to invent more explicit proof that a drastic shift has taken place. Instead of defining wealth as land, land is defined as not-wealth, and something else is now defined as wealth in its place.

That is evidence of not the reformation of received categories but the formation of new ones, not continuous with the old. And the representation of matters is quite articulated in the contrast between wealth as real estate and wealth as Torah. Then how do we turn real estate into Torah? That transvaluation of values is worked out, once more quite explicitly, in the statement (Y. [=Yerushalmi or Talmud of the Land of Israel] Megillah 4:1.IV.P-Q: "'I can write the whole Torah for two hundred copper coins.' What did he do, he went and bought flax seed worth two hundred copper coins, sowed it, reaped it, made it into ropes, caught a deer, and wrote the entire Torah on the deer hide." The three operative components here are money, land, and Torah. As we recall, the definition of real wealth was real estate. So we transform money into land. But then the definition of wealth is shifted, and the symbolic shift is blatant: turn money into real wealth, then real wealth produces the wherewithal of making a Torah. And with that rather stunning symbolic transformation, we find ourselves in a world wholly different from the one in which scarce resources are identified with matters of material, palpable value, and in which economics is the theory of the rational disposition of scarce resources of capital, labor, movables, real estate, and the like.

What we see therefore is not the revision, let alone the expansion, of a received category, but adumbrations of the transformation of the category into a counterpart-category, one that systemically addresses the same issue but presents a mirror-image of the received category's meanings and doctrines. How does the

---

endorsed their view and preserved it as part of their official writing. For critical, historical purposes, what later authorities and compilers put into the mouths of people who lived hundreds of years earlier provides facts about those later authorities' and compilers' opinions. The sole fact in hand is that the compilers of a fifth-century writing endorsed the views at hand by including them in their compilation, and that suffices to make the point that the representation of matters speaks for the fifth century sages. What we know about the views of first century figures depends on how we evaluate the attribution to them of sayings that first surface in documents redacted many hundreds of years later. For our purpose, such attributions possess no interest whatsoever.

received economics change as a continuing category? In my view, the received economics does not undergo categorical revision at all. Have we found, beyond the valuation of land, the conception of true value, and other traits of Aristotelian economics, appreciation of other media of material wealth and value, e.g., market place, capital, and the like? I think not. I can identify in the documents under examination no new thinking on economic questions at all. For instance, I can locate no interest in the market, in production of goods and services, in addition to produce of land, such as would signify reflection on the limitations of philosophical economics and the expansion of the range of concern beyond the theoretically-constricted limits of the Mishnah's economics. There simply is no new thinking on economics. Instead, as we shall see in due course, a new "scarce resource" essentially beyond the limits of the old, that is, a supernatural resource, defined a category, and a new rationality superseded the received one. But before following the new, let us examine the third component of the initial system, its politics. Here too we shall see that dual process of amplification of the literary expression of the given system and also the utter reformulation of its category-formation.

IV. THE TRANSVALUATION OF VALUE

Consideration of the transvaluation of value brings us to the successor-system's counterpart category, that is, the one that in context forms the counterpart to the Mishnah's concrete, this-worldly, material and tangible definition of value in conformity with the familiar, philosophical economics. We have now to ask, what, in place of the received definition of value and the economics thereof, did the new system set forth?

The transformation of economics involved the redefinition of scarce and valued resources in so radical a manner that the concept of value, while remaining material in consequence and character, nonetheless took on a quite different sense altogether.[7] The counterpart category of the successor-system, represented by the authorships responsible for the final composition of the Yerushalmi, Genesis Rabbah, Leviticus Rabbah, and Pesiqta deRab Kahana, concerned themselves with the same

---

[7] Does that fact then suggest the new system's theory of the social order set forth no economics at all? After all, there is no reason that a theory of the social order required an economics at all, since a variety of theories of the social order of the same time and place other than Aristotle's and the Mishnah's — Plato's for one, the Gospels' for another, the Essene Community at Qumran's for a third — managed to put forth a compelling theory of society lacking all sustained and systematic, systemically pertinent attention to economics at all. I insist, however, that the successor-system put forth a theory of the way of life that must be characterized as an economics, not as a theology that made reference, by the way, to topics of economic interest but an economics. It was, however, one involving a different value from the ultimate value, real property, characteristic of Aristotle's and the Mishnah's economics.

questions as did the conventional economics, presenting an economics in function and structure, but one that concerned things of value other than those identified by the initial system. So indeed we deal with an economics, an economics of something other than real estate.

But it was an economics just as profoundly embedded in the social order, just as deeply a political economics, just as pervasively a systemic economics, as the economics of the Mishnah and of Aristotle. Why so? Because issues such as the definition of wealth, the means of production and the meaning of control thereof, the disposition of wealth through distributive or other media, theory of money,reward for labor, and the like — all these issues found their answers in the counterpart-category of economics, as much as in the received and conventional philosophical economics. The new "scarce resource" accomplished what the old did, but it was a different resource, a new currency. At stake in the category meant to address the issues of the way of life of the social entity, therefore, were precisely the same considerations as confront economics in its (to us) conventional and commonplace, philosophical sense. But since the definition of wealth changes, as we have already seen, from land to Torah, much else would be transformed on that account.

That explains why, in the formation of the counterpart-category of value other than real value but in function and in social meaning value nonetheless, we witness the transformation of a system from philosophy to religion. We err profoundly if we suppose that in contrasting land to Torah and affirming that true value lies in Torah, the framers of the successor-system have formulated an essentially spiritual or otherwise immaterial conception for themselves, that is, a surrogate for economics in the conventional sense. That is not what happened. What we have is an economics that answers the questions economics answers, as I said, but that has chosen a different value from real value — real estate, as we have already seen — as its definition of that scarce resource that requires a rational policy for preservation and enhancement. Land produced a living; so did Torah. Land formed the foundation of the social entity, so did Torah.

The transvaluation of value was such that an economics concerning the rational management and increase of scarce resources worked itself out in such a way as to answer, for quite different things of value from real property or from capital such as we know as value, precisely the same questions that the received economics addressed in connection with wealth of a real character: land and its produce. Systemic transformation comes to the surface in articulated symbolic change. The utter transvaluation of value finds expression in a jarring juxtaposition, an utter shift of rationality, specifically, the substitution of Torah for real estate. We recall how in a successor-document (but in none prior to the fifth century compilations) Tarfon thought wealth took the form of land, while Aqiba explained to him that wealth takes the form of Torah-learning. That the sense is material and concrete is explicit: land for Torah, Torah for land.

Let us begin with a simple definition of "value." While bearing a variety of inchoate meanings, associated with belief, conviction, ideal, moral preference, and the like, the word to begin with bears an entirely concrete sense. Value means that which people value, under ordinary circumstances, what they hold to be of concrete, tangible, material worth. In the nature of things, I regard "value" as another way of referring to "scarce resources." What is "of value" conventionally is what provides a life of comfort and sustenance and material position. In commonplace language, "value" (as distinct, therefore, from the vague term, "values") refers to those scarce resources to the rational management and increase of which economics devotes its attention: real wealth.[8] This means, in our contemporary context, capital, and in the context of Aristotle's and the Mishnah's economics, real estate.[9] Then when I speak of the transvaluation of value, I mean that the material and concrete things of worth were redefined — even while subjected to an economics functioning in the system as the counterpart to the initial economics of the Mishnah and of Aristotle. In the successor-writings ownership of land, even in the Land of Israel, contrasts with wealth in another form altogether, and the contrast that was drawn was material and concrete, not merely symbolic and spiritual. It was material and tangible and palpable because it produced this-worldly gains, e.g., a life of security, comfort, ease, as these too found definition in the systemic context of the here and the now.

It follows that, while in the successor system's theory of the component of the social order represented by the way of life, we find an economics, it is an economics of scarce resources defined as something other than particular real estate. Why do I insist that these questions are economic in character? It is because they deal with the rules or theory of the rational management of scarce resources, their preservation and increase, and do so in commonplace terms of philosophical economics, e.g., the control of the means of production, the definition of money and of value, the distribution of valued goods and services, whether by appeal to the market or to a theory of distributive economics, the theory of the value of labor and the like. But while the structure remained the same, the contents radically would differ, hence the transvaluation of value. It was as if a new currency were issued to replace the old, then declared of no value, capable of purchasing nothing worth having. In such an economics, there is far more than a currency-reform, but rather a complete economic revolution, a new beginning, as much as a shift from

---

[8] I use "real" in the technical sense, meaning, landed wealth or property, real estate. Any other usage draws me into questions of theology or philosophy, with which economics does not deal. I shall presently argue that there is no spiritualizing or moralizing or philosophizing "value," which bears concrete meanings and material consequences in the documents considered here.

[9] For Aristotle, land could be anywhere; for the Mishnah's economics, the ultimate value was a particular piece of land, which was the Land of Israel occupied by holy Israel. But, then, Aristotle was a philosopher, and, in the end, "our sages of blessed memory" were theologians. The one seeks general rules, the other, the generalizations yielded by revelation.

socialism to capitalism. But the transvaluation, in our case, was more thorough-going still, since involved was the very reconsideration of the scarcity of scarce resources. Both elements then underwent transvaluation: the definition of resources of value, the rationality involved in the management of scarcity. In a word, while real estate cannot increase and by definition must always prove scarce, the value represented by Torah could expand without limit. Value could then increase indefinitely, resources that were desired and scarce be made ever more abundant, in the transformed economics of the successor-system.

While responding to the same questions of that same part of the social order with which the received category concerned itself, the economics that emerged in no way proves discontinuous with the received economics. Why not just another economics than the philosophical one we have considered? The reason is that so abrupt and fundamental a reworking will be seen to have taken place that the category — way of life — *while yet an economics* — nonetheless is now a wholly-other economics, one completely without relationship to the inherited definition of way of life (manner of earning a living) as to both structure and system.

For at stake is not merely the spiritualization of wealth, that is to say, the re-presentation of what "wealth" *really* consists of in other-than-material terms. That would represent not an economics but a theology. For example, the familiar saying in tractate Abot, "Who is rich? One who is happy in his lot," simply does not constitute a statement of economics at all. Like sayings in the Gospels that denigrate wealth, this one tells nothing about the rational management (e.g., increase) of scarce resources, it merely tells about appropriate moral attitudes of a virtuous order: how life is worth living, not answering an economic question at all. On the other hand, the tale that contrasts wealth in the form of land and its produce with wealth in the form of Torah (whatever is meant by "Torah") does constitute a statement of economics. The reason is that the story-teller invokes precisely the category of wealth — real property — that conventional economics defines as wealth. If I have land, I have wealth, and I can support myself; if I have Torah, I have wealth, and I can support myself. Those form the two components of the contrastive equation before us. But then wealth is disenlandised, and the Torah substituted for real property of all kinds. That forms not a theology, nor an economics in any conventional sense, bur, rather, an anti-economics. The same will be seen to be so in politics.

Take, for example, the as in the following explicit statement that a sentence of the Torah is more valuable than a pearl:

Y Peah 1:1 XVII (trans. by Roger Brooks)

E.   Ardavan sent our holy Rabbi a priceless pearl and said to him, "Send me something as valuable as this."

F.   He sent him a doorpost-scroll (mezuzah] containing words of Torah].

G. Ardavan said to him, "I sent you an item beyond price, but you send me something worth but a few cents."

H. Rabbi said to him, "Your precious things and my precious things are not equivalent.' You sent me something I have to guard, but I sent something that guards you while you sleep: 'When you walk along, [the words of Torah] will lead you, when you lie down, they will watch over you' (Prov. 6:22)

If I have words of the Torah in hand, there are scarce resources in my possession that I otherwise do not have: security, for example, against whatever demons may want to harm me in my sleep.

Why do I insist that these kinds of stories deal with scarce resources in a concrete sense? Because in both cases cited to this point the upshot of the possession of Torah is this-worldly, concrete, tangible, and palpable. The rewards are not described as "filling treasuries in the heart," nor do they "enrich the soul," nor are they postponed to the world to come (as would be the case in a kind of capitalistic theology of investment on earth for return in heaven). The tale concerning Aqiba and Tarfon, like the one involving Rabbi and Ardavan, insists upon precisely the same *results* of the possession of wealth of value in the form of "Torah" as characterize wealth or value in the form of real estate. The key-language is this: "Go, buy us a piece of land, *so we can get a living from it* and labor in the study of Torah together." Tarfon assumes owning land buys leisure for Torah-study; Aqiba does not contradict that assumption, he steps beyond it.

Then one thing forms the counterpart and opposite of the other — anti-economics, economics, respectively — but both things yield a single result: wealth to sustain leisure, which any reader of Xenophon's handbook on economics (estate management, in his context) will have found an entirely commonplace and obviously true judgment. That explains why the form that wealth in the successor-system now takes — Torah rather than real estate — presents a jarring contrast, one that is, of course, the point of the story. And as a matter of fact, as we shall see in just a moment, that jarring contrast will have proved unintelligible to any authorship prior to the second stage in the formation of the canonical writings and explicitly contradicts the sense of matters that predominates in the first stage: the Torah is not to be made "a spade to dig with" (whatever that can have meant). In Tarfon's mind, therefore, real (in the theological sense) value is real (in the economic sense) wealth, that is, real estate, because if you own land, you can enjoy the leisure to do what you really want to do, which (as every philosopher understood) is to study (in the sages' case) the Torah together. But to Aqiba, in the tale, that is beside the point, since the real (in the theological sense) value (in the economic sense, that is, what provides a living, food to eat for instance) is Torah (study), and that, in itself, suffices. The sense is, if I have land, I have a living, and if I have Torah, I have a living, which is no different from the living that I have from land — but which, as a matter of fact, is more secure.

Owning land involved control of the means of production, and so did knowing the Torah. But — more to the point — from land people derived a living, and from Torah people derived a living in *precisely* the same sense — that is to say, in the material and concrete sense — in which from land they could do so. That is alleged time and again, and at stake then is not the mere denigration of wealth but the transvaluation of value. Then the transvaluation consisted in [1] the disenlandisement of value, and [2] the transvaluation of (knowing or studying) the Torah, the imputation to Torah of the value formerly associated with land. And that is why it is valid to claim for Torah the status of a counterpart-category: the system's economics, its theory of the way of life of the community and account of the rational disposition of those scarce resources that made everyday material existence possible and even pleasant: an economics of wealth, but of wealth differently defined, while similarly valued and utilized.

For like Aristotle, when the authorship of the Mishnah conducted discourse upon economic questions, they understood wealth in entirely this-worldly terms. The Torah formed a component in the system of hierarchical classification, not a unit of value or a measure of worth. By contrast, as we shall see, in the successor-system portrayed by the Talmud of the Land of Israel, Genesis Rabbah, Leviticus Rabbah, and their companions, the concept of scarce resources was linked to the conception of Torah and so took on altogether fresh meanings, but in exactly the same context and producing exactly the same material consequences, e.g., having food to eat and a dwelling for shelter, with the result that we have to redefine that which serves the very category, "economics," altogether. Why is this necessary? It is because of those stunning transvaluations, already cited, of value stated explicitly and baldly in the contrast between land and Torah. When the successor-documents contrast the received value with the value they recognize, then we must ask about the formation of the counterpart-category and consider how to make sense of that category.

Accordingly, I have now to show that when our authorship spoke of Torah, they addressed the issues of scarce resources in the way in which, when the authorship of the Mishnah or Aristotle spoke of real wealth, they addressed those same issues. Then we require an account of the goods and services assigned the status of "scarce resources," and thence we shall define the theory of rational disposition that in the successor-system constitutes the economics. The questions are the same. But they are addressed to different things of value, different scarce resources altogether, and the systemic goal is to make abundant what has been scarce.

Since Torah — left undefined for the moment — now forms the definition of wealth, the question immediately confronts us: has that sense of the word really changed so considerably from its representation in the first stratum of the literature that we must impute to the word meanings that are represented as both fresh and simply not considered in the initial economics of the first Judaism? That is to say, was Torah in the Mishnah not that same ultimate value that it became in the successor-system? If it was, then any claim that Torah has replaced real estate as the definition of value and worth — the transvaluation of value in a very concrete sense — is simply beside the point. In the initial system — it may be claimed — Torah stood for something of ultimate worth, right alongside real property and its equivalents, each in its own context, each for its own purpose. I have now therefore to turn back to the issue of the standing and meaning of Torah in the Mishnah and to demonstrate that in the Mishnah, Torah, now to be defined as Torah-learning, in no way functions as a scarce resource; in no way occupies the position, as a statement of real worth and value, that it gained in the successor-system and in the writings that adumbrate it. In the Mishnah, if I know Torah, I enter a certain status, since knowledge of Torah forms part of the taxic structure of the Mishnah's social system. But if I know the Torah, I have still to earn a living, and scarce resources are defined, we already know, by real estate and equivalents.

To make that point stick, I have now to show that, in the Mishnah, Torah stands for status but produces no consequences of a material order, or, as a matter of fact, even for one's caste-status. It is the simple fact that studying the Torah is deemed an action to which accrues unlimited benefit. This is made explicit:

M. Peah. 1:1A-E
(trans. Brooks, in Neusner, *Mishnah*, pp. 14-15).

A.   These are things that have no specified measure: the quantity of produce designated as *peah;* the quantity of produce given as firstfruits, the value of the appearance offering, the performance of righteous deeds, and time spent in study of Torah.

B.   These are things the benefit of which a person enjoys in this world, while the principal remains for him in the world to come: deeds in honor of father and mother, performance of righteous deeds, and acts which bring peace between a man and his fellow.

C.   But the study of Torah is as important as all of them all together

The study of Torah, or knowledge of the Torah, is equivalent to a variety of other meritorious actions, e.g., designating produce as "corner of the field" for use by the scheduled castes; bringing an offering of high cost; honoring parents. Among these comparable deeds, study of the Torah enjoys pride of place. But the rewards are not worldly, not material, not palpable. If I know the Torah, I enjoy a higher status than if I do not; but I have still to work for a living.

This underlines the simple fact that in the Mishnah it is not assumed that a disciple of a sage gets support on account of his Torah-study, and it also is not assumed that the sages makes his living through Torah-study, or other Torah-activities. Knowledge of the Torah or the act of study enjoys no material value. For instance, an act of betrothal requires an exchange of something of value; among the examples of value the act of study or teaching of the Torah is never offered, e.g., "Lo, thou art betrothed to me in exchange for my teaching you [or your brother or your father] a teaching of the Torah" is never suggested as a possibility. So Torah-learning is not material and produces no benefits of a material character. Sages' status may derive from knowledge of Torah, but that status is not confused with the material consideration involved in who may matter whom. In M Qid. 4:1 sages do not form a caste. "Ten castes came up from Babylonia," but the "status" of sage has no bearing upon his caste status. Then what difference does Torah-study or Torah-knowledge make? It is, as I have stressed, one of taxic consequence and one of status, but with no bearing whatsoever upon one's livelihood.

What about knowledge of Torah as a way of making one's living? In the list of professions by which men make a living we find several positions. First is that of Meir and Simeon:

Mishnah Qiddushin 4:14

E. R. Meir says, "A man should always teach his son a clean and easy trade. And let him pray to him to whom belong riches and possessions.

G. "For there is no trade which does not involve poverty or wealth.

H. "For poverty does not come from one's trade, nor does wealth come from one's trade.

I. "But all is in accord with a man's merit."

J. R. Simeon b. Eleazar says, "Have you ever seen a wild beast or a bird who has a trade? Yet they get along without difficulty. And were they not created only to serve me? And I was created to serve my Master. So is it not logical that I should get along without difficulty? But I have done evil and ruined my living."

One's merit makes the difference between poverty and wealth, or one's sinfulness. A more practical position is that which follows in the continuation of the passage:

K. Abba Gurion of Sidon says in the name of Abba Gurya, "A man should not teach his son to be an ass driver, a camel driver, a barber, a sailor, a herdsman, or a shopkeeper For their trade is the trade of thieves."

L. R. Judah says in his name, "Most ass drivers are evil, most camel drivers are decent, most sailors are saintly, the best among physicians is going to Gehenna, and the best of butchers is a partner of Amalek."

The third view is that of Nehorai, who holds that Torah suffices as a means for making a living:

M.   R. Nehorai says, "I should lay aside every trade in the world and teach my son only Torah.

N.   "For a man eats its fruits in this world, and the principal remains for the world to come.

0.   "But other trades are not that way.

P   "When a man gets sick or old or has pains and cannot do his job, lo, he dies of starvation.

Q.   "But with Torah it is not that way.

R.   "But it keeps him from all evil when he is young, and it gives him a future and a hope when he is old.

S.   "Concerning his youth, what does it say? 'They who wait upon the Lord shall renew their strength' (Is. 40:31). And concerning his old age what does it say? 'They shall still bring forth fruit in old age" (Ps. 92:14).

T.   "And so it says with regard to the patriarch Abraham, may he rest in peace, 'And Abraham was old and well along in years, and the Lord blessed Abraham in all things (Gen. 24:1).

U.   "We find that the patriarch Abraham kept the entire Torah even before it was revealed, since it says, Since Abraham obeyed my voice and kept my charge, my commandments, my statutes, and my laws (Gen. 26:5)."

Does Nehorai tell us that if we study the Torah, we will have all our worldly needs met, as Aqiba tells Tarfon that Torah is the counterpart of real estate but a more secure investment? I think not. Quite to the contrary, precisely why Torah works as it does is made explicit at R: "It keeps him from evil when he is young." That is to say, the position of Meir and Simeon is repeated, only in a fresh way. If I know the Torah, I will not sin. The conception that, if I study Torah, I automatically get the food I need to eat and the roof I need for shelter is not at issue here, where our concern is with being kept from evil in youth and enjoying God's blessing in old age on account of keeping the Torah — a very different thing, as we shall see presently.

The first apologia for the Mishnah, tractate Abot, takes the view that one should not make one's living through study of the Torah. That is made explicit in Torah-sayings of tractate Abot, where we find explicit rejection of the theory of Torah-study as a means of avoiding one's obligation to earn a living. Torah-study without a craft is rejected, Torah-study along with labor at a craft is defined as the ideal way of life. The following sayings make that point quite clearly:

M. Abot 2:2 and 3:17

2:2 A.   Rabban Gamaliel, a son of Rabbi Judah the Patriarch says: Fitting is learning in the Torah along with a craft, for the labor

put into the two of them makes one forget sin. And all learning
of the Torah which is not joined with labor is destined to be null
and causes sin.

3:17 A. R. Eleazar b. Azariah says, "...If there is no sustenance [lit.:
flour], there is no Torah-learning. If there is no Torah-learning,
there is no sustenance."

Here there is no contrast between two forms of wealth, one less secure, the other
more. The way of virtue lies rather in economic activity in the conventional sense,
joined to intellectual or philosophical activity in sages' sense. Again, Xenophon
will not have been surprised. The labor in Torah is not an economic activity and
produces no solutions to this-worldly problems of getting food, shelter, clothing.
To the contrary, labor in Torah defines the purpose of human life; it is the goal; but
it is not the medium for maintaining life and avoiding starvation or exposure to the
elements.

Yohanan ben Zakkai speaks of Torah-study as the goal of a human life, on
the one side, and a reward paid for Torah study, clearly in a theological sense and
context, on the other. That the context of Torah-study is religious and not economic
in any sense is shown by Ḥananiah's saying, which is explicit: if people talk about
the Torah, the Presence of God joins them to participate:

M. Abot 2:8

2:8 A. Rabban Yohanan ben Zakkai received [the Torah] from Hillel
and Shammai. He would say: If you have learned much Torah,
do not puff yourself up on that account, for it was for that purpose
that you were created.

Do worldly benefits accrue to those who study the Torah? The rabbi cited in the
following statement maintains that it is entirely inappropriate to utilize Torah-
learning to gain either social standing or economic gain:

M. Abot 4:5

B. R. Sadoq says, "Do not make [Torah-teachings] a crown in which
to glorify yourself or a spade with which to dig. So did Hillel
say, "He who uses the crown perishes. Thus have you learned:
Whoever derives worldly benefit from teachings of the Torah
takes his life out of this world."

I cannot think of a statement more likely to startle the author of the story involving
Aqiba and Tarfon than this one, since Aqiba's position is precisely the one rejected
here. It is the simple fact that the bulk of opinion in the Mishnah and in tractate
Abot identifies Torah-learning with status within a system of hierarchical

classification, not with a medium for earning a living. Admittedly that is not the only position that is represented. The following seems to me to contrast working for a living with studying Torah and to maintain that the latter will provide a living, without recourse to hard labor:

M. Abot 3:15

A.   R. Nehunia b. Haqqaneh says, "From whoever accepts upon himself the yoke of the Torah do they remove the yoke of the state and the yoke of hard labor. And upon whoever removes from himself the yoke of the Torah do they lay the yoke of the state and the yoke of hard labor."

But the prevailing view, represented by the bulk of sayings, treats Torah-study as an activity that competes with economic venture and insists that Torah-study take precedence, even though it is not of economic value in any commonplace sense of the words. That is explicitly imputed to Meir and to Jonathan in the following:

M. Abot 4:10

4:10 A.   R. Meir says, "Keep your business to a minimum and make your business the Torah. And be humble before everybody. And if you treat the Torah as nothing, you will have many treating you as nothing. And if you have labored in the Torah, [the Torah] has a great reward to give you."

4:9 A.   R. Jonathan says, "Whoever keeps the Torah when poor will in the end keep it in wealth. And whoever treats the Torah as nothing when he is wealthy in the end will treat it as nothing in poverty."

Torah-study competes with, rather than replaces, with economic activity. That is the simple position of tractate Abot, extending the conception of matters explicit in the Mishnah. If I had to make a simple statement of the situation prevailing at ca. 250, sages contrast their wealth, which is spiritual and intellectual, with material wealth; they do not deem the one to form the counterpart of the other, but only as the opposite.

And that brings us to consider the re-presentation of wealth in the successor-documents and to seek a richer sample of opinion than the story that ended the preceding chapter and that, I maintain, frames the new economics of the successor system. A system that declares forbidden using the Torah as a spade with which to dig, as a means of making one's living, will have found proof for its position in the numerous allegations in Wisdom literature that the value of wisdom, understood of course as the Torah is beyond price: "Happy is the man who finds wisdom...for the gain from it is better than gain from silver, and its profit better than gold; she is more precious than jewels, and nothing you desire can compare with her...." (Prov. 3:13-15). That and numerous parallels were not understood to mean that if people devoted themselves to the study of the Torah and the teaching thereof, they would not have to work any more. Nor do the praises of wisdom specifically contrast Torah-learning with land-ownership. But in the successor-writings, that is precisely what is commonplace. And the conclusion is drawn that one may derive one's living from study of the Torah: then a spade with which to dig, as much as a real spade served to dig in the earth to make the ground yield a living.

But there are passages that are quite explicit: land is wealth, or Torah is wealth, but not both; owning land is power and studying Torah permits (re)gaining power. To take the first of the two propositions in its most explicit formulation:

Leviticus Rabbah XXX:I.4.

A. R. Yohanan was going up from Tiberias to Sepphoris. R. Hiyya bar Abba was supporting him. They came to a field. He said, "This field once belonged to me, but I sold it in order to acquire merit in the Torah."

B. They came to a vineyard, and he said, "This vineyard once belonged to me, but I sold it in order to acquire merit in the Torah."

C. They came to an olive grove, and he said, "This olive grove once belonged to me, but I sold it in order to acquire merit in the Torah."

D. R. Hiyya began to cry.

E. Said R. Yohanan, "Why are you crying?"

F. He said to him, "It is because you left nothing over to support you in your old age."

G. He said to him, "Hiyya, my disciple, is what I did such a light thing in your view? I sold something which was given in a spell of six days [of creation] and in exchange I acquired something which was given in a spell of forty days [of revelation].

H. "The entire world and everything in it was created in only six days, as it is written, 'For in six days the Lord made heaven and earth' [Ex. 20:11].

I. "But the Torah was given over a period of forty days, as it was said, 'And he was there with the Lord for forty days and forty nights' [Ex. 34:28].

J. "And it is written, 'And I remained on the mountain for forty days and forty nights'" (Deut. 9:9).

.5 A. When R. Yohanan died, his generation recited concerning him [the following verse of Scripture]: "If a man should give all the wealth of his house for the love" (Song 8:7), with which R. Yohanan loved the Torah, "he would be utterly destitute" (Song 8:7)....

C.   When R. Eleazar b. R. Simeon died, his generation recited concerning him [the following verse of Scripture]: "Who is this who comes up out of the wilderness like pillars of smoke, perfumed with myrrh and frankincense, with all the powders of the merchant?" (Song 3:6).

D.   What is the meaning of the clause, "With all the powders of the merchant"?

E.   [Like a merchant who carries all sorts of desired powders,] he was a master of Scripture, a repeater of Mishnah traditions, a writer of liturgical supplications, and a liturgical poet.

The sale of land for the acquisition of "merit in the Torah" introduces two principal systemic components, merit and Torah.[10] For our purpose, the importance of the statement lies in the second of the two, which deems land the counterpart — and clearly the opposite — of the Torah.

Now one can sell a field and acquire "Torah," meaning, in the context established by the exchange between Tarfon and Aqiba, the opportunity to gain leisure to (acquire the merit gained by) the study of the Torah. That the sage has left himself nothing for his support in old age makes explicit the material meaning of the statement, and the comparison of the value of land, created in six days, and the Torah, created in forty days, is equally explicit. The comparison of knowledge of Torah to the merchandise of the merchant simply repeats the same point, but in a lower register. So too does the this-worldly power of study of the Torah make explicit in another framework the conviction that study of the Torah yields material and concrete benefit, a political desideratum, and not just spiritual renewal. Thus R. Huna states, "All of the exiles will be gathered together only on account of the study of Mishnah-teachings."[11]

In alleging that the pertinent verses of Proverbs were assigned a quite this-worldly and material sense, so that study of the Torah really was worth more

---

[10] In a well-crafted system, of course, principal parts prove interchangeable or closely aligned, and that is surely the case here. But I have already observed that the successor-system is far more tightly constructed than the initial one, in that the politics and the economics flow into one another, in a way in which, in the initial, philosophical system, they do not. The disembedded character of the Mishnah's economics is discussed at some length in my *Rabbinic Political Theory: Religion and Politics in the Mishnah.* Chicago, 1991: The University of Chicago Press. Here again, Aristotle's deeply-embedded economics show the character of his thought as philosophical, while that of "our sages of blessed memory" once more marks them as theological system-builders.

[11] *Pesiqta deRab Kahana* VI:III.3.B.

than silver, I say no more than the successor-compilations allege in so many words. Thus we find the following, which faces head-on the fact that masters of the Torah are paid for studying the Torah, so confirming the claim that the Torah now served as a spade with which to dig:

Pesiqta deRab Kahana XXVII:I

.1 A. R. Abba bar Kahana commenced [discourse by citing the following verse]: *Take my instruction instead of silver, and knowledge rather than choice gold* (Prov. 8:10)."

B. Said R. Abba bar Kahana, "*Take the instruction of the Torah instead of silver.*

C. "Take the instruction of the Torah and not silver.

D. "*Why do you weigh out money? [Because there is no bread]* (Is. 55:2).

E. "'Why do you weigh out money to the sons of Esau [Rome]? [It is because] *there is no bread,* because you did not sate yourselves with the bread of the Torah.

F. "*And [why] do you labor? Because there is no satisfaction* (Is. 55:2).

G. "*Why do you labor* while the nations of the world enjoy plenty? *Because there is no satisfaction,* that is, because you have not sated yourselves with the bread of the Torah and with the wine of the Torah.

H. "For it is written, *Come, eat of my bread, and drink of the wine I have mixed* (Prov. 9:5)."

.2 A. R. Berekhiah and R. Hiyya, his father, in the name of R. Yosé b. Nehorai: "It is written, *I shall punish all who oppress him* (Jer. 30:20), even those who collect funds for charity [and in doing so, treat people badly], except [for those who collect] the wages to be paid to teachers of Scripture and repeaters of Mishnah traditions.

B. "For they receive [as a salary] only compensation for the loss of their time, [which they devote to teaching and learning rather than to earning a living].

C. "But as to the wages [for carrying out] a single matter in the Torah, no creature can pay the [appropriate] fee in reward."

The obvious goal, the homily at 1.E, surely stands against my claim that we deal with allegations of concrete and material value: the imputation to the learning of the Torah of the status of "scarce resources." But, as a matter of fact, the whole of No. 2 makes the contrary position explicit: wages are paid to Torah-teachers.

That ultimate value — Torah-study — surely bears comparison with other foci of value, such as prayer, using money for building synagogues, and the like. It is explicitly stated that spending money on synagogues is a waste of money, while spending money supporting Torah-masters is the right use of scarce resources. Further, we find the claim, synagogues and school houses — communal real estate — in fact form the property of sages and their disciples, who may dispose of them just as they want, as any owner may dispose of his property according to his unfettered will. In Y. Sheqalim we find the former allegation, Y. Megillah the latter:

Y. Sheqalim 5:4.II.

A. R. Hama bar Haninah and R. Hoshaia the Elder were strolling in the synagogues in Lud. Said R. Hama bar Haninah to R. Hoshaia, "How much money did my forefathers invest here [in building these synagogues]!"

B. He said to him, "How many lives did your forefathers invest here! Were there not people who were laboring in Torah [who needed the money more]?"

C. R. Abun made the gates of the great hall [of study]. R. Mana came to him. He said to him, "See what I have made!"

D. He said to him, "'For Israel has forgotten his Maker and built palaces'! (Hos. 8:14). Were there no people laboring in Torah [who needed the money more]?"

Y. Sotah 9:13.VI.

C. A certain rabbi would teach Scripture to his brother in Tyre, and when they came and called him to do business, he would say, "I am not going to take away from my fixed time to study. If the profit is going to come to me, let it come in due course [after my fixed time for study has ended]."

Y. Megillah 3:3:V.

A. R. Joshua b. Levi said, "Synagogues and schoolhouses belong to sages and their disciples."

B. R. Hiyya bar Yosé received [guests] in the synagogue [and lodged them there].

C. R. Immi instructed the scribes, "If someone comes to you with some slight contact with Torah learning, receive him, his asses, and his belongings."

D. R. Berekhiah went to the synagogue in Beisan. He saw someone rinsing his hands and feet in a fountain [in the courtyard of the synagogue]. He said to him, "It is forbidden to you [to do this]."

E. The next day the man saw [Berekhiah] washing his hands and feet in the fountain.

F.   He said to him, "Rabbi, is it permitted to you and forbidden to me?"

G.   He said to him, "Yes."

H.   He said to him, "Why?"

I.   He said to him, "Because this is what R. Joshua b. Levi said: 'Synagogues and schoolhouses belong to sages and their disciples.'"

Not all acts of piety, we see, are equal, and the one that takes precedence over all others (just as was alleged at Mishnah-tractate Peah 1:1) is study of the Torah. But the point now is a much more concrete one, and that is, through study of the Torah, sages and their disciples gain possession, as a matter of fact, over communal real estate, which they may utilize in any way they wish; and that is a quite concrete claim indeed, as the same story alleges.

No wonder, then, that people in general are expected to contribute their scarce resources for the support of sages and their disciples. Moreover, society at large was obligated to support sages, and the sages' claim upon others was enforceable by Heaven. Those who gave sages' disciples money so that they would not have to work would get it back from Heaven, and those who did not would lose what they had:

Y. Sotah 7:4.IV.

F.   R. Aha in the name of R. Tanhum b. R. Hiyya: "If one has learned, taught, kept, and carried out [the Torah], and has ample means in his possession to strengthen the Torah and has not done so, lo, such a one still is in the category of those who are cursed." [The meaning of "strengthen" here is to support the masters of the Torah.]

G.   R. Jeremiah in the name of R. Hiyya bar Ba, "[If] one did not learn, teach, keep, and carry out [the teachings of the Torah], and did not have ample means to strengthen [the masters of the Torah] [but nonetheless did strengthen them], lo, such a one falls into the category of those who are blessed."

H.   And R. Hannah, R. Jeremiah in the name of R. Hiyya: "The Holy One, blessed be he, is going to prepare a protection for those who carry out religious duties [of support for masters of Torah] through the protection afforded to the masters of Torah [themselves].

I.   "What is the Scriptural basis for that statement? 'For the protection of wisdom is like the protection of money'" (Qoh. 7:12).

J.   "And it says, '[The Torah] is a tree of life to those who grasp it; those who hold it fast are called happy'" (Prov. 3:18).

Such contributions form the counterpart to taxes, that is, scarce resources taken away from the owner by force for the purposes of the public good, that is, the ultimate meeting point of economics and politics, the explicit formation of distributive, as against market, economics. Then what is distributed and to whom and by what force forms the centerpiece of the systemic political economy, and the answer is perfectly simple: all sorts of valued things are taken away from people and handed over for the support of sages.

The disenlandisement of economics, the transvaluation of value so that Torah replaced land as the supreme measure of value and also, as a matter of fact, of social worth — these form (an) economics. It is, moreover, one that is fully the counterpart of the philosophical economics based upon real estate as true value that Aristotle and the framers of the Mishnah constructed, each party for its own systemic purpose. If we have not reviewed the components of the economics of the Torah — the theory of means of production and who controls the operative unit of production of value, the consideration of whether we deal with a market- or a distributive economics, the reason is that we have not had to. It is perfectly obvious that the sage controlled the means of production and fully mastered the power to govern them; the sage distributed valued resources — supernatural or material, as the case required — and the conception of a market was as alien to that economics as it was to the priestly economics revised and replicated by the Mishnah's system. Enough has been said, therefore, to establish beyond reasonable doubt the claim that in the Torah we deal with the system's counterpart category, its economics.

And yet that very fact calls into question my insistence that what we have is not (merely) another economics, with a different value, but a counterpart economics. For I claim that what we have is a systemic counterpart, not the same thing in another form: an anti-economics and the transvaluation of value, not merely the redefinition of what is to be valued. Obviously, I have reservations that have led me to insist that the systemic economics forms a counterpart to, but not a parallel and a mere replication of, another economics. A shift from valuing land to valuing liquid capital, or from valuing beads to valuing conches, for that matter, would not require the invention of the category, counterpart-economics, or the rather protracted argument offered earlier concerning the movement from the subject to the predicate of the operative language of definition. Why, then, my rather odd claim that we have an economics that is transvalued, not merely redefined?

It is because economics deals with scarce resources, and the disenlandisement of economics in the successor-Judaism has turned upon its head the very focus of economics: scarcity and the rational confrontation with scarcity. To land rigid limits are set by nature, to the Holy Land, still more narrow ones apply. But to knowledge of the Torah no limits pertain. So we find ourselves dealing with an economics that concern not the rational utilization of scarce resources, but the very opposite: the rational utilization of what can and ought to be the opposite of scarce. In identifying knowledge and teaching of the Torah as the ultimate value, the successor-system has not simply constructed a new economics in place of an old one, finding of value something other than had earlier been valued; it has redefined economics altogether. It has done so, as a matter of fact, in a manner that is entirely familiar, by setting forth in place of an economics of scarcity an economics of abundant productivity.

Disenlandising value thus transvalues value by insisting upon its (potential) increase as the definition of what is rational economic action. The task is not preservation of power over land but increase of power over the Torah, because one can only preserve land, but one can increase one's knowledge of the Torah. So, to revert to the theoretical point that in context seemed so excessive, the economics of the initial system concerns the rational disposition of the scarce resource comprised by particular real property; the rational increase of the potentially-abundant resource comprised by Torah-learning is — serves and functions as — the economics of the successor-system.

v. FROM THE CASE TO THE GENERALIZATION

Let us now broaden the framework of discussion, explaining what happened after the Mishnah in more general terms. What we shall see is that the case of economics represents in a small way a much broader process of systemic transformation that was underway, specifically, the re-formulation of a philosophical law code into a theological formulation. The entire theory of the social order, of which the Mishnah's treatment of economics forms one important component, was recast, as modes of thought moved from the philosophical and generalizing to the theological and exegetical.

To gain access to the theory of the social order that a religious system wishes to set forth, we turn to its canon, since the canon recapitulates the system, not the system, the canon. In the case of the description of successive Judaic systems — theories of the social order made up of a world view, a way of life, an a theory of the social entity, "Israel" — we have therefore first of all to gain perspective upon the canon of the Judaism that emerged from ancient times and governed to our own day. When we have grasped the stages in the unfolding of the canonical writings of that single Judaism, we shall find it possible also to characterize the Judaic systems to which each subset among the group of documents attests. That canon, called "the Torah," in two parts, written and oral, consisted of the Hebrew Scriptures of ancient Israel ("the Old Testament"), called in this Judaism "the written Torah," and a set of writings later on accorded the status of Torah as well and assigned origin at Sinai through a process of oral formulation and oral transmission, hence, "the oral Torah."

As we have seen, the first of those writings that came to comprise the oral Torah, the the single most important one, was the Mishnah, ca. 200. That document carried in its wake two sustained amplifications and extensions called talmuds, the one produced in the Land of Israel, hence the Talmud of the Land of Israel, ca. 400, the other in Babylonia, in the Iranian Empire, hence the Talmud of Babylonia, ca. 600.

The other important part of the Torah, the written part, served analogously to define a framework for (formally) continuous discourse and so received a variety of sustained amplifications, called Midrash-compilations. These form three sets, corresponding to the Mishnah, the Talmud of the Land of Israel, and the Talmud of Babylonia. In this paper I concentrate on the first two, that is, the Judaism adumbrated by the Mishnah and its Midrash-compilations, which I classify as philosophical, and the Judaism attested by the Yerushalmi and its Midrash-compilations, which I characterize as religion. In future work I shall show that the third set adumbrates a transformation from a religious to a quintessentially theological system, terms to be explained in due course.

1. THE MISHNAH'S COUNTERPARTS IN MIDRASH-COMPILATIONS: The first, within the orbit of the Mishnah, ca. 200-300, addressed the books of Exodus, Leviticus, Numbers, and Deuteronomy, in Mekhilta Attributed to R. Ishmael for Exodus, Sifra, for Leviticus, one Sifré to Numbers, another Sifré, to Deuteronomy.

2. THE YERUSHALMI'S COUNTERPARTS IN MIDRASH-COMPILATIONS: The second, ca. 400-500, associated with the first of the two Talmuds. took up the books of Genesis and Leviticus, in Genesis Rabbah and Leviticus Rabbah, and the latter begat Pesiqta deRab Kahana in its model.

3. THE BAVLI'S COUNTERPARTS IN MIDRASH-COMPILATIONS: The third, ca. 500-600, identified with the second Talmud, addressed a lectionary cycle of the synagogue, dealing with the books of Lamentations (read on the ninth of Ab), Esther (read on Purim), Ruth (read on Pentecost), and Song of Songs (read on Passover), in Lamentations Rabbah, Esther Rabbah I (the first two chapters only), Ruth Rabbah, and Song of Songs Rabbah.

The first of the three groups presents marks of transition and mediation from one system to the next.[12] The second, Genesis Rabbah and Leviticus Rabbah, joined by Pesiqta deRab Kahana, with the Talmud of the Land of Israel, attest to that system that I classify as religious. The third, the final Rabbah-compilations, together with the Talmud of Babylonia, point to the one I classify as theological, and in a moment I shall define the indicative traits of each classification.

Now, as is clear, the documentary evidence set forth a system of a very particular kind: one that laid out the components of the social order and explained how they formed a cogent whole. From beginning to end, the Judaic systems attested by the successive parts of the canon defined as their problem the construction of a social world. The categorical structure of each, in succession, framed intelligible

---

[12] That is the thesis of my *The Canonical History of Ideas. The Place of the So-called Tannaite Midrashim, Mekhilta Attributed to R. Ishmael, Sifra, Sifré to Numbers, and Sifré to Deuteronomy.* Atlanta, 1990: Scholars Press for Brown Judaic Studies.

thought by appeal to the issues of the world framed, first of all, by a particular ethnos, the social entity (the most neutral language I can find), which was called (an) "Israel." Every Judaic system, moreover, would take as its task the definition of the shared life of (an) Israel: its way of life or (broadly speaking) ethics, its world view or ethos. So each set forth the account of the social entity or the "Israel" that realized in its shared and corporate being the ethics (again, broadly construed),and explained that ethos by appeal to the ethos. As a matter of definition, it must follow, a Judaic system is a system that derives its generative categories from the (theoretical) requirements of framing a social order: who are "we," what do we do together, and why are we the corporate body that we are, thus, ethnos, ethics, ethos. And that brings us back to the first of the great Judaic systems that in the end formed Judaism, the system to which the authorship of the Mishnah refer in framing their writing.

The Mishnah, set forth in the form of a law code a highly philosophical account of the world ("world view"), a pattern for everyday and material activities and relationships ("way of life"), and a definition of the social entity ("nation," "people," "us" as against "outsiders," "Israel") that realized that way of life and explained it by appeal to that world view. Then the successor-documents, closed roughly two centuries later, addressed the Mishnah's system and recast its categories into a connected, but also quite revised, one.

Why call them "successors"? Because, in form, the writings of the late fourth and fifth centuries were organized and presented as commentaries on a received text, the Mishnah for the Talmud, Scripture for the Midrash-compilations. So the later authorships insisted, in their own behalf, that they (merely) explained and amplified the received Torah. Whn these documents attached themselves to the Mishnah, on the one side, and the Hebrew Scriptures, on the other, they gave literary form to the theory that the one stood for the oral, the other, the written, revelation, or Torah, that God gave to Moses at Mount Sinai.

Specifically, the Talmud of the Land of Israel, formed around thirty-nine of the Mishnah's sixty-two tractates, and Genesis Rabbah and Leviticus Rabbah (joined by Pesiqta deRab Kahana), addressed the first and third books of Moses, respectively, along with some other documents. The very act of choosing among the Mishnah's tractates only some and ignoring others, of course, represents an act of taste and judgment — hence system-building through tacit statement made by silence. But, as a matter of fact, much of the Talmud as well as of the principal Midrash-compilations do amplify and augment the base-documents to which they are attached.[13] In choosing some passages and neglecting others, and, more to the point, in working out their own questions and their own answers, in addition to those of the Mishnah, the authorships[14] attest to a system that did more than merely extend and recast the categorical structure of the system for which the Mishnah stands. They took over the way of life, world view, and social entity, defined in the Mishnah's system. And while they rather systematically amplified details, framed a program of exegesis around the requirements of clerks engaged in enforcing the rules of the Mishnah, they built their own system.

VI. The Mishnah: Judaism as a Philosophy in the First and Second Centuries

The Mishnah set forth a Judaism that is to be classified as philosophical — both in method and also in message. The Judaism of the Mishnah portrayed an economics in the model of Aristotle's, and a politics closely akin to his. An economics in this context must likewise present a theory of the rational disposition of scarce resources that (other) philosophers of the same age will have recognized as familiar, therefore philosophical. A politics along these same lines must exhibit the traits of a philosophical politics as other philosophers of the age will have defined philosphical politics. Since the Mishnah reached closure in ca. 200, my definition of philosophy and what may be characterized as philosophical derives from that same age, the Greco-Roman one, and as a matter of fact, within the vast and varied Greco-Roman philosophical tradition, a specific figure emerges as paradigmatic.

---

[13] My estimate for the Talmud of the Land of Israel, in the tractates I probed, is that, in volume, as much as 90% of the Talmud serves to amplify passages of the Mishnah, and not much more than 10% contains intellectual initiatives that are fundamentally fresh and unrelated to anything in the Mishnah-passage under discussion, see my *Talmud of the Land of Israel. XXXV. Introduction. Taxonomy* (Chicago, 1983: The University of Chicago Press). Then my *Judaism in Society. The Evidence of the Yerushalmi. Toward the Natural History of a Religion* (Chicago, 1983) aims to show that even the passages that (merely) clarify words or phrases of the Mishnah in fact set forth a considerable, autonomous program of their own, cf. especially pp. 73-112. But what is clearly distinct from the Mishnah is set forth on pp. 113-254.

[14] This term is meant to take account of the collective and social character of much of the literary enterprise. I have already underlined the anonymous character of the canonical evidence. Not a single authoritative book of Judaism in late antiquity bears the name of an identified author, and the literary traits of not a single piece of writing may securely be imputed to a private person. The means for gaining acceptance was anonymity, and the medium of authority lay in recapitulating collective conventions of rhetoric and logic, not to mention proposition. To speak of "authors" in this context is confusing, and hence the resort to the word at hand.

Aristotle for the present purpose defines the model of philosophical method. As to a philosophical proposition of considerable weight, I appeal to an important proposition of Middle Platonism, coming to full expression to be sure only in the writings of Plotinus's neo-Platonism two generations after the closure of the Mishnah. If I can show that the method of the Mishnah corresponds to that of Aristotle, and a fundamental message of the Mishnah restates within the appropriate idiom a proposition of Middle Platonism, I may fairly characterize the Mishnah's system as philosophical in context, that is, as a system that other philosophers can (with proper education) have recognized as philosophical. As to economics and politics, Aristotle likewise serves to set forth the standard for defining an economics that is philosophical and a philosophical politics as well. The Mishnah was philosophical both in its method, which is Aristotelian, and in its message, which is the one of Middle Platonism, and fully realized later on in Plotinus.[15]

---

[15] It would require more space than I have to spell out the details of the philosophical character of the Judaism of the Mishnah. I have published a variety of books to substantiate the statements of this section, including the following:

FOR PHILOSOPHY: The operative proposition in these monographs and books is that the Mishnah's the method is Aristotelian, the proposition, Middle or Neo-Platonic:

The Philosophical Mishnah. Volume I. *The Initial Probe.* Atlanta, 1989: Scholars Press for Brown Judaic Studies.

The Philosophical Mishnah. Volume II. *The Tractates' Agenda. From Abodah Zarah to Moed Qatan.* Atlanta, 1989: Scholars Press for Brown Judaic Studies.

The Philosophical Mishnah. Volume III. *The Tractates' Agenda. From Nazir to Zebahim.* Atlanta, 1989: Scholars Press for Brown Judaic Studies.

The Philosophical Mishnah. Volume IV. *The Repertoire.* Atlanta, 1989: Scholars Press for Brown Judaic Studies.

Judaism as Philosophy. The Method and Message of the Mishnah. Columbia, 1991: University of South Carolina Press.

FOR ECONOMICS: The operative proposition here is that the Mishnah presents an Aristotelian economics, which bears an important part of its systemic message. The economics is distributive, just as is Aristotle's, and the systemic message is congruent, in its context, to the systemic place of economics in Aristotle's larger system.

The Economics of the Mishnah (Chicago, 1989: THe University of Chicago Press).

FOR POLITICS: The operative thesis here is that the politics of the Mishnah and the politics of Aristotle bear important points of correspondence. But there is an important difference, which is that the political actor of Aristotle's politics is the same as his principal in economics, specifically, the householder, while in the Mishnah, the principal economic actor, the householder, in no way forms a political category at all, and even in language, the word for householder never appears in the political tractates of the Mishnah, e.g., Sanhedrin-Makkot. In context I explain the systemic difference that accounts for the disjuncture between the Mishnah's economics and its politics, in the comparison with Aristotle's. This is spelled out in the following study.

Rabbinic Political Theory. Religion and Politics in the Mishnah (Chicago, 1991: The University of Chicago Press).

VII.   THE TALMUD OF THE LAND OF ISRAEL, GENESIS RABBAH, AND LEVITICUS RABBAH: FROM JUDAISM AS A PHILOSOPHY TO JUDAISM AS A RELIGION IN THE FOURTH AND FIFTH CENTURIES

We turn to the modes of thought of the successor-writings and ask principally about how methodologically the later documents compare with the rhetorical and logical modes of thought that, in the Mishnah, are to be classified as philosophical. What we see is that the literary evidence is consistent for both the Yerushalmi and the pertinent Midrash-compilations in pointing toward rhetoric and logic of an other-than-philosophical character. So as to modes of thought and argument expressed in rhetoric and logic (and, as a matter of fact, proposition as well) a philosophical system is set forth by the Mishnah and faithfully preserved but not replicated in the philosophical manner by the successor-documents. These writers make connections and draw conclusions and portray the result in a way vastly different from the way of the Mishnah. That sets the stage for the movement from worldview, expressed through philosophy, to way of life and definition of the social entity, that is, for the Mishnah, economics and politics, respectively.

Two questions clarify the issue of continuity in category-formation. What we want to know is simple: have the successor-authorships revised or redefined the received categories? Do we find in the Yerushalmi and its companions a considerable extension and reformation of the philosophical economics and politics set forth by the Mishnah? In fact the philosophers whose ideas are presented by the Mishnah will have been surprised and also informed by what they found in the Yerushalmi's re-presentation of the Mishnah. A continuing, philosophical reading of an essentially philosophical economics and politics was not underway. The Yerushalmi's reading of the Mishnah served purposes other than those of clarification, extension, and above all, practical application. That proves that the Yerushalmi and related writings have undertaken a considerable labor of category-reformation. Not philosophers but something else, they have given to the Mishnah a decent burial and gone on to other matters.

The criteria for knowing how the Mishnah's system has been received then are clear. On what problems do the successor-authorships concentrate — theoretical or exegetical? And whence do they derive their continuing intellectual program — the tasks of reconsideration and criticism, or the work of practical application? Exemplary discourses, time and again show a range of questions deriving from not philosophers and theorists but clerks and judges: people who have to know one thing from something else in material reality.

In the case of economics we find rules governing cases, not definitions of abstractions. In the case of politics we come up with not the extension and elaboration of the received structure but the portrayal of a quite different one. When speaking of the Mishnah, the successor-writers paraphrase and clarify its sentences. When moving beyond the limits of the Mishnah, they make matters their own and set forth, side by side with the Mishnah and its message, a quite different account of economics and politics.

In other-than-exegetical passages of the Yerushalmi scarce resources, so far as these are of a material order of being, e.g., wealth defined as the Mishnah and Aristotle did, are systemically neutral. A definition of scarce resources emerges that explicitly involves a symbolic transformation, with the material definition of scarce resources set into contradiction with an other-than-material one. So we find side by side clarification of the details of the received category and adumbration of a symbolic revision and hence a categorical transformation in the successor-writings. The representation of the political structure of the Mishnah undergoes clarification, but alongside, a quite separate and very different structure also is portrayed. The received structure presents three political classes, ordered in a hierarchy; the successor-structure, a single political class, corresponding on earth to a counterpart in Heaven. Here too a symbolic transaction has taken place, in which one set of symbols is replicated but also reversed, and a second set of symbols given instead.

This I may express in a simple way: a structure comprising a hierarchical composition of foci of power gives way to a structure made centered upon a single focus of power. That single focus, moreover, now draws boundaries between legitimate and illegitimate violence, boundaries not conceived in the initial system. So in all three components of the account of the social order — politics, economics, and philosophy — the philosophical system gives way to one of another classification. The worldview comes to expression in modes of thought and expression — the logic of making connections and drawn conclusions — that are different from the philosophical ones of the Mishnah. The way of life appeals to value expressed in other symbols than those of economics in the philosophical mode. The theory of the social entity comes to concrete expression in sanctions legitimately administered by a single class of persons (institution), rather than by a proportionate and balanced set of classes of persons in hierarchical order, and, moreover, that same theory recognizes and defines both legitimate and also illegitimate violence, something beyond the ken of the initial system. So, it is clear, another system is adumbrated and attested in the successor-writings. And the classification of that other system is not within philosophy but within religion.[16]

---

[16] Works of mine in which these matters are substantiated include the following:

> *The Talmud of the Land of Israel. A Preliminary Translation and Explanation.* Chicago: The University of Chicago Press: 1983. XXXV. *Introduction. Taxonomy.*
>
> *The Integrity of Leviticus Rabbah. The Problem of the Autonomy of a Rabbinic Document.* Chico, 1985: Scholars Press for Brown Judaic Studies.
>
> *Comparative Midrash: The Plan and Program of Genesis Rabbah and Leviticus Rabbah.* Atlanta, 1986: Scholars Press for Brown Judaic Studies.
>
> *From Tradition to Imitation. The Plan and Program of Pesiqta deRab Kahana and Pesiqta Rabbati.* Atlanta, 1987: Scholars Press for Brown Judaic Studies. [With a fresh translation of Pesiqta Rabbati *Pisqaot* 1-5, 15.]

VIII. COUNTERPART CATEGORIES

The social order by definition attends to the way of life, world view, and definition of the social entity, that a system puts forth. But by "way of life" or "world view" one system need not mean exactly the same category of data that another system adopts for itself, and, it goes without saying, we cannot claim functional equivalency, for obvious reasons as irrelevant as the judgment of relativism. A system selects its data to expose its systemic categories; defines its categories in accord with the systemic statement that it wishes to set forth; identifies the urgent question to which the systemic message compellingly responds. To understand a system, we begin with the whole and work our way inward toward the parts; the formation of categories then is governed by the system's requirements: the rationality of the whole dictates the structure of the categorical parts, and the structure of the parts then governs the selection of what fits into those categories.[17]

The philosophical character of the initial system's world-view, way of life, and theory of the social entity, that is, its philosophy, economics, and politics. We have then to wonder how these same categories fared in the successor-system's documentary evidence. As a matter of simple fact, while sharing the goal of presenting a theory of the social order, as to their categorical formations and

---

Judaism in Society: The Evidence of the Yerushalmi. Toward the Natural History of a Religion. Chicago, 1983: The University of Chicago Press. *Choice*, "Outstanding Academic Book List, 1984-1985."

Judaism and Scripture: The Evidence of Leviticus Rabbah. Chicago, 1986: The University of Chicago Press. [Fresh translation of Margulies' text and systematic analysis of problems of composition and redaction.] Jewish Book Club Selection, 1986.

The Foundations of Judaism. Method, Teleology, Doctrine. Philadelphia, 1983-5: Fortress Press. I-III. I. *Midrash in Context. Exegesis in Formative Judaism.* Second printing: Atlanta, 1988: Scholars Press for Brown Judaic Studies.

The Foundations of Judaism. Method, Teleology, Doctrine. Philadelphia, 1983-5: Fortress Press. I-III. II. *Messiah in Context. Israel's History and Destiny in Formative Judaism.* Second printing: Lanham, 1988: University Press of America. Studies in Judaism series.

The Foundations of Judaism. Method, Teleology, Doctrine. Philadelphia, 1983-5: Fortress Press. I-III. III. *Torah: From Scroll to Symbol in Formative Judaism.* Second printing: Atlanta, 1988: Scholars Press for Brown Judaic Studies.

Judaism in the Matrix of Christianity. Philadelphia, 1986: Fortress Press. British edition, Edinburgh, 1988, T. & T. Collins.

Judaism and Christianity in the Age of Constantine. Issues of the Initial Confrontation. Chicago, 1987: University of Chicago Press.

[17] None of these points intersects with either relativism or functionalism; the issues are wholly other. At stake in systemic description, analysis, and interpretation, after all, ultimately is the comparative study of rationalities. But this conclusion carries us far beyond the argument of this part of the book — and indeed of the book as a whole.

structures, the initial, philosophical Judaic system and the successor system differ in a fundamental way. Stated very simply, the successor-system held up a mirror to the received categories and so redefined matters that everything was reversed, left becoming right, down becoming up, power turned into weakness, things of real value transformed into intangibles. A free-standing document, the Mishnah, reverently received for merely exegetical purposes by the authorship of the first Talmud, the Talmud of the Land of Israel, served to precipitate the transvaluation of all of the values of that document's initial statement.

The categorical transformation that was underway, signaling the movement from philosophy to religion, comes to the surface when we ask a simple question: precisely what do the authorships of the successor-documents speaking not about the Mishnah but on their own account, mean by economics, politics, and philosophy? That is to say, to what kinds of data do they refer when they speak of scarce resources and legitimate violence, and exactly how — as to the received philosophical method — do they define correct modes of thought and expression, logic and rhetoric, and even the topical program worthy of sustained inquiry? The questions arise because in consequence of the results of Part I we now know that the received categories were in no way subjected to redefinition.

The components of the initial formation of categories were examined thoughtfully and carefully, paraphrased and augmented and clarified. But the received categories were not continued, not expanded, not renewed. Preserved merely intact, as they had been handed on, the received categories hardly serve to encompass all of the points of emphasis and sustained development that characterize the successor-documents — or, as a matter of fact, any of them. On the contrary, when the framers of the Yerushalmi, for one example, moved out from the exegesis of Mishnah-passages, they also left behind the topics of paramount interest in the Mishnah and developed other categories altogether.[18] In these other categories, the framers of the successor- system defined theiir own counterparts. These counterpart-categories, moreover, redefined matters, following the main outlines of the structure of the social order manifest in the initial system. The counterpart-categories set forth an account of the social order just as did the ones of the Mishnah's framers. But they defined the social order in very different terms altogether. In that redefinition we discern the transformation of the received system, and the traits of the new one fall into the classification of not philosophy but religion.

For what the successor-thinkers did was not continue and expand the categorical repertoire but set forth a categorically-fresh vision of the social order — a way of life, world view, and definition of the social entity — within appropriate

---

[18] That fact is demonstrated in my *Talmud of the Land of Israel. A Preliminary Translation and Explanation. 35. Introduction. Taxonomy* (Chicago, 1983: The University of Chicago Press). There I show that when Mishnah-exegesis is concluded, a quite separate agendum takes centerstage, the emphases of which find no counterpart in the Mishnah. That seems to me to justify the consideration of counterpart-categories, such as I introduce here.

counterpart-categories. And what is decisive is that these served as did the initial categories within the generative categorical structure definitive for all Judaic systems. So there was a category corresponding to the generative component of worldview, but it was not philosophical; another corresponding to the required component setting forth a way of life, but in the conventional and accepted definition of economics it was not an economics; and, finally, a category to define the social entity, "Israel," that any Judaic system must explain, but in the accepted sense of a politics it was not politics.

Addressing the issues ordinarily treated by the method and message of philosophy, economics, or politics, the counterpart categories nonetheless supplied for the social order a worldview, way of life, and definition of the social entity. And, as a matter of fact, the Judaism that emerged from late antiquity adopted as its categorical structure the counterpart categories we are going to define and explore and recast the Mishnah within them. The formation of Judaism took place through the transformation of Judaism from an account of the social order that was essentially philosophical to one that was fundamentally religious was accomplished by the system-builders whose conceptions came to literary expression in the Talmud of the Land of Israel, Genesis Rabbah, Leviticus Rabbah, and Pesiqta deRab Kahana.

IX. The Foundations of Systemic Reformation

Exactly how was this categorical reformation accomplished? To state matters first in the most abstract way, it was done by reversing the flow of language, specifically taking the predicate of a sentence and moving it to the position of the subject, that is, commencing not from subject but from predicate. Since we have taken the case of the Mishnah's philosophical economics and how it was reworked into the Talmud's theological redefinition of the very sense of "scarce resources" as part of a revision of the systemic rationality, we turn directly the case of economics.

From "[1] economics is [2] the rational disposition of scarce resources," the category of way of life was rephrased into, "[2] the rational disposition of scarce resources is [1] (their, in context, systemic) economics." The reverse reading therefore yields the counterpart category, defined by this sentence: *"a (any) theory of rational action with regard to scarcity...,* then: is (for the system at hand) its economics." The same procedure serves, too — *mutatis mutandis* — for discerning systems' politics and science or learning or philosophy. This transvaluation of values, through not merely the re-formation but the utter transformation of categories, set forth an essentially fresh answer to a fundamentally new urgent question.

Let me make more concrete this matter of the reverse-definition of economics, placing the predicate as the subject. The Judaism of the Mishnah presents a theory of economics. The Mishnaic system addresses the definition of rational action with regard both to the allocation of scarce resources, on the one side, and to the increase and disposition of wealth, on the other. It was a specifically philosophical economics because, in structure and in doctrine, it conformed with that of Aristotle. Now in the successor-system, can we identify what is meant by scarce resources and can we define the rationality required for the disposition, in the systemic context at hand, of such resources? When we say, "a (or any) theory of rational action with regard to scarcity *is* (an) economics," we mean, any account of what is deemed scarce and therefore to require rational action as to allocation, increase, and disposition, functions to define the category that is the counterpart, in the philosophical system of the Mishnah, to economics. It answers the same question, but it utterly recasts the terms of the question.

In the Mishnah, as in other philosophical systems, the way of life finds definition in economics, the worldview in philosophy (both as to method and as to proposition), and the account of the social entity in a politics. But that is simply not the case in the successor-documents, and what serves as way of life, world view, and definition of the social entity in no way conforms to what had defined these same categories. That fact is hardly surprising, for there are quite elaborate and well-composed systems of the social order, fully spelling out the way of life, worldview, and definition of the social entity, in which — to concentrate on the case at hand — in the received and accepted sense of economics as a theory of the rational disposition of scarce resources, we simply have no economics at all. Augustine's design and account of the City of God, for example, introduces its own categories in response to the same requirements of definition and articulation of the social order. The history of salvation, deriving from the Christian's great creation, the Bible, for instance, forms the critical center, and philosophy, while profoundly influential on his thought, hardly generates the primary categorical structures. And the first twelve hundred years of Christian system-builders found it entirely possible to set forth the Christian social order's way of life without defining an economics for themselves.[19]

It follows that for failing to present an economics, accounts of the social order do not define a way of life. To the contrary, the simple fact is that, when they do define a way of life in terms of scarce resources, what they mean is not what we ordinarily mean by economics. True, such systems omit all reference to, or treat as systemically inert and inconsequence, such topics as wealth and money, production and distribution, work and wage, ownership and conduct of economic entities.

---

[19] As with the sages of Judaism, so with the first important Christian economics, it was the encounter with Aristotle (and not with Scripture) that made urgent the formation of a Christianity encompassing, for the way of life of its social order, elaborate attention to the expression of theological truth in economics and rules for the Christian management and preservation of scarce resources, defined in the conventional sense of philosophical economics.

The entire repertoire of subjects comprising conomic action in all its forms simply are lacking. But the issues of tangible wealth and materials goods do emerge — must emerge, and, it follows, the systems will have to identify for themselves something other than real wealth (real estate, capital, for instance) when they design those societies that express the respective systems' messages: urgent question, self-evidently valid answer, integrating the whole and rendering the system cogent and coherent.

But how to deal with such accounts of the social order that lack an economics or a politics or a philosophy in the familiar senses of these categories? To answer that question of method in the analysis of category-formation, I have to discover and define what serves, in such a system, the task of economics in a philosophical system. To do so — as stated in abstract form just now — I propose the notion that, "[2] a (any) theory of rational action with regard to scarcity *is* [1] economics." Matters that hardly fall into the category of economic theory at all may yield points of congruency. As a matter of fact they may also validate those systemic comparisons and contrasts that permit us to trace the history of an on-going system from its philospohical to its religious formulation.

Let me now spell out why I find critical this two-directional reading — first, "*economics is* [or, encompasses] the theory of rational action with regard to scarcity," second, "a theory of rational action with regard to scarcity *is encompassed by economics.*" To state matters negatively, if one system presents a conventional economics and another does not, then I cannot compare the one to the other (beyond the observation that one has, the other does not have, an economics). But — on the positive side — if I can show how one body of coherent thought in one system addresses the same question that another body of equally coherent thought takes up in the other, then the comparability — at the point of not detail but of the main beams of structure — of the two systems becomes possible. The sole undemonstrated premise of argument is that any system must explain in its account of the social order what people are to think and do and how they are to define themselves as a social entity. But in the very language, social order, are embedded these three components: society and order in both intellect and practice. So at stake is the comparison of systems.

X. THE COMPARISON OF SYSTEMS, THE CONTRAST OF RATIONALITIES

In this context, by the comparison of systems, I mean the contrast of one rationality to another.[20] The comparison of rationalities then is made possible by

---

[20] I of course allude to the great conception of Max Weber in his studies of China, India, and ancient Israel. In asking why capitalism here, not there, he founded the comparative study of rationalities. Many present themselves as his successors, some with more reason than others, but, in the aggregate, I have not found a rich theoretical literature vastly to revise Weber's definition of issues concerning Judaism, China, and India. In this regard philosophy

the dual and reciprocal definition of [1] economics as the theory of rational action with regard to scarcity, and of [2] the theory of rational action with regard to scarcity as economics. The same is so, of course, for philosophy and politics.[21] When we understand the particular rationality of the economics of — to take the case at hand — the Judaism of the Mishnah, we find the way to translate into categories of rationality that we can grasp that Judaism's to us familiar category with the to us alien and odd rationality of the Yerushalmi's counterpart, which, as we shall see, covers matters we do not conceive to fall into the rubric of economics at all but that answered the same questions to which, for us and for the philosophical economics of the Mishnah, economics attends.

That is to say, when we see that a category for an alien system and its rationality constitutes *its* economics and therefore forms a counterpart to economics as we understand that subject within our rationality, we learn how in a critical component to translate system to system. We may then make the statement, "In that system, within their rationality, that category of activity forms a component of economic theory, while in our system, within our rationality, we do not think of that category of activity as a component of economic theory at all." And this we do without assuming a posture of relativism, for example claiming that their economics, and, with it, their rationality, is pretty much the same, or as at least as valid, as ours. Framing the relativist judgment in that way, we see that relativism is simply not relevant to what is at stake. That kind of interpretation of matters is not pertinent to my exercise in translation and comparison carried out through the definition and examination of counterpart-categories in this larger analysis of the formation of Judaisms, seen as statements of social systems. Quite to the contrary, at stake is not relativism but the comparative study of religions: how each composes for itself an account of the social world. And in the case of the movement of Judaism from philosophy to religion, a natural comparison is at hand: Augustine's and the rabbis' cities of God. For Augustine did his work in the same age as did the Judaic sages represented by the Talmud of the Land of Israel, Genesis Rabbah, and Leviticus Rabbah. But what they had in common is far more than shared existence in a time

---

has gone far beyond the limits of theory in social science. That is not to suggest important work on Weber's rationality is lacking. Mentioning the names of Anthony Giddens and Jeffrey Alexander suffices to underline that the tradition of Weber has gone forward in the theoretical realm.

[21] Would I extend the matter to, let us say, medicine, technology, city-planning, mathematics, the provision of a water-supply, a department of defense, or any of the other diverse components of the social order and its culture, whether intellectual or institutional? At this moment, I should have to decline an invitation to descend into such unbounded relativism, for then everything is the equivalent of something, and nothing is to be defined in itself. So for the moment I leave matters at the basic components of any and all social orders, as I have identified them.

of upheaval, the fall of Rome for Augustine, the conversion of Rome to Christianity for the Judaic sages. They shared, also, a single response: a profound reconsideration of the social order.

XI. THE COMPARISON OF RELIGIOUS THEORIES OF THE SOCIAL ORDER: [1] FROM A PHILOSOPHICAL TO RELIGIOUS JUDAISM

The Mishnah's God can scarcely compete with the God of the Yerushalmi and the Midrash-compilations.[22] For the God of the philosophers, the apex of the hierarchy of all being as the framers of the Mishnah have positioned God, has made the rules and is shown by them to form the foundation of order. All things reach up to one thing, one thing contains within itself many things: these twin-propositions of (philosophical) monotheism, which the philosophical system of Judaism to which the Mishnah attests demonstrates in theory and proposes to realize in the facts of the social order, define a God who in an orderly way governs all the palpable relationships of nature as of supernature — but who finds a place, who comes to puissant expression, in not a single one of them. The God of the philosophers assures, sustains, supports, nourishes, guarantees, governs. But the way that God responds to what we do is all according to the rule. That is, after all, what natural philosophy proposes to uncover and discern, and what more elevated task can God perform than the nomothetic one accomplished in the daily creation of the world.

But God in the successor-system gains what the philosophical God lacks, which is personality, active presence, pathos and empathy. The God of the religious system breaks the rules, accords an entitlement to this one, who has done some one remarkable deed, but not to that one, who has done nothing wrong and everything right. So a life in accord with the rules — even a life spent in the study of the Torah — in Heaven's view is outweighed by a single moment, a gesture that violates the norm, extending the outer limits of the rule, for instance, of virtue. If the God of the philosophers' Judaism makes the rules, the God of the religious Judaism breaks them. The systemic difference, of course, is readily extended outward from the personality of God: the philosophers' God thinks, the God of the religious responds, and we are in God's image, after God's likeness, not only because we through right thinking penetrate the principles of creation, but through right attitude replicate the heart of the Creator. Humanity on earth incarnates God on high, the Israelite family in particular, and, in consequence, earth and Heaven join — within.

What precipitated deep thought upon fundamental questions of social existence was a simple fact. From the time that Christianity attained the status of a licit religion, the Jews of Palestine witnessed the formation of circumstances that

---

[22] My initial comments on that matter are in *The Incarnation of God: The Character of Divinity in Formative Judaism* (Philadelphia, 1988: Fortress Press).

had formerly been simply unimaginable: another Israel, in the same place and time, competed with them in their terms, quoting their Scriptures, explaining who they were in their own categories but in very different terms from the ones that they used. We need not explain the profundities of religious doctrine by reducing them to functions and necessities of public policy. But it is, a matter of simple fact, that the Jews in the fourth century had witnessed a drastic decline in their power to exercise legitimate violence (which is to say, violence you can make stick), as well as in their command of the real estate of Palestine that they knew as the Holy Land and its wealth. The system's stress upon matters of intentionality and attitude, subject to the governance of even the most humble of individuals, even the most insignificant of nations, exactly corresponded to the political and social requirements of the Jews' condition in that time. The transformed Judaism made of necessity a theological virtue, and, by the way, the normative condition of the social order.

The sages who wrote the Talmud of the Land of Israel, Genesis Rabbah, Leviticus Rabbah, and Pesiqta deRab Kahana, did not stand alone in their profound reflection on how earth and Heaven intersect, the issue to which their system devoted itself, and how the here and the now forms a moment in history. As it happens, at the same time and, as a matter of fact, under similar circumstances of historical crisis, another system-builder was at work. When we appreciate the commonalities of the task facing each party and the dimensions that turn out to take the measure of the results of each, we realize how different people, speaking each to their own world, delivering each their own statement, turn out in the same time to answer the same question in what is, as a matter of fact, pretty much the same cosmic dimensions, and, it would turn out, with the same enduring results for the formation of Western civilization.[23]

XII. THE COMPARISON OF RELIGIOUS THEORIES OF THE SOCIAL ORDER: [2] THE TWO CITIES OF GOD OF LATE ANTIQUITY, AUGUSTINE'S THE RABBIS'

Augustine of Hippo's life, in North Africa and Italy, (354-430) coincided with the period in which, to the east, the sages of the Land of Israel produced their Talmud in amplification of the Mishnah as well as their Midrash-compilations in extension of Moses's books of Genesis and Leviticus. But he comes to mind, for comparison and contrast, not merely because of temporal coincidence, but rather because, like the sages of Judaism, he confronted the same this-worldly circumstance, one in which the old order was coming to an end — and was acknowledged to be closing. In 410 the Goths took Rome, refugees of Alaric's

---

[23] One need not exaggerate the influence of either St. Augustine or our sages of blessed memory to claim that the Christianity and the Judaism framed by each, respectively, defined norms and set the course for the two great religions of the West.

conquest fleeing to North Africa (as well, as a matter of fact, as to the Land of Israel/Palestine, as events even early in the story of Jerome in Jerusalem tell us[24]). At the very hour of his death, some decades later, Augustine's own city, Hippo lay besieged by the Vandals. So it was at what seemed the twilight of the ancient empire of Rome that Augustine composed his account of the theology of the social order known as the *City of God.* Within his remarkable *oeuvre,* it was that work that renders of special interest here the sages' contemporary and their counterpart as a system-builder.

Like the critical issue of political calamity facing sages in the aftermath of the triumph of Christianity and the failure of Julian's brief restoration of both paganism and (as to Jerusalem) Judaism, the question Augustine addressed presented a fundamental challenge to the foundations of the Christian order, coming as it did from Roman pagan aristocrats, taking refuge in North Africa.[25] What caused the fall of Rome, if not the breaches in its walls made by Christianity? The first three books of *The City of God* responded, in 413, and twenty-two books in all came to

---

[24] I refer to J. N. D. Kelly, *Jerome: His Life, Writings, and Controversies* (N.Y., 1975: Harper & Row).

[25] The bibliography for this chapter lists the books I have consulted. In no way claiming to know first hand and in a thorough way the scholarship on Augustine, even in the English language, I chose to rely mostly upon a single work, consulting others mostly for my own illumination. It is the up-to-date and, I think, universally respected account by Peter Brown,*Augustine of Hippo* (Berkeley and Los Angeles, 1967: University of California Press). The pertinent passage is on p. 302. All otherwise unidentified page references to follow are to this work. My modest generalizations about the intersection of the two systems on some points important to each rests, for Augustine, entirely on Brown. I found very helpful the outline of the work presented by John Neville Figgis, *The Political Aspects of S. Augustine's 'City of God'* (London, 1921: Longmans Green and Co.), pp. 1-31, and the characterization of Augustine's thought by Herbert A. Deane, *The Politican and Social Ideas of St. Augustine* (New York & London, 1963: Columbia University Press). In Deane's lucid account, anyone in search of specific doctrinal parallels between sages' system and that of Augustine will find ample evidence that there is none of consequence. As will become clear, what I find heuristically suggestive are structural and functional parallels, not points of doctrinal coincidence of any material importance. My sense is that the success of Brown's book overshadowed the important contribution of Gerald Bonner, *St. Augustine of Hippo. Life and Controversies* (London, 1963: SCM Press, Ltd.), a less dazzling, but more systematic and (it seems to me) useful presentation. A brief and clear account of the two cities is in Eugene Teselle, *Augustine the Theologian* (N.Y., 1970: Herder and Herder), pp. 268-278, who outlines the variety of approaches taken to the description and interpretation of the work: polemical, apologetic; philosophy or theology of history; analysis of political ideology; source of principles of political and moral theory; and of ecclesiastical policy; and the like. The achievement of F. Van der Meer, *Augustine the Bishop. Religion and Society at the Dawn of the Middle Ages* (New York, 1961: Harper & Row). Translated by Brian Battershaw and G. R. Lamp, is not to be missed: a fine example of the narrative-reading of religion by a historian of religion of one useful kind. Precisely what Augustine means by "the city of

a conclusion in 426: a gigantic work.[26] While *The City of God* (re)presents Christian faith "in the form of biblical history, from Genesis to Revelation,[27] just as sages present important components of their system in historical form of narrative, I see no important doctrinal points in common between the program of Israel's sages in the Land of Israel and that of the great Christian theologian and philosopher. Each party presented in an episodic way what can be represented as an orderly account of the social order,[28] each for the edification of its chosen audience; neither, I think, would have understood a line of the composition of the other, in writing or in concept. And that unbridgeable abyss makes all the more striking the simple fact that, from one side of the gap to the other, the distance was slight. For each party addressed questions entirely familiar, I think, to the other, and the gross and salient traits of the system of the one in some striking ways prove symmetrical to those of the other.[29]

God" is worked out by John O'Meara, *The Charter of Christendom: The Significance of the City of God* (New York, 1961: The Macmillan Co.), who says (p. 43) that "the city of God exists already in heaven and, apart from certain pilgrim men who are on their way to it while they are on this earth, in heaven only." When I speak of sages' having extended the boundaries of the social system from earth to Heaven, I mean to suggest something roughly parallel, in that, when women and men on earth conform to the Torah, they find themselves in the image and after the likeness of Heaven. The sense of the concept "history," then, is "the story of two cities," so Hardy, pp. 267ff. (cf. Edward R. Hardy, Jr., "The City of God," in Roy W. Battenhouse, *A Companion to the Study of St. Augustine* (New York, 1955: Oxford University Press), pp. 257-286. I find the story of Israel among the nations as the equivalent, unifying and integrating conception of history in the doctrine(s) of history in the Yerushalmi and Leviticus Rabbah; this then means Israel forms the counterpart to the city of God, and I think that is the beginning of all systemic comparison in this context (and, I should suspect, in all others).

[26] p. 303.

[27] John H. S. Burleigh, *The City of God. A Study of St. Augustine's Philosophy. Croall Lectures, 1944* (London, 1949: Nisbet & Co. Ltd.), p. 153.

[28] But the two parties have in common the simple fact that the representation of their respective systems is the accomplishment of others later on, indeed, in the case of sages, much later on indeed. Note the judgment of Deane, Augustine "was not a system-builder...Virtually everything that Augustine wrote...was an occasional piece" (Herbert A.Deane, *The Political and Social Ideas of St. Augustine* (New York & London, 1963: Columbia University Press, p. viii). Sages' documents, it is quite obvious, do not utilize the categories for the description of the social order that I have imposed: ethos, ethics, ethnos; worldview, way of life, doctrine of the social entity. But systemic description in its nature imputes and of necessity imposes system, and that is so, whether the system is deemed social or theological in its fundamental character. I have no difficulty in defending the proposition that sages' system was in its very essence a system of society, that is, of the holy people, Israel, and the union of social and theological thought in Augustine is signalled by the very metaphors he selected for his work, in his appeal to "the city."

[29] My choice of Augustine is by no means capricious, based merely on the temporal coincidence of our sages of blessed memory in the Yerushalmi and related writings and

The relationship of the opposing cities of God and the devil, embodied in the pilgrim Church and the empirical state, presents the chief systematic problem of *The City of God*.[30] Augustine covered, in five books, "those who worshipped the gods for felicity on earth;" in five, "those who worshipped them for eternal felicity;" and twelve, the theme of the origin of "two cities, one of God, the other of the world," "their unfolding course in the part," "their ultimate destinies."[31] True, sages reconsidered the prior disinterest in history, but they did not then produce a continuous account of everything that had every happened, and Augustine did. Nor do the two literary monuments, Augustine's and sages', bear anything in common as to form, style, sources, mode of argument, selection of audience, literary convention of any kind. Then why treat the system of sages and the systematic statement of Augustine as so connected as to warrant comparison? For the obvious reason that the authorship of Israel and the Christian author not only responded to the same circumstance but also framed the question deemed posed by that common circumstance in the same terms: a recasting, in historical terms, of the whole of the social order, a rethinking, in the image of Augustine, of God's city.

What then was the value of the polis, which I have rendered in this article as "the social order," and exactly who lived in the city of the earth? It was "any group of people tainted by the Fall," any that failed to regard "the 'earthly' values

---

Augustine. What I think more compelling is the fact that sages inherited a Middle Platonic doctrine concerning the unity of all being and reworked it in historical-narrative terms, therefore finding in (among other concepts) the notion of *zekhut* a medium for the unification of the generations, past and present. (I have spelled out the centrality of that notion in my article, "Zekhut," to appear in *Journal of the American Academy of Religion*.) Augustine, for his part, is everywhere described as a reworking the heritage of Platonism, drawing chiefly from Plotinus, so for instance Burleigh, p. 157. As a guess, therefore, I would venture that the principal shift in the large-scale modes of thought from the Mishnah through to the Yerushalmi along with Genesis Rabbah, Leviticus Rabbah, and Pesiqta deRab Kahana, was the movement away from Aristotelian modes of thought, such as characterized the Mishnah, to those of Middle Platonism. But not being a historian of philosophy in antiquity, I am able only to suggest that hypothesis as a subject for further inquiry. In any event one did not have to adopt the inheritance of Plato, in the formulation of Middle Platonism, Neo-Platonism, or Plotinus, to focus upon the social order as the centerpiece of philosophical, systematic thought and system-building. Aristotle (much less influential in this period, to be sure) provided an equally accessible model for anyone who might wish to rethink the foundations of the polis or of the social being of Israel, the holy people, in the Land of Israel, the holy land.

[30] So Teselle, p. 270.

[31] pp. 303-304. Cf.. also Burleigh, pp. 166ff., on Augustine's attitude toward "the concrete political structures of history."

they had created as transient and relative."[32] To this Augustine responds, "Away with all this arrogant bluffing: what, after all, are men but men!"[33] The rise of Rome is reduced, in Brown's words, "to a simple common denominator...the 'lust for domination.'" The Romans were moved by "an overweening love of praise: 'they were, therefore, "grasping for praise, open-handed with their money; honest in the pursuit of wealth, they wanted to hoard glory.""[34] But the true glory resides not in Rome but in the city of God: "the virtues the Romans had ascribed to their heroes would be realized only in the citizens of this other city; and it is only within the walls of the Heavenly Jerusalem that Cicero's noble definition of the essence of the Roman Republic could be achieved."[35] The Judaic sages — we now realize — assuredly concurred on whence comes glory, whence shame: the one from humility, the other, pride.

      The system of Augustine addresses the crisis of change with an account of history, and it is, therefore, in the same sense as is the system of the Judaic sages, a deeply historical one: "The whole course of human history...could be thought of as laden with meanings which might be seized, partially by the believer, in full by the seer."[36] So Brown: "In his *City of God*, Augustine was one of the first to sense and give monumental expression to a new form of intellectual excitement." God communicates through both words and events. Specifically, history proves the presence of a division between an earthly and a heavenly city.[37] Why do I find this historical interest pertinent to my picture of a Judaism's social order? Because, in Brown's words, "there is room, in Augustine's view of the past, for the

---

[32] p. 309.

[33] p. 309.

[34] p. 310.

[35] pp. 311-312.

[36] p. 317.

[37] p. 319. See Burleigh, pp. 185ff., "A philosophy of history." He cites the following: "St. Augustine's De Civitate Dei...may be regarded as the first attempt to frame a complete philosophy of history...It was...a singularly unsuccessful attempt; for it contained neither philosophy nor history, but merely theology and fiction." Whether or not so of Augustine, that statement seems to me an apt description of the form of history as invented in the pages of the Talmud of the Land of Israel. My presentation of sages' thought on history is in my *The Foundations of Judaism. Method, Teleology, Doctrine.* Philadelphia, 1983-5: Fortress Press. II. *Messiah in Context. Israel's History and Destiny in Formative Judaism.* Second printing: Lanham, 1988: University Press of America. Studies in Judaism series. This matter has not played a principal role in my exposition of the successor-system, because it seems to me ancillary and not categorically-definitive. Burleigh describes the dominant philosophy of the age, characteristic of Augustine as well, as anti-historical. But Augustine's "Platonic Biblicism in effect brings them [history and philosophy] into the closest relation. Biblical History is Platonic idealism in time." That statement seems to me to run parallel to the characterization of the rabbinic uses of history in the form of persons and events as exemplary and cyclical, rather than unique and linear.

consideration of whole societies...."[38] But the building block of society is relationship, and the whole of human history emerges out of the relationship of Cain and Abel, natural man after the fall, citizen of this world, against a man who built no city, "by hoping for something else...he waited upon the name of the Lord."[39] Brown says:

> Augustine treats the tension between Cain and Abel as universal, because he can explain it in terms applicable to all men. All human society...is based on a desire to share some good. Of such goods, the most deeply felt by human beings is the need for 'peace:' that is, for a resolution of tensions, for an ordered control of unbalanced appetites in themselves, and of discordant wills in society...the members of the [city of earth[, that is, fallen men, tend to regard their achievement of such peace in society as sufficient in itself...[40]

The city of Heaven is "the consecrated commonwealth of Israel," the city of earth, everybody else.[41] Brown's summary of Augustine's main point with slight alteration serves as epitome of sages' views:

> What was at stake, in the City of God and in Augustine's sermons, was the capacity of men to 'long' for something different, to examine the nature of their relationship with their immediate environment; above all, to establish their identity by refusing to be engulfed in the unthinking habits of their fellows.[42]

How alien can sages, concerned as they were with the possibilities of extraordinary conduct or attitude, have found Augustine's interest in establishing identity by reflection on what others deemed routine? The obvious answer justifies juxtaposing the two systems as to not only their ineluctable questions, but also their self-evidently valid answers.

Two further rhetorical questions seem justified: if Augustine spoke of "resident aliens" when referring to the citizens of God's city,[43] then how difficult can sages have found interpreting the identity of their social entity, their Israel, in the same way: here now, but only because of tomorrow: the pilgrim people, *en route* to somewhere else. And why should we find surprising, as disciples of Israel's sages, a city of God permeated, as was Augustine's, by arguments for hope:[44]

---

[38] p. 320.
[39] p. 320.
[40] p. 322.
[41] p. 322.
[42] p. 322.
[43] p. 323
[44] p. 328.

"'Lord, I have loved the beauty of Thy house.' From his gifts, which re scattered to good and bad alike in this, our most grim life, let us, with His help, try to express sufficiently what we have yet to experience."[45]

Two systems emerged from the catastrophes of the fifth century, Augustine's[46] for the Christian, sages' for the Judaic West. Constructed in the same age and in response to problems of the same character and quality, the systems bore nothing in common, except the fundamentally same messages about the correspondence of the individual's life to the social order, the centrality of relationship, the rule of God, and the response of God to what transcended all rules.

By both systems, each in its own way, God is joined to the social order because it is in relationships that society takes shape and comes to expression, and all relationships, whether between one person and another or between mortals and God, are wholly consubstantial.[47] That is why, for Augustine, the relationship between the individuals, Cain and Abel, can convey and represent the relationships characteristic of societies or cities, and that is why, for sages, the relationships between one person and another can affect God's relationship to the village needing rain or the householder needing to shore up his shaky dwelling-place.

XIII. DIFFERENT PEOPLE TALKING ABOUT DIFFERENT THINGS TO DIFFERENT PEOPLE, BUT SAYING THE SAME THING

True, we deal with the two utterly unrelated systems of the social order, fabricated by different people, talking about different things to different people, each meant to join the society of humanity (or a sector thereof) with the community

---

[45] p. 328.

[46] Note Burleigh, p. 218: "The Fifth Century...was a period of radical historical change." But just as Augustine expressed no sense of "the end of an era," so in the pages of the documents surveyed here I find no world-historical foreboding, only an optimistic and unshakeable conviction that Israel governed by its own deeds and attitudes its own destiny every day. That seems to me the opposite of a sense that all things are changing beyond repair. I can find no more ample representation of the historical convictions of our sages of blessed memory than Burleigh's representation of Augustine's: "Rome might pass away. The protecting fostering power of her emperors might be withdrawn. But God endured. His purpose of gathering citizens into His Eternal City was not frustrated by transient circumstances. St. Augustine had no anxiety for the Empire or for civilization, even 'Christian' civilization, because he found a better security in God." It is interesting to note that Burleigh gave his lectures in 1944, responding it seems to me to the impending dissolution of the British Empire in his rereading of Augustine — and dismissing an interest in the fate of Empires as essentially beside the point for Augustine. So I think it was for our sages.

[47] Burleigh characterizes matters in this way: "He seems to have been satisfied to show...that the exposition and defence of the Christian faith necessitates a survey of all History, which is in its essence God's providential government of the human race" (p. 202).

of Heaven. But both formed quite systematic and well-craftged responses to one and the same deep (and in my judgment, thoroughly merited) perception of disorder, a world that has wobbled, a universe out of line. Rome fallen, home besieged, for Augustine, corresponding to the end of autonomy and the advent of another (to be sure, *soi-disant*) "Israel," for sages, called into question orders of society of very ancient foundation. And that produced a profound sense that the rules had been broken, generating that (framing matters in contemporary psychological terms) alienation that was overcome by Augustine in his way, by sages in theirs.[48]

How, in the language of Judaism as our sages formulated it, may we express the answer to the question of the times? The shaking of the foundations of the social order shows how Israel is estranged from God. The old rules have been broken, therefore the remarkable and the exceptional succeeds. What is unnatural to the human condition of pride is humility and uncertainty, acceptance and conciliation. Those attitudes for the individual, policies for the nation, violate the rule. Then let God respond to transcending rules. And when — so the system maintains — God recognizes in Israel's heart, as much as in the nation's deliberation, the proper feelings, God will respond by ending that estrangement that marks the present age. So the single word encompassing the question addressed by the entire social system of the successor-Judaism must be *alienation.* The human and shared sense of crisis — whether Augustine reflecting on the fall of Rome, or sages confronting the end of the old order — finds its response in the doctrine of God's assessment, God's response. God enters the social order imagined by sages because God in the natural order proves insufficient, a Presence inadequate to the human situation. God must dwell in the city of humanity, and Israel in the city of God. So what in secular terms we see as a historical crisis or in psychological terms as one of alienation, in religious terms we have to identify as a caesura in the bounds of eternity. The psychological theology of the system joins the human condition to the fate of the nation and the world — and links the whole to the broken heart of God.

And yet that theological observation about the incarnate God of Judaism does not point us toward the systemic center, which within my definitions of what a system is must be social and explain the order of things here and now. For in the end, a religious theory of the social order describes earth, not Heaven.[49] It simply begs the question to claim that the system in the end attended to the condition of God's heart, rather than humanity's mundane existence. For a religious system is

---

[48] The basic motif of alienation, personal, cosmic, political, theological, as much as affective characterizes the two systems, because it defines the condition that provokes for each system the generative question, and because it is in the mode of reintegration that each system finds its persistent statement. True, alienation defines a purely contemporary category and forms a judgment made by us upon the circumstance or attitude of ancients. But the category does serve to specify, for our own understanding, what is at stake.

[49] To be sure, earth in the model of Heaven, or, as we might prefer, Heaven in the model of earth.

not a theological one, and questions about the way of life, world-view, and social entity, admittedly bearing theological implications or even making theological statements, in the end find their answers in the reconstruction of the here and now. So I have not identified the central tension and the generative problematic, nor have I specified the self-evident answer to that question that the system, in every sentence and all details means to settle. It is for identifying that generative problematic of the religious Judaism of the fifth century that the comparison between the Judaism of our sages of blessed memory and the Christianity of Augustine in his *City of God* proves particularly pertinent.

To state matters very simply, as we now realize, Augustine's personal circumstance and that of our sages correspond, so do Augustine's central question and the fundamental preoccupation of our sages. Augustine's *City of God* and the Talmud of the Land of Israel took shape in times that were changing, and both systemic statements accommodated questions of history. But we see the answer, therefore the question, when we realize that, as a matter of fact, both did so in the same way.

Specifically, Augustine, to be sure bringing to fruition the tradition of Christian historical thought commencing with Eusebius, provided for Christianity a theory of history that placed into the right perspective the events of the day. And our sages did the same, first of all affirming that events required recognition, second, then providing a theory of events that acknowledged their meaning, that is, their historicity, but that also subordinated history to considerations of eternity. The generative problematic of the successor-system concerned history: vast changes in the political circumstance of Israel, perceived mutations in the tissue of social relationship, clearly an interest in revising the plain meaning of ordinary words: value, power, learning. And the systemic answer for its part addressed questions of long-term continuity, framed in genealogical terms for the now-genealogically-defined Israel: the past lives in us, and the system explains in very precise and specific terms just how that takes place, which is through the medium of inherited entitlement or attained entitlement. The medium was indeed the same. Power was weakness, value was knowledge, and knowledge was power: all things formed within the Torah.

But if that was the message by way of answer to the historical question of change and crisis, then what how had the question of history come to be formulated? It was, of course, precisely what events should be deemed to constitute history, what changes matter, and what are we to do. The answer — our sages' and Augustine's alike — was that only certain happenings are eventful, bear consequence, require attention. And they are eventful because they form paradigms, Cain and Abel for Augustine, Israel's patriarchs and matriarchs for our sages.[50]

---

[50] But while I think they are primary, as the formation of Genesis Rabbah at this time indicates, they are not alone; Israel at Sinai, David on the throne, and other historical moments serve

Then what has happened to history as made by the barbarians at Rome and Hippo, the Byzantine Christians at Tiberias and Sepphoris? It has ceased to matter, because what happened at Rome, what happened at Tiberias, is no happening at all, but a mere happenstance. The upshot is not that history follows rules, so we can predict what will be, not at all.

Augustine did not claim to know what would happen tomorrow morning, and our sages interpreted events but did not claim to shape them, except through the Torah. The upshot is that what is going on really may be set aside in favor of what is really happening, and the story that is history has already been told in (for Augustine) the Bible and (for our sages) the Torah. But, then, that is no longer history at all, but merely, a past made into an eternal present. So, if I may specify what I conceive to be the systemic answer, it is, there are some things that matter, many that do not, and the few that matter echo from eternity to eternity, speaking in that voice, the voice of God, that is the voice of silence, still and small.

The systemic question, urgent and immediate and critical, not merely chronic, then, concerned vast historical change, comprising chains of events. The answer was that, in an exact sense, "event" has no meaning at all. Other than historical modes of organizing existence governed, and history in the ordinary sense did not form one of them. Without the social construction of history, there also is no need for the identification of events, that is, individual and unique happenings that bear consequence, since, within the system and structure of the successor-Judaism, history forms no taxon, being replaced by *zekhut,* the conception of a heritage of entitlement that can be received from the past, that is, merit deriving from the ancestors (rather than guilt and sin), a historical category that was — we now realize — in the deepest sense anti-historical. So, it must follow, no happening is unique, and, on its own, no event bears consequence.

Neither Augustine nor our sages produced narrative history; both, rather, wrote reflections *on* history, a very different matter. For neither did narrative history, ordinarily a sustained paraphrastic chronicle, serve as a medium for organizing and explaining perceived experience. True, both referred to events in the past, but these were not strung together in a continuing account. They were cited because they were exemplary, not because they were unique. These events then were identified out of the unlimited agenda of the past as what mattered, and these occasions of consequence, as distinct from undifferentiated and unperceived happenings were meant to explain the things that mattered in the chaos of the everyday.

In responding as they did to what we conceive to be historical events of unparalleled weight, Augustine and our sages took positions that, from our

---

as well. It is a mere impression, not a demonstrable fact, that the patriarchs and matriarchs provide the primary paradigm.

perspective, prove remarkably contemporary. For we now understand that all histories are the creation of an eternal present, that is, those moments in which histories are defined and distinguished, in which events are identified and assigned consequence, and in which sequences of events, "this particular thing happened here *and therefore...*," are strung together, pearls on a string, to form ornaments of intellect. Fully recognizing that history is one of the grand fabrications of the human intellect, facts not discovered but invented, explanations that themselves form cultural indicators of how things are in the here and now, we may appreciate as far more than merely instrumental and necessary the systemic responses to the urgent questions addressed in common by our sages and by Augustine.

Shall we then represent the successor-Judaism is a historical religion,[51] in that it appeals for its world-view to not myth about gods in heaven but the history of Israel upon earth — interpreted in relationship to the acts of God in heaven to be sure? And shall we characterize that Judaism as a religion that appeals to history, that is, to events, defined in the ordinary way, important happenings, for its source of testing and establishing truth? I think not. That Judaism identifies an event through its own cognitive processes. Just as the canon that recapitulates the system, so events — things that happen given consequence — recapitulate the system. Just as the system speaks in detail through the canon, so too through its repertoire of events granted recognition the system delivers its message. But just as the canon is not the system, so the recognition of events does not classify the system as historical.

XIV. THE AHISTORICISM OF THE JUDAISM OF THE DUAL TORAH

This brings me directly to the final question of systemic description: what exactly does the successor-Judaism — the Judaism put forth by an essentially religious system — mean by events? To answer that question succinctly is simple. In the canonical literature of the the the successor-Judaism, events find their place, within the science of learning of *Listenwissenschaft* that characterizes this literature, along with sorts of things that, for our part, we should not characterize as events at all. Events have no autonomous standing; events are not unique, each unto itself; events have no probative value on their own. Events form cases, along with a variety of other cases, making up lists of things that, in common, point to or prove one thing.

Events of other kinds, even those that seem to make an enormous, and awful, difference in Israel's condition, will appear on the same list as persons, places, things. And the contrary lists — very often in the form of stories as we have seen — tell us events that in and of themselves change biography (the life and fate of an ass-driver) and make history. That means that events not only have no

---

[51] I leave for Augustine-scholarship the counterpart-question on him.

autonomous standing on their own, but also that events constitute no species even within a genus of a historical order. For persons, places, and things in our way of thinking do not belong on the same list as events; they are not of the same order. Within the logic of our own minds, we cannot classify the city, Paris, within the same genus as the event, the declaration of the rights of man, for instance, nor is Sinai or Jerusalem of the same order of things as the Torah or the Temple, respectively. But in the logic of the Judaism before us, Jerusalem stands for sanctity and for Temple; it is of precisely the same taxic order.

What then shall we make of a list that encompasses within the same taxic composition events and things? Answering that question shows us how our sages sort out what matters from what does not, and events, by themselves, do not form a taxon and on their own bear no means and therefore do not matter. For one such list made up of events, persons, and places, is as follows: [1] Israel at the sea; [2] the ministering angels; [3] the tent of meeting; [4] the eternal house [=the Temple]; [5].Sinai. That mixtures an event (Israel redeemed at thje sea), a category of sensate being (angels), a location (tent of meeting, Temple), and then Sinai, which can stand for a variety of things but in context stands for the Torah. In such a list an event may or may not stand for a value or a proposition, but it does not enjoy autonomous standing; the list is not defined by the eventfulness of events and their meaning, the compilation of matters of a single genus or even a single species (tent of meeting, eternal house, are the same species here). The notion of event as autonomous, even unique, is quite absent in this taxonomy. And once events lose their autonomy, that process of selection gets under way that transforms one event into history bearing meaning and sets aside as inconsequential in the exact sense all other events.

Since this point is systemically so fundamental, let me give the case of another such list, which moves from events to other matters altogether, finding the whole subject to the same metaphor, hence homogenized. First come the events that took place at these places or with these persons: Egypt, the sea, Marah, Massah and Meribah, Horeb, the wilderness, the spies in the Land, Shittim, for Achan/ Joshua and the conquest of the Land. Now that mixture of places and names clearly intends to focus on particular things that happened, and hence, were the list to which I refer to conclude at this point, we could define an event for the successor-Judaism as a happening that bore consequence, taught a lesson or exemplified a truth, in the present case, an event matters because it the mixture of rebellion and obedience. But there would then be no doubt that "event" formed a genus unto itself, and that a proper list could not encompass both events, defined conventionally as we should, and also other matters altogether.

But the literary culture at hand, this textual community proceeds, in the same literary context, to the following items: [1] the Ten Commandments; [2] the show-fringes and phylacteries; [3] the *Shema* and the Prayer; [4] the tabernacle and the cloud of the Presence of God in the world to come. Why we invoke, as our candidates for the metaphor at hand, the Ten Commandments, show-fringes and phylacteries, recitation of the *Shema* and the Prayer, the tabernacle and the cloud of the Presence of God, and the mezuzah, seems to me clear from the very catalogue. These reach their climax in the analogy between the home and the tabernacle, the embrace of God and the Presence of God. So the whole is meant to list those things that draw the Israelite near God and make the Israelite cleave to God. And to this massive catalogue, events are not only exemplary — which historians can concede without difficulty — but also subordinated.

They belong on the same list as actions, things, persons, places, because they form an order of being that is not to be differentiated between events (including things that stand for events) and other cultural artifacts altogether. A happening is no different from an object, in which case "event" serves no better, and no worse, than a hero, a gesture or action, recitation of a given formula, or a particular locale, to establish a truth. It is contingent, subordinate, instrumental.[52] And why find that fact surprising, since all history comes to us in writing, and it is the culture that dictates how writing is to take place; that is why history can only paraphrase the affirmations of a system, and that is why events recapitulate in acute and concrete ways the system that classifies one thing that happens as event, but another thing is not only not an event but is not classified at all. In the present instance, an event is not at all eventful; it is merely a fact that forms part of the evidence for what is, and what is eventful is not an occasion at all, but a condition, an attitude, a perspective and a viewpoint. Then, it is clear, events are subordinated to the formation of attitudes, perspectives, viewpoints — the formative artifacts of not history in the conventional sense but culture in the framework of Sahlin's generalization, "history is culturally ordered, differently so in different societies, according to meaningful schemes of things."[53]

Events not only do not form a taxon, they also do not present a vast corpus of candidates for inclusion into some other taxon. Among the candidates, events that are selected by our documents are few indeed. They commonly encompass Israel at the Sea and at Sinai, the destruction of the first Temple, the destruction of the second Temple, events as defined by the actions of some holy men such as Abraham, Isaac, and Jacob (treated not for what they did but for who they were), Daniel, Mishael, Hananiah and Azariah, and the like. It follows that the restricted repertoire of candidates for taxonomic study encompasses remarkably few events, remarkably few for a literary culture that is commonly described as quintessentially historical!

---

[52] I can think of no more apt illustration of Geertz's interesting judgment: "an event is a unique actualization of a general phenomenon, a contingent realization of the cultural pattern." But my principal master in the present matter is Sahlin, cited in the next note.

[53] See his *Islands of History* (Chicago, 1985: The University of Chicago Press).

Then what taxic indicator dictates which happenings will be deemed events and which not? What are listed throughout are not data of nature or history but of theology: the issue of history is one of relationship, just as with Augustine. Specifically, God's relationship with Israel, expressed in such facts as the three events, the first two in the past, the third in the future, namely, the three redemptions of Israel, the three patriarchs, and holy persons, actions, events, what-have-you — these are facts that are assembled and grouped. What we have is a kind of recombinant theology given narrative form through tales presented individually but not in a sustained narrative. This recombinant theology through history is accomplished when the framer ("the theologian") selects from a restricted repertoire a few items for combination. What we have is a kind of subtle restatement, through an infinite range of possibilities, of the combinations and recombinations of a few essentially simple facts (data).

The net effect, then, is to exclude, rather than to include: the world is left outside. The key to systemic interpretation lies in the exegesis of that exegetical process that governs selection: what is included, what is excluded. In this context I find important Jonathan Z. Smith's statement:

> An almost limitless horizon of possibilities that are at hand...is arbitrarily reduced...to a set of basic elements....Then a most intense ingenuity is exercised to overcome the reduction...to introduce interest and variety. This ingenuity is usually accompanied by a complex set of rules.[54]

If we know the complex set of rules in play here, we also would understand the system that makes this document not merely an expression of piety but a statement of a theological structure: orderly, well-composed and proportioned, internally coherent and cogent throughout.

The canonical, therefore anything but random, standing of events forms a brief chapter in the exegesis of a canon. That observation draws us back to Smith, who observes:

> the radical and arbitary reduction represented by the notion of canon and the ingenuity represented by the rule-governed exegetical enterprise to apply the canon to every dimension of human life is that most characteristic, persistent, and obsessive religious activity....The task of application as well as the judgment of the relative adequacy of particular applications to a community's life situation remains the indigenous theologian's task; but the study of the process, particularly the study of comparative systematics and exegesis, ought to be a major preoccupation of the historian of religions.[55]

---

[54] "Sacred Persistence: Towards a Redescription of Canon," in William Scott Green, ed., *Approaches to Ancient Judaism* 1978, 1:11-28. Quotation: p. 15.
[55] *ibid.* p. 18.

Smith speaks of religion as an "enterprise of exegetical totalization," and he further identifies with the word "canon" precisely what we have identified as the substrate and structure of the list. If I had to define an event in this canonical context, I should have to call it merely another theological thing: something to be manipulated, combined in one way or in another, along with other theological things.

In insisting that the successor-system remains connected to the initial one, I have until now left open the identification of the joining threads of thought. But now I scarcely need to elaborate. The systems are connected because the successor-system sustains the generative mode of thought of the initial one, which was list-making. But now the lists derive from data supplied by Scripture (as with the bulk of Augustine's historical events of paradigmatic consequence), rather than by nature. Now as before, list-making is accomplished within a restricted repertoire of items that can serve on lists; the list-making then presents interesting combinations of an essentially small number of candidates for the exercise. But then, when making lists, one can do pretty much anything with the items that are combined; the taxic indicators are unlimited, but the data studied, severely limited. So the systems connect because the successor-system in mode of thought and medium of expression has recapitulated the initial system.

The radical shift in category-formation, the utterly-fresh systemic composition and construction — these turn out to carry forward received modes of thought. So far as the two systems may both be called Judaisms, and so far as these Judaisms so join as to form one on-going Judaism, continuity is in not message but method. The history of religion is the exegesis of exegesis, and, for the case before us, the transformation of Judaism likewise tells two stories. The one portrays successive and essentially distinct, free-standing systems. The other narrates that enduring process that sustains and unites and nourishes — and, therefore, also defines.

And, by the way, that shift in category-formation also accounts for the Talmudic re-working of the very sense and meaning of the word, "economics." So I have answered the question of my esteemed colleague, Professor Elzinga, in a way in which, I hope, his wonderful invention, the detective who teaches me economics more effectively than all the textbooks except for Aristotle's, might find plausible. Then again, he might now.

PART TWO

DEBATES ON THEOLOGY:
HISTORICAL, CONSTRUCTIVE,
AND APOLOGETIC

II

IS THERE A THEOLOGY OF RABBINIC JUDAISM?

What is at stake in the problem of theology?[1] It is whether or not, out of a given body of authoritative writings, we may appeal to that 'ism, that (for the present case) "Judaism," that all of us assume forms the matrix for all the documents all together. That is to say, the issue of theology bears consequence because upon the result, in the end, rests the question of whether we may speak of a religion, or only of various documents that intersect here and there. The conception of "Judaism," or "Christianity," or "Buddhism," serves the purpose of holding together in a coherent philosophically harmonious and proportionate construction diverse and otherwise inchoate facts, e.g., writings, artifacts of material culture, myths and rites, all of them, without distinction as to provenience or origin, deemed to contribute to an account of one and the same systematic composition, an -ity or an -ism; and, further, all of them — beliefs, rites, attitudes and actions alike — are assumed to animate each. So when we speak of a religion as a whole, not simply a body of texts — documents or archaeological findings or contemporary social scientific description — of a particular group of people who confess a single set of beliefs, we take for granted that beyond the social facts there is a system of thought that can be defined in a systematic way.

That assumption serves to clarify and organize otherwise chaotic facts. The reason is that, assuming all facts pertain to one whole and cogent construction of ideas, one thing, we form an account, frequently framed in terms of propositional beliefs, of that one thing, assumed to encompass everything in its classification

[1] Keynote Address, *Den judaistiska dagen,* Åbo Akademi. May 3, 1995

and, I stress, also to infuse each item of its class. That is what happens when we define a religion, in the present instance, Judaism. We then define a religion not only in terms of its social order — the way of life, world view, and theory of the social entity of people who believe certain things and consequently form a community that does things in one way, rather than some other — but in terms of its abstract system of belief and behavior. This we view out of all context, imputing the presence of this -ism at all points at which any of its characteristic data turn up.

Having formed such a definition, we therefore take for granted that a datum that falls into the classification of that systematic statement or that -ism bears within itself not only its own facts but a large body of other facts imputed to the datum by reason of the character of the classification that encompasses it. When we speak of "Judaism," for example, we take for granted that beyond a given datum we define as "Judaic" lies an entire structure, one that imparts context and meaning to each of its data in turn and that both encompasses transcends them all. On that basis, we may speak of Judaism: the Judaic view of this, that, and the other thing, and so too with Buddhism, Hinduism, Christianity and a variety of other -isms and -ities. When, therefore, in the study of religion, we invoke the conception of an -ism that transcends its own data and organizes them, much is at stake. Precisely what we study when we study religion comes under discussion.

When we ask not merely for a compendium of what a given religion alleges, e.g., about God, the world, and the human person, but for a systematic and philosophically coherent formulation of convictions in a statement that is not only true but also harmonious and genuinely cogent (one part connecting with another and all holding together), then our problem in answering the question at hand proves not so readily resolved. For if we take all of the components of the canon of the Judaism of the dual Torah as matters had unfolded in late antiquity — that is, the Mishnah and Tosefta, the two Talmuds, and the Midrash-compilations of that early period — and we ask how we are to find out whether these several documents all together present a cogent theological system, the correct method for theological inquiry hardly presents itself in a prompt and unambiguous manner. For once we take as our criterion for identifying the presence of theology the clear marks of system, structure, and order, matters prove chaotic.

The source of the confusion lies in the state of the written evidence of the religion, Rabbinic Judaism, or the Judaism of the dual Torah, or Classical Judaism, or Normative Judaism, as people may prefer to call it. When I refer to the state of the evidence, I refer not to problems of philology or textual tradition, but to the diversity of conviction, and, even more, to the episodic character in which convictions are set forth. To state matters simply: the various documents that comprise the canon of Judaism scarcely cohere in more than formal ways. That is not because the various writings contradict one another, but because each of the documents pursues its own program, and all together, the components of the canon scarcely intersect at the deepest layers of premise and presupposition. Consequently, we may readily set forth the theologies of the various testimonies to that single Judaism of the Rabbinic species, but we face obstacles in defining the single theology to which all the diverse documents appeal, and upon which each of them builds its particular statement. That the documents stand autonomous of one another in conviction, focus, and points of emphasis, does not mean they contradict one another, but it does mean we cannot readily figure out how diverse positions hold together. We do not know what is primary and generative, what is secondary and derivative. Hence we have theological statements but no clear system. But to maintain there is a theology of Rabbinic Judaism is to claim for the matter systemic, not merely random and notional, standing.

The written evidence comes to us in a variety of compilations or documents, all of them rather carefully crafted, but none of them brought into clear relationship with any other of its genre (the two Talmuds, for instance, stand in total isolation from one another). Now, by definition, that fact — the autonomy of the score and a half of major compilations — need not set an insuperable obstacle in the way of investigating the theological structure and order of the canon all together. Much theological work begins with the definition of structure and order and proceeds to utilize the historical, canonical writings to fill in the blanks of the questionnaire prepared out of that definition. Whether the dogmatic theology of George F. Moore in his *Judaism. The Age of the Tannaim* (1927), and in the continuators and imitators of Moore such as E. P. Sanders's *Judaism: Practice and Belief. 63 BCE-66 CE* (1992),[2] or the systematic-historical theology of Solomon Schechter or of Abraham Heschel in his *Torah min hashshamayim,* the problem is the same. Categories formed outside of the canon impose upon the canon a structure and a system that the canonical writings themselves have not yielded — and to which they conform only with difficulty. We are left with theology that is neither systematic — being limited to authoritative writings of the long-ago past — nor historical — being formed in isolation from the category-formation of the sources themselves. The result succeeds as neither theology — lacking the autonomous intellect of the theologian — nor historical — imposing contemporary categories upon the theology of another age altogether.

Clearly, the data to be sorted out in the study of whether Rabbinic Judaism rested upon a coherent theology must derive from the sources, read within their categories — but for our purposes. That the categories must find definition in the documents, not in our program, takes priority. If we bring our categories, for example, God's love for Israel, or God's election of Israel, the theology we impute to the documents turns out to sustain the theology we deem critical. But to describe the theology of Rabbinic Judaism in its formative documents, we make a historical

---

[2] On Sanders's methodological dependence upon Moore, see William Scott Green, "Introduction: The Scholarly Study of Judaism," in J. Neusner, ed., *Judaism in Late Antiquity.* (Leiden, 1995), I. *The Literary and Archaeological Sources,* pp. 1-12.

claim: in those days, in these writings, this category took priority. And to make such a claim, we have to allow the documents to dictate their categorical formation and stand in judgment upon our hypothetical definition of it.

To take up our purpose next: it is to determine whether a cogent and internally coherent body of ideas forms the foundation for the specific propositions as to religious truth that the documents set forth, severally but also jointly. If we can uncover such a theological system that forms the structure upon which sayings that episodically take theological positions depend, then we may affirm, Rabbinic Judaism sets forth not only religious convictions and attitudes, but also a coherent, philosophically founded theology. But if the sources on their own do not stand upon or appeal to a single system of ideas that hold together in a consistent and proportionate way, then we must conclude, Rabbinic Judaism, as portrayed by its foundation-documents, sets forth religious truth but no theological structure worthy of the name.

Now let me spell out the principal obstacle to a documentary theological category-formation. It is that the canonical documents do not coalesce. They not only are to be distinguished from one another in the indicative traits of rhetoric, topic, and logic.[3] They also do not come together at the deep structures of presupposition. Each document stands for not only its own program, but also its own deepest, most pervasive and implicit premises. None intersects with any other when we move beneath the surface of detail to penetrate into the main point and the ubiquitous and generative problematic. So each document goes its own way, investigating the problems its authors or compilers deem urgent, and rarely do two or more documents intersect anywhere but in convictions or principles that for them all prove inert and in none of them provoke deep and systematic thought.

To make this point clear: we may take for granted all documents concur that God revealed the Torah to Moses; but in none of the documents does that point precipitate sustained exegetical inquiry. Much that would characterize all documents would elicit agreement beyond the limits of Rabbinic Judaism, even beyond the boundaries of all Judaisms, since Christianity in all of its systems would agree, to take one obvious point, that God created heaven and earth and upon much else. So the areas of shared conviction prove either systemically neutral for all the religious systems that emerge from the Hebrew Scriptures of ancient Israel, on the one side, or quite beside the main point that a given piece of writing wishes to make in its own terms. A simple example will clarify matters by way of contrast. All of the Gospels intersect in fundamental ways, sharing convictions of program and problematic, so that we may indeed produce not only a theology of the school of Matthew but a Gospels' theology. Common premises, concerning for instance the

---

[3] My complete statement is in my *Introduction to Rabbinic Literature.* N.Y., 1994: Doubleday. The Doubleday Anchor Reference Library.

standing as to divinity of Jesus Christ (to use the Christian language), infuse the whole; a common program of exegesis — the life and teachings of God Incarnate upon earth — governs throughout.

So we may say that the Gospels at the level of premise and presupposition stand together and set forth, beyond difference, an area of common convictions concerning a single coherent theological program. If the Gospels present us with diverse groups writing about a common topic, appealing to a set of convictions held in common, conceiving of a common audience, then the Rabbinic canonical writings by the same criteria profoundly differ. That is because they do not write about common topics that pervade the entire corpus; they do not appeal to a set of convictions that govern throughout but only to different convictions, each shaped within the limits of a single document; and if, beyond the circle of sages themselves, a single audience is contemplated, it is difficult to identify that audience in terms that transcend the merely platitudinous.

Let me briefly summarize the results of an inquiry into the Judaism that the various canonical documents presuppose, the Judaism that encompasses them all and holds together the concerns and convictions of each.[4] Through a systematic inquiry into the premises and presuppositions of the data of the canonical documents, I have reached a negative conclusion. It is that all we know concerning the Judaism that the rabbis take for granted in a long sequence of basic writings concerns diverse documents' specific propositions and the presuppositions they yield, the premises of various writings. These need not be found internally contradictory, but they also do not coalesce into a coherent systemic statement. The sources at hand do not validate the conception of an encompassing Judaism that underpins everything every document states and that reaches expression, in one detail or another, in one document or another. On the basis of the evidence in hand, we cannot describe the "Judaism" that the rabbis of the Judaism of the dual Torah took for granted. What we can describe is only what the authors of the various documents, respectively, took for granted, and the result of that description proves local and topical: particular to the various documents, respectively.

---

[4] I refer to *The Judaism the Rabbis Take for Granted.* Atlanta, 1995: Scholars Press for South Florida Studies in the History of Judaism. That book summarizes the systematic source-analysis in the following seven works: *The Judaism Behind the Texts. The Generative Premises of Rabbinic Literature.* Atlanta, 1994: Scholars Press for South Florida Studies in the History of Judaism. I. *The Mishnah.* A. *The Division of Agriculture;* I. *The Mishnah.* B.*The Divisions of Appointed Times, Women, and Damages (through Sanhedrin).* I. *The Mishnah* C. *The Divisions of Damages (from Makkot), Holy Things and Purities;* II. *The Tosefta, Tractate Abot, and the Earlier Midrash-Compilations: Sifra, Sifré to Numbers, and Sifré to Deuteronomy;* III. *The Later Midrash-Compilations: Genesis Rabbah, Leviticus Rabbah and Pesiqta deRab Kahana;* IV. *The Latest Midrash-Compilations: Song of Songs Rabbah, Ruth Rabbah, Esther Rabbah I, and Lamentations Rabbati. And The Fathers According to Rabbi Nathan;* V. *The Talmuds of the Land of Israel and Babylonia.*

When we examine the premises and presuppositions of sages' writings, we find sherds and fragments of this and that, not a complete and coherent theology of this Judaism; and, moreover, propositions in the form of premises or presuppositions do not circulate from document to document at all. Some form the foundations of one document or a set of documents, others prove critical elsewhere. Few presuppositions play an active, provocative role in the formation of writings in all canonical documents treated here, that is, everything except for the two Talmuds. Generalizing on the cases we are given, whether of law or of exegesis, we produce generalizations that remain particular to their documents or to the genre of their documents. So if there was a Judaism that formed the ground of thought and speculation for sages, we do not have much evidence of its character or contents.

Until now I have taken for granted that there certainly was one cogent Rabbinic Judaism, with a coherent corpus of myths, symbols, and rites, and deriving from a linear, unitary history, such as I have outlined in a variety of works, most notably, *The Transformation of Judaism. From Philosophy to Religion.*[5] That history struck me as incremental and harmonious; that impression guided me through more than a quarter-century of systematic work. But now, having addressed a question about considerations of premise and presupposition and asked how the Rabbinic writings reveal what their authors take for granted, I have to call into doubt what I had taken for my generative principle. It is that the writers of the Rabbinic documents take little for granted, and nothing for granted that matters very deeply in the formation of any one of those documents. We do not now know very much about that Judaism that the rabbis took for granted, because the documents that comprise their canon for late antiquity provide only very limited access to the general conceptions that underlie the specific writings in hand.[6]

To make this point concrete: If we accept the challenge of E. P. Sanders, who says, "One must press behind the contents of the Mishnah and attempt to discover what the contents of the Mishnah presuppose," [7] we find the premises and presuppositions of the Mishnah. We cannot show that these form generative

---

[5] Champaign, 1992: University of Illinois Press.

[6] For a long time, then, I have assumed that, while we cannot define a single Judaism characteristic of all ancient Judaists (Jews who practice a religion they call Judaism), we certainly may speak of a single, coherent Rabbinic Judaism. That is, I understood as a matter of premise that all of the Rabbinic documents hold together in a single corpus, one that is not only coherent because of its organization as exegeses of received writings (Scripture, the Mishnah), but also cogent in its principal points of belief. But now I find that that is not the case; there is no positive evidence, deriving from the documents examined here, that sustains the conception of a single cogent Rabbinic Judaism. We have little reason based on internal evidence to explain why a given document finds its place in the canon of that Judaism as it had reached definition at the end of ancient times.

[7] E. P. Sanders, "Puzzling Out Rabbinism," in William Scott Green, ed., *Approaches to Ancient Judaism* 1980, 2:73

conceptions for other documents. We can demonstrate that most of them do not. We may dismiss as particular to its task the entire corpus of legal premises and presuppositions. Those of the Mishnah prove tied to the context of law, and the other documents have none of consequence that are comparable.

The same is true of the Midrash-compilations, with their rich heritage of theological premises. The two densest conceptions, concerning Israel and the nations and the meaning of history, do not lie at the foundations or form the presuppositions of the Mishnah or Tosefta. When it comes to the law, a single proposition strikes me as important, that the law preserves the example of the patriarchs and matriarchs or embodies what God did and does. That broadly circulated proposition then maintains that, in conforming to the law, holy Israel imitates God. As to the Mishnah's philosophical and theological premises, the most important philosophical givens functions only in the Mishnah. The paramount matter — hierarchical classification serves only there. More to the point, no other document works out its ideas along the lines of philosophical thought. And that leaves theology. So, in the aggregate, premises appear bound to the documents that rest upon them, and those that circulate through the canonical writings examined here are vastly outweighed in volume and impart by those that do not. True, as we noted at the outset, certain premises "surely" or "obviously" are everywhere taken for granted, e.g., the unity of God, the importance of the Torah, and the like. But these remain inert, or, when they generate thought, accommodate themselves to context, e.g., the Mishnah's use of monotheism is distinctive to the Mishnah's interest in hierarchical classification.

True, the picture is somewhat more complicated, since all documents rest upon theological convictions of one sort of another. And we have no basis on which to suppose that the convictions important in one document and absent in another will have elicited objections among the authors of the writings in which they play no role. Nonetheless, when we raise the question of whether important theological conceptions unify all of the documents, providing the substrate of conceptions or attitudes for each one, the results prove somewhat puzzling. An idea that takes priority in one set of writings attracts slight attention elsewhere; premises that prove pressing here scarcely appear elsewhere. Two absolutely critical premises show what is at stake. The emotions, sentiments, and attitudes of God and humanity correspond. With the centrality of intentionality throughout the Mishnah — along with the method of hierarchical classification the generative premise of that document — simply does not prepare us for the fact that, beyond the Mishnah, intentionality does not define an area of exploration, not at all. The rabbis not only take the centrality of intentionality for granted, they build upon it. Then if they take it for granted throughout but neglect that same idea, we have to wonder whether that enormous premise of thought makes much impact where it is not urgent for a given document's larger program; then the premise follows the documentary program and gains entry only where the document requires it.

The upshot is that we cannot show many ideas that run from document to document, or group to group, and that enter into the definition of how a document finds its place in the canon. Then, it would appear, no traits tell us why one book would gain its place in the canon of the Judaism of the dual Torah examined here, and another would not. That is not to suggest the identification of writings for the canon is arbitrary, only that on the basis of what documents appear to have taken for granted, we do not know what the criteria for admission might have been. I find myself unable to point to a setting in the exegetical compilations, early, middle, and late, in which intentionality plays a part in the formation of a concrete idea, on the one side, or itself presents a critical consideration, on the other.

What is presupposed and also generative in one set of writings plays no role in others, with the one important exception of the general themes of covenant, commandment, Torah, and God's dominion; but these, we now realize, are topical: subjects that form premises quite particular to documents where they play a role, no more than that. Contrast the remarkable cogency of the presentation of premises particular to documents, e.g., history in the later Midrash-compilations, intentionality and hierarchical classification in the earlier legal ones, with the diffuse character of presuppositions with respect to covenant, commandment, Torah, and God's dominion. Our results point to a different conclusion from the one I had anticipated. Specifically, these represent themes that move from one document to another, rather than propositional premises that form the intellectual foundations of any one of them. Indeed, a closer look at my formulation of matters shows that I have joined as a single rubric matters that may well be differentiated, and, when differentiated, prove as particular to documents as hierarchical classification, intentionality or the meaning and structure of history.

Take covenant, commandment, and Kingdom of God, for example. While assuredly at the foundation of every Judaic writing that appeals to Scripture, the notion that Israel is covenanted with God, and that the Torah defines the terms of the covenant, is surely more critical in the Midrash-compilations than in the Mishnah and the Tosefta. There, when we speak of God's kingdom, we formulate matters not in mythic terms but in the definition of the realm of the sacred. But I was the one to identify the realm of the sacred — space and time in the interplay on Sabbath and festival, Israel's space in God's time in their interpenetration — with the kingdom of God. The notion of God's rule expressed through the space-and-time continuum does not surface in later writings, where the kingdom of God bears quite a different set of meanings.

The presuppositions or premises that form the foundations of a document's exegesis of its propositions prove particular to the document even when themes or topics or symbols or ideas appear to be shared with other writings or to have moved from document to document. For at stake are not merely opaque symbols, e.g., the Torah, the covenant, the kingdom of Heaven, but the shaping of these topics for some propositional or at least provocative purpose. And, more to the point, when we take a closer look at those premises that do appear to circulate beyond the narrow limits of a single compilation or set of compilations (e.g., Genesis Rabbah, Leviticus Rabbah, and Pesiqta de Rab Kahana, or the late Rabbah-compilations), what we define as premises in all their concreteness prove specific to the document, or set of documents, in which the ubiquitous idea is treated. A second glance at the treatment of the topic of the Torah leaves no doubt about that fact.

Some themes or ideas or images or symbols recur here and there. But when they do, they reach the level of premise and presupposition of concrete compositions in formulations that prove specific to the document that uses them. It follows that the premises of the canonical documents of Judaism do not transcend their documentary setting. That result calls into question the conception that a corpus of ideas at the deepest structure of the canonical writings hold those writings together and form of them all a single coherent statement. The opposite is the fact. In substance, we are unable to find ideas that are both active, not inert, and ubiquitous, not specific to a kind of writing (e.g., law or exegesis) or a set of closely related writings (e.g., the Mishnah and the Tosefta, or some of the subsets of the Midrash-compilations). If, therefore, we had to explain what accounts for the inclusion, in a single coherent canon, of both the Mishnah and, e.g., Song of Songs Rabbah or the Tosefta and Leviticus Rabbah, on the strength of matters of substance — premises that circulate throughout, givens of conviction or conception, attitude or sentiment — we should be unable to answer that question.

When we "press behind the contents of the Mishnah and attempt to discover what the contents of the Mishnah presuppose," we do not find "Judaism," in the sense that by "Judaism" we mean a coherent body of ideas that form the structure of a variety of authoritative documents. That is to say, we cannot show that a canon of writings — all of which, all together, comprise "Judaism" — takes shape around a coherent body of premises. When we "press behind the contents of the Mishnah and attempt to discover what the contents of the Mishnah presuppose," we find the presuppositions of the Mishnah. And those presuppositions form the basis for the very particular conceptions of the Mishnah. On what basis, then, we link the Mishnah to Leviticus Rabbah and allege that at their foundations, both documents lay out the same -ism, that is, the same systematic and cogent set of ideas and attitudes that form a coherent and entire account of the social order of holy Israel — way of life, world view, theory of the social entity — I cannot say. There is no substantive basis at the level of premises and presuppositions that run from here to there and play a provocative role throughout for the conception of the canon of the dual Torah.

Where then are we to turn for the cogent, authoritative, and coherent statement that our sages proposed to set forth? The answer, obviously, is the Talmud of Babylonia, on the one side, and its rationality, on the other. In that writing, which stands at the end and absorbs and recasts whatever of the prior heritage the Talmud's framers — the authors of its compositions, the compilers of its composites, but particularly the later — deemed consequential, we may expect to find that answer. For that is the final document of the Judaism of the dual Torah in its formative age, the piece of writing that, from its closure to this very morning, has been identified by Judaism as authoritative, normative, and ultimately, compendious and comprehensive. To state the matter somewhat loosely, the tradition is not only its own best historian, it is also its own authoritative theologian.

The Bavli comes at the end of the formation of the Rabbinic canon in late antiquity, but it also stands at the beginning of all that was to follow, which would take the form of commentary upon the Bavli or which would refer to the Bavli as the court of final appeal. So for perfectly simple, formal reasons, we are on firm ground in asking the Bavli to make a coherent statement. But there is a substantive basis as well. The Bavli for its part takes the form of a systematic search for cogent and harmonious statements, everywhere pursuing inconsistency and proposing to iron out disharmony. The Bavli's hermeneutics begins with the very criterion I have set forth for distinguishing religious ideas from theological systems: its close and careful attention to what is implicit, its search beneath the surface of things for ultimate unity, rigorous coherence, balance, order, proportion. Not only so, but as a matter of fact, the Bavli is the sole document of Rabbinic Judaism that holds together the two principal literary categories of that Judaism, halakhah, law, and aggadah, lore, inclusive of exegetical tradition. Other documents contain mostly the one or mostly the other; this one incorporates a large component of both. So the Bavli stands at the apex for formal, substantive, and literary reasons.

This leads me to address two questions, one of method, the other of substance. Where do we commence our inquiry into Rabbinic theology? The theology of Rabbinic Judaism must find its definition in what is prior to proposition and takes precedence over premises of thought. Our sages' "Judaism" must commence in the ways in which we make connections and draw conclusions. That is where all thought begins, and that is the point at which the social order dictates the wherewithal of rationality. If we know how people connect one thing to something else, making connections that yield a "therefore," we can follow onward and upward to the surface of the social order the processes that yield premises and define presuppositions, and so onward into the here and now of cows that gore and empires that reign but for a moment. So while we cannot set forth a theology of Rabbinic Judaism, we can and should now undertake to set forth a theology of the Talmud of Babylonia. And that will constitute the authoritative theology of Judaism — as faithful Jews have affirmed from the time of the closure of the Talmud to our own day. The one whole Torah of Moses our Rabbi, oral and written, reaches us in the pages of The Talmud, as generations of sages have expounded it, onward to this morning.

But what of the substance? Earlier I argued that we cannot impose our category-formation upon the ancient documents. Doing so violates the simplest rules of historical inquiry, because it forms an act of brutal anachronism. We cannot say, what mattered most to them is what concerns us most of all, for we have no way of determining out of the sources whether or not our judgment conforms to theirs. But what categories of their must define our inquiry? In my view the answer is dictated by those matters upon which our sages lavished their best energies, their most sustained critical capacities. If we ask at what point harmony is besought, coherence pursued, disharmony and inconsistency rigorously investigated and disposed of, the answer is clear to all familiar with the document. It is at the statement of the law, whether practiced or theoretical, that our sages insist upon exposing cogency and resisting inconsistency. When they investigate the premise of a rule and compare said premise with that of another rule, that is the point at which they penetrate into the depths of the structure of the law of the Torah. There they insist they will find the solid granite on which they will construct their system.

What they deemed subject to the most rigorous standards of coherence, when they resisted easy answers and facile harmonizations, there we must follow in our search for the propositions that must dictate the category-formation of Rabbinic theology. To know what categories engaged our sages, we have to define the law behind the laws, the one statement the sages wished to make through diverse cases. Let me give a single concrete example of what I mean. When I examined the Talmud's elaborate and protracted reading of Mishnah-tractate Zebahim 5:3ff. to the end, I find that nearly the entire chapter addresses the question of the connection between rules recorded in the Mishnah and rules presented in Scripture. The metaproposition that encompasses the numerous specific propositions is simple: how do we make connections between rules and their point of origin. Every time we ask, "what is the source [in Scripture] for this statement," we find an answer that is left to stand. So one fundamental and ubiquitous metaproposition of the Bavli may be set forth in this language:

    1. it is important to link laws that occur in one source to those that occur in another;

    2. among the compilations [components of "the one whole Torah of Moses, our rabbi," in later mythic language] that enjoy canonical status [in our language], the premier is Scripture;

    3. so whenever we find a statement of a rule in the Mishnah and ask for its source, the implicit criterion of success will be, "the rule is founded on language of Scripture, properly construed;"

    4. so, consequently, the proposition implicit in numerous propositions, common to them all and holding them all together, is this: all rules cohere, and the point of origin of nearly all of them is the written part of the Torah revealed by God to Moses at Sinai.

The metapropositional program contributed by the Bavli's framers concerns how series are made, which is to say, whether connections yield static or dynamic results, which is to say, at the deepest layers of intellect, how thought happens. Now, at the end, we ask the framers of the Mishnah to address the question before us. And in answer, they give us silence. So we know that here we hear what is distinctive to, and the remarkable discovery of, the authorship of the Bavli. Since, it is clear, that discovery has taken place within the words of the written Torah, and, since their deepest metaproposition maintained that the words of the written Torah are the words of God to Moses, our rabbi, at Sinai, — the words, not just the gist — we have to conclude with what I conceive to be the bed-rock of the metapropositional program before us: the Torah teaches us not only what God said, but how God thinks. When we understand the Torah rightly, we engage in thinking about thought. And that is how we know God: through thought. So Spinoza was not so heretical after all.

Now, one may wonder, have we crossed the boundary from theology to philosophy, allowing the hermeneutics of the law to divert us from our original destination altogether? The answer is, we have to allow the philosopher-theologians of the Bavli to lead us where they will — if we propose to set forth what we conceive to be their theology. Once we affirm the priority of the Bavli, then the Bavli's hermeneutics dictates the direction in which we are to venture. But we need not conclude our inquiry with their definition of matters. I argued that in its quest for coherence of diverse matters the Bavli insists upon the priority of law, halakhah; that is where inconsistency attracts attention. Then, it must follow, a sustained effort to investigate the theology of the Bavli will direct itself toward the way in which the law contains and conveys theological judgments.

Some excellent beginnings of inquiry provide guidance even now, for example, Ephraim Urbach's correlation of the laws of inheritance and the conviction of eternal life and his essay on law and prophecy.[8] These papers point the way to the concrete and detailed research on the theological premises of the law of the Talmud that, in the end, will make possible a valid category-formation, on the one side, and well-criticized theological propositions, displayed in all their coherence and encompassing conviction, on the other. But if I had to select the model of the work of theological inquiry, I could do no better than turn to Maimonides, who insisted to begin with that law and philosophy cohere, the one making its statement in its way, the other in its manner, and both of them saying the same thing.

We have then to shift our theological inquiry in three ways. First, we must allow Rabbinic Judaism to define its own theological source, and, for reasons I have now spelled out, I regard the Talmud of Babylonia as the designated statement of all that is coherent and compelling.

---

[8] "Hilkhot Yerushah vehayye olam," *Fourth World Congress of Jewish Studies Papers* (Jerusalem, 1967) 1:133-141; "Law and Prophecy," *Tarbis* 1958, 23:1-25.

Second, we have to permit the category-formation to emerge from the selected source, paying close attention to its points of recurrent concern and emphasis, its foci, its principal concerns, and its generative principles. Where the document exposes its premises, we have the beginnings of the category-formation we seek.

Third, since the document makes its statement mainly through law, we have to learn to listen to that statement when it is made through the laws. There, I maintain, we shall uncover a rich and remarkably purposive theological system, one that contains within itself all that matters in religion: what it means to be humanity, "in our image, after our likeness," and what God has in mind when he speaks of holy Israel as "the kingdom of priests and the holy people." That is to say, out of theological anthropology, on the one side, and theological politics and sociology, on the other, we shall find ourselves contemplating that system and structure that, in its own terms, sets forth the theology of Rabbinic Judaism: our sages' conception of God with us.

III

Where, When and How Does Holy Israel Meet God?

Holy Israel meets God in the Torah, which is God's self-manifestation to Israel and humanity.[1] The encounter takes place in song, when holy Israel sings the words of the Torah, affirming, "This is the Torah that Moses presented to the children of Israel upon the instruction of the Lord." The moment of the always-sung proclamation frames the occasion of meeting, knowing God as God wishes to be known From antiquity onward, music carried the words, and, sometimes, melody without words bore meaning too. Holy Israel assembles to sing the Torah in two places: synagogue and yeshiva or center for the study of Torah for God's sake. It follows that the conduct — the singing — of holy Israel in the synagogue and academy or yeshiva in hour of the giving and the receiving of the Torah marks the moment and the locus at which Israel meets God. In the words and music, gesture and movement, dance and drama and sentiment, attitude, and emotion of that moment, God is made manifest in the congregation of Israel. That is where God has chosen to become known to humanity — so the Torah says, so holy Israel affirms.

Now to answer the question that heads this essay: God sings to Israel. The Torah is God's song. In secular, descriptive language, in Judaism, God is made manifest in the Torah: *in the Torah holy Israel meets God.*

Israel's God is a God who sings, neither in the storm nor in the thunder, but in the voice that pierces the silence, the thin voice, the urgent voice. The halting, nervous, quavering chirping of the bar or bat mitzvah, the boy or girl at puberty called for the first time to read the Torah to the community assembled for prayer in the synagogue, is the voice that Moses heard from the cleft in the rock.

---

[1] This essay goes over some of the main propositions of my *Judaism's Theological Voice: The Melody of the Talmud.* Chicago, 1995: The University of Chicago Press.

Moses, denied the vision he sought, heard instead the voice to proclaim the name: "I will proclaim before you my name, 'The Lord.'" It is the thin voice of silence that Elijah heard — that same Elijah present at the circumcision of the bar mitzvah, that same Elijah who at the end of time will announce the coming of the Messiah. Through song eternity breaks through into the here and now of time.

I say, "God sings," because, when received with reverence by holy Israel, the Torah always is sung;[2] I call the Torah God's song, because the Torah is given ("revealed") by God in the act of self-manifestation. So the Torah itself proclaims its own origins in Heaven: "I am the Lord your God...," "The Lord spoke to Moses, saying, Speak to the children of Israel and say to them...," "I will make all my goodness pass before you and will proclaim before you my name, 'The Lord,' and I will be gracious to whom I will be gracious and will show mercy on whom I will show mercy. But you cannot see my face." These and companion proclamations leave no doubt for holy Israel that in the Torah is God: the record of God's call to humanity through holy Israel. Israel receives the Torah to meet God and in the Torah Israel's encounter with God takes place.

But to take place is to locate in ordinary space an event of utopian potentiality. Where in particular is the locative event of encounter to be found? This act of self-revelation and therefore encounter in the Torah takes place before living Israel in two places, synagogue and academy. In both meetings the Torah is not read but sung, and the singing serves to transform secular study into sacred service. Thus — in line with these facts of the faith as practiced every day and everywhere — the theology of Judaism finds its voice in the singing of the Torah. Israel sings God's song on its way across the ages — song without end — through eternity, to Heaven.

Then to describe the theology of Judaism we have to identify its melody. Three propositions consequently form the burden of this essay.

1. ISRAEL RECEIVES THE TORAH WHERE AND WHEN IT IS SUNG: we return, now, with a clear understanding of what is at stake in these public places, the synagogue and the house of study. These are the locations in which the Torah takes place. That is so because the Torah is given to holy Israel, so in the location in which the individual becomes the community, the place in which the quorum forms and words are said in public and therefore put up for public disputation and exposition, there and then God calls to Israel. Precisely what happens in these places? How in them does God speaking in the present tense, give the Torah? All that has been said to this point prepares the way for the final solution to the mystery of how Israel takes place, how the Torah is given, how the gift is received by Israel, when and where

---

[2] That in ancient times books ordinarily were sung aloud, not read silently, is a fact not germane to our inquiry. For, speaking within the framework of the Torah, we may note that those books, when sung, belonged solely to this world, while the Torah — words, some in books, some not — when sung echoes out of eternity. In more secular terms, facts of history play no probative role in the theological inquiry into our meeting with God.

God is made manifest — all ways of saying one thing. That thing in secular words is, here is the theology of Judaism, its theological voice.

2. ISRAEL MEETS GOD IN SONG: In the Torah, specifically when and where it is sung, Israel meets God. That meeting is in the synagogue and in the academy, where, received with song and dance, blessing and petition, God's pronouncement, the Torah, comes in words and sentences to Israel, God's people. Assembled as all Israel in synagogue or as the particular disciples of the Torah in the academy or yeshiva, God's people hears the sung words: receives and determines to obey, to dance to the compelling rhythms, to sing with the forceful melody. And in the song without end, the never-finished symphony, there is how the covenant with the founders, Abraham and Sarah, Isaac and Rebecca, Jacob and Leah and Rachel, continues: the covenant in the flesh, the covenant in the Torah, wholly one in Israel.

3. GOD SINGS: the Torah manifests God, and the Torah is sung, so God's self-manifestation takes place in the Torah, which is God's song; the simple point is, in the Torah it is God who does the singing. That proposition at the outset, I find in the simple fact of the faith as it is lived the theological verities that govern. I deal with the facts of the faith of Judaism as the religion is practiced. These facts of the living faith form the data for theological construction: in the synagogue the Torah is sung; in the academy, the Torah is sung. In the synagogue and in the academy Israel takes place in the here and now. In the synagogue and in the academy Israel stands at Sinai to receive the Torah. In the synagogue when the Torah is declaimed, the blessings is said, "...who gives the Torah." In the academy, when the Torah is studied, the solemn Qaddish for the sages, sanctifying God's name, accompanies the act of learning.

God never talks to Israel, rather shouting, commanding, insisting, compelling, or whispering, cajoling, pleading: all very operatic. To invoke the world we know, God is not a TV sports announcer on the late night news, saying what happened this afternoon (which everybody knows), but a sports reporter, commenting on the event as it takes place; then, even the instant reply evokes excitement. Prose cannot contain the presence, but only poetry; not theology of merely well-worded propositions, but sung theology alone suffices. In synagogues we sing all our prayers because we sing the Torah. We do not sing the Torah because we are praying. We sing those prayers in loud voices, because we do not deem it proper to mumble and slur our words when we speak to God. We recite the Torah in three declaimed word, the precise word, because that is the sole right way of pronouncing what God has said to say.

All this are we supposed to learn from a simple fact? Do I attach so much consequence to the data that the words of the Torah in the synagogue are not read, not recited, not narrated or acted out or represented in a ritual ("in remembrance") or declaimed in ordinary voice but sung out? Indeed we are, indeed I do. For it is a given in the holy life that when any day we receive the Torah in the synagogue or academy, receiving the Torah takes place just as if it were on the very day on which the words were first sung out. Here is no act of historical memory. It is a proclamation of a present event.

That explains the paradigm I find in synagogue and academy life. In both localities' encounters it is music — singing out the words — that forms the medium for the message. Then what conclusions are we supposed to draw from the actualities of the lived faith and its sung theology? I find here the resolution of the paradoxes, the solution of the mysteries, that I set forth a moment ago. Once more we move rapidly along, four more propositions stating the implications of now-established facts of the practiced, living faith, the faith of the Torah in vital, holy Israel:

1. THE IMMEDIACY OF REVELATION, THE HERE AND NOW OF SONG: How do Sinai at one time in the past and the giving of the Torah in the here and now? What chemistry of the present moment unites them so as to surpass the paradox of past and present in one and the same moment? Music comes into being at the moment of performance; written out notes are not music. Music is intensely present; that is its only used tense. That is why music forms the sole right medium for that message, because God's self-manifestation in the Torah takes place in the immediate and acutely present tense. Music then matches the moment: it is not merely an event remembered out of the long-ago past, a paradigm to be reenacted; nor is the Torah imitated or acted out, as though there merely to be recapitulated. To the contrary, these ways of recovering the past are hardly appropriate, since the Torah in the synagogue and academy comes not out of the past but out of the very present, as God is present. Our sages of blessed memory have a way of dismissing the mere facts of history: "So what was, was." The sense in the Talmud is, so what? Facts out of the past bear no consequence for the here-and-now of eternal encounter with God. That is why the Torah forms anything but an inert fact of history. To the Torah, that is, the life of holy Israel, the Torah forms the truth concerning how things are and Who is here: the whole in the acutely present, continuing tense.

2. THE SONG IS A VERY SPECIFIC ONE: Specific words are sung and made to sing in a particular way; here is not singing in general — mere exuberance, an invention of the moment, *la di da, la la, la la* — but a tradition of music matching the circumstance and the sentiment. When we meet God in the singing of the Torah, we encounter not only music but also words. The Torah's song is a very specific one: these words match these sounds. So the Torah tells us much more than that there is a god. It tells us that there is this one and only God, the Lord who speaks to us through the Torah, and who tells us what we are supposed to do and how we are created to live our lives. Why do I insist that that song, that revelation, is specific and propositional, not general and merely the revelation that there is the Presence?

To state matters in concrete and secular terms: the way the words are sung is closely prescribed by ancient tradition; the melodies are very old, the conventions of punctilious sound and precise matching of word to music bearing the authority of the ages. Nothing so captures the union of tradition and the present than the fact that the musical modes come from ancient tradition, but are recreated in age succeeding age as though made up that morning. I can think of no more accurate a metaphor then for the realization of the Torah in the here and now than music; absent the performer, the notes lie dead on the page, black marks on white paper. Performed properly, the notes carry us into the mind of the composer, but they also recreate the mind of the composer in our very presence. Without Israel to sing, there are no words, there is no melody, and the encounter has not taken place and cannot happen. God, Torah, and Israel are one, each essential to the being of the others. Israel contributes the here and now, God, eternity, the Torah, the link from there to here and all time to one moment.

3. Sᴜɴɢ Tʜᴇᴏʟᴏɢʏ: So that is how it is with the sung theology of Judaism, the theological voice of the Torah at that very place, in that very moment, at which the Torah is pronounced. When the words are rightly sung, pronounced with precision, in proper rhythm and vocal pattern, then the Torah's message comes in the words and in the music, both. Without song, with the Torah merely read, revelation does not take place; there is no reason then to recite a blessing, as we do to revere the act. For the Torah read, not sung, is a mere book, with inert information. Indeed, it is a document that is danced with. On the festival of the Rejoicing of the Torah, holy Israel takes the Torah from its ark and dances with the Torah, each person in turn, into well into the night and the day beyond. The Torah is the lord of our dance, just as, in time to come, God and the Messiah will be lords of the dance. On the Sabbath when the Torah is read, it is carried through the congregation, accompanied by the singing of psalms of praise and prayer. As music is made physical in dance, so in the rites of proclaiming the Torah Israel responds to the encounter, like Miriam and the women at Sinai, with not only song but also dance.

When with sacred choreography and measured song the Torah is proclaimed, declaimed, then and only then it is Torah — revelation. And that transformation of writing on parchment into the meeting with God cannot serve merely as an act of remembrance; the moment of revelation can never be merely reenacted nor recapitulated, but only renewed in the freshness of the song — not new but always renewed, just as music when played realizes its eternal present. It is not played so that we may remember how Mozart made up and played this music, but so that we may encounter this music, this very music, in the here and now of the living moment.

4. Gᴏᴅ Sɪɴɢs: So come to a synagogue on a Sabbath, Monday, or Thursday, or on a holy day or festival, and you will hear the Torah not read but sung, loud and clear, in ancient chant, melody matching natural sounds of the very words God says. The song of the Torah — I cannot stress too much — ordinarily is sung with great punctiliousness. Where that is not the case, it is a disgrace to the community that receives God in a slovenly way, or not at all. It is solely to hear the Torah declaimed that holy Israel is summoned to the synagogue. Most of the rest of the liturgy may be recited at home, in private, in thick silence. The Torah defines the

sole, obligatory public event. This is so not only for what the Torah says in God's behalf, but what Israel says in response. Specifically, once the Torah is removed from its holy ark, carried in choreographed parade around the synagogue, the scroll is held up. At that sight of the unfurled columns of the scroll displayed before it, in response the congregation sings back, "This is the Torah that Moses set before the children of Israel at the command of the Lord." Then, and only then, holy Israel have announced itself as present, the Torah is sung out to the people. So it goes week by week, through the year: "in the beginning God created the heaven and the earth..." through "And there arose not a prophet since in Israel like unto Moses, whom the Lord knew face to face...." So goes the song of the Torah from Genesis through Deuteronomy, song out of the scroll of the Torah. To that, everything else forms massive commentary.

So much for the written part of the Torah, sung as God's song in the synagogue. It is easy to witness or at least to imagine how the written Torah is sung in the synagogue. What about singing the oral part of the Torah in the academy?

5.   ISRAEL RESPONDS IN SONG: If the written part of the Torah is God's statement in the synagogue, what of that other, oral part of the Torah? For the Torah, for holy Israel, comes in two media, the written, known to the Christian world as "the Old Testament," and the oral, the part unique to holy Israel. This other, orally-formulated and orally transmitted component of the one whole Torah of Moses our rabbi, is now preserved in the documents of our sages of blessed memory, in the Mishnah (ca. 200 C.E. [=A.D.]), the statement of the oral Torah as an account of Holy Israel's impalpable existence in the form of a philosophical law code, and then in the Mishnah's principal commentaries and amplifications, the two Talmuds, the one of the Land of Israel (ca. 400 C.E.) and the other of Babylonia, ca. 600 C.E.), and various compilations of amplifications of the Torah produced by the sages represented in the Mishnah and Talmuds and called "Midrash," or explanation and extension, of Scripture. These documents all together, form the starting point of the oral part of the Torah, extending upward to Sinai and outward to us. And, for our purposes, what makes the oral part of the Torah equal in importance to the written is, in the careful study of the writings of our sages of blessed memory, through which the Torah, oral and written, joins together and comes to us, we hear God's word and respond to it — and talk back. And the location at which Israel not only hears the Torah proclaimed but joins in the song with words of its own is the yeshiva, or holy academy, where the Torah is studied night and day. And there, too, the theological music takes shape in its own, distinctive melody.

But in the academy the music is less readily imagined, and, in the ordinary circumstance, people not part of the yeshiva-world are not likely to find their way to hear the music. The world at large knows the power of sacred music sung in a holy place, whether the great choirs of the churches, singing into vast rooms filled with mysterious light, or in the community of Israel, every one a member of the choir, singing out the words of prayer and Scripture. But the picture of a school house where people sing their studies finds no obvious analogue in everyday experience. And yet, only when we understand that other kind of singing — we whom God has made singing out our song to our maker in response to God's song to us — do we truly know God as the Torah, oral as much as written, makes God known to us.

A few words of description will have to suffice to explain how the oral part of the Torah is sung as well. One fact is essential at the outset: that the Talmud and related writings, which form the curriculum of the academy or yeshiva, themselves form parts of the Torah. How they are read and discussed, as much as how the Torah scroll in the synagogue is read and discussed, then tells us about how the Torah is re-presented. Everything that follows, then, rests on the simple fact that just as the written Torah, the Pentateuch, is sung in the synagogue, so the Talmud, the oral Torah, is sung in the yeshiva. That is to say, the part of the Torah that is studied in the yeshiva is the oral part, written down, finally in the Talmud of Babylonia (and related writings). So how learning is carried on in the academy, as much as how the Pentateuch is read in the synagogue, tells us how in Judaism Israel meets God in the Torah. In the walls of the academy deep silence falls only at the moment of prayer at which praying Israel addresses God directly, in the You of The Prayer par excellence.[3] Then, if you stand outside the open window of a yeshiva in Jerusalem or Efrat, you will hear a silence so perfect that the sole sound is birds' chirping — or the falling of a single feather from an angel's wing.

Go to an academy and stand against the wall and listen to the cacophony, as men young and old shout at each other in animated (also ritualized) argument, and you will soon hear the inner rhythm of the shouts and grasp that they are not yelling at one another but singing to one another. In fact there is a pattern, a sing-song, not an array of civil arguments, calmly put forth for reasoned argument and decision, but an explosion of violent sound, crescendos of phrases, rivers of words, all of them flowing in a powerful current, deeply felt, sincerely meant: the stakes are high. So the men shout at one another, singing to one another, the chant bearing the signals of the sort of argument that is being mounted, the conventions of thought that are being replayed.

But shouting and shrieking mark the location and shape sound all the rest of the time. This one proposes, that one disposes. This one forms a proposition in response to what the Torah (here: the Mishnah, the Talmud, or a later commentator) says, and that one says why what this one says is wrong: here are the flaws. If you are right, then I shall show the absurd consequence that follows. If you maintain

---

[3] I refer here to the Eighteen Benedictions of obligatory daily worship, and their counterpart for Sabbaths and Festivals, which are recited in solitary silence, each worshipper speaking directly to God. These some call "the amidah," the prayer said standing, and others call "the shemoneh esré, or eighteen benedictions.

thus-and-so, I shall demonstrate the disharmonies that result. Your music is my cacophony, your melody, my disharmony. And then you sing back, No, because, or Yes, but, and I sing back: an endless exchange of voices. All the time, we are held together in our argument by shared conviction that what is at stake is truth, not power, nor personalities, nor even the merely formal rituals of an empty academicism such as we may see acted out on an academic stage here or there.

And that is the Talmudic melody: the exchange of powerfully-held convictions, formed as rational propositions, set forth by appeal to evidence and argument, in behalf of perfectly secular truth: how things are and how they are supposed to be. Sustained, serious conflict over truth, for stakes exceeding measure, on the part of mature minds, forms holy Israel's response to the Torah, its song within the Torah. For, in Torah-study in a yeshiva, argument takes the form of song, reasoning is reenforced in the upward and the downward movement of the melodic line, and conclusions are drawn in crescendo. Tables are pounded, hands swing about, a choreography not so gentle as the synagogues, but as formed and in context also as graceful and expressive. The antiphonal sound of argument carries music for not only debate but dance, with much physicality and many fixed gestures, as much of body as of voice.

True, what you would hear in a yeshiva would be music of an other-than-conventional sort is hot music, not cool music. You need listen only briefly to grasp that the sound is organized, with rhythms, with measures and beats, with upward and downward passages, with hesitations and movement, words spoken largo, allegro, adagio, sostenuto, then agitato — yes, always *agitato*. But it is composed music, not chaos; the alternation of sound and silence such as music requires appeals follows an aesthetic of its own, one that, as we shall see, conveys theological truth in its way, as much as words do in theirs.

So if in the synagogue boys and girls chirp, in the academy, adults shout. In the synagogue God speaks to Israel. In the Yeshiva Israel talks back to God. To the secular eye, from the educated, academic perspective, the yeshiva is a strange place: it in variably encompasses a large room, full of tables, where bearded men sit chattering at one another, vehemently arguing, banging hands on tables or on books, throwing violent words at one another. That shows they care; the stakes are high. Each brings honor to the other. For argument forms the highest gesture of respect: it means each takes the other seriously. Argument becomes possible only when minds meet, becomes palpable when general agreement leaves space for particular points of contention. And contention for the sake of Heaven forms an act of sanctification, by the intellect, through passion. In the yeshiva people argue about problems that may appear remote from the world in which they make their lives. But they are studying Torah, specifically, the Talmud, together with its commentaries of more than a thousand years, the codes of law that govern proper conduct, the exegeses of words and phrases that make sense of the elliptical text at hand.

What gives the yeshiva the sound of a symphony — Charles Ives is the composer who comes to mind for the occasion, but, in his way, John Cage will have found himself at home — is simple: when this oral part of the Torah is studied, it too is sung, not read, recited in its own singsong, not repeated like any other book. The phrasing of the recitations correspond to measures of music, the recitative of the Mishnah or the questions and answers of the Talmud to melodic lines, the shouting to operatic declamation, the rapid-fire exchanges to duets, trios, quartets. The sound comes in waves, never in unison, rarely in harmony, but yields always a single piece of music. All serious learning in yeshivas takes the form of antiphonal argument, — if you say this (voice up), then how about that (voice down). Then bang the table. It is organized sound, shouted theology.

By repeating a line or a sound-pattern, or by reprise and development, prose becomes poetry, sound becomes music. Sound that is no longer random carries its own signals; when we know what to expect, or know to expect surprise, we have music. In yeshiva-study the repetitions of lines and the rhythm create the singsong that is song, and if you stood against the wall and listened, you would soon enough pick out the rhythms and the melodies of learning; if you stood in the corridors of a learned society or a faculty, you would hear sound, but not music; it would be whispering, mostly, or joking; when stakes are high, people argue; when they take one another seriously, they contend; some shout.

These are the sounds of battle, the clashing of the swords of reason and the cymbals of argument in the Torah. But conflict for the sake of aggression, not God, takes over, and no world of intellect exceeds that of the yeshivas in the venom that can poison argument. If for theology in Christianity men would kill or die, in Judaism, they do more than yell and scream, gesticulate and stamp their feet. They isolate, ignore, dismiss, condemn, shun, boycott, and avoid. Blood shed in the Christian theological wars, lives spent in silent isolation from the contentious other in the Judaic theological battles, "this book I will not read because he wrote it, that idea I will not consider because it comes from the proscribed location" — whether God can love the hatred committed in God's name only God can tell us. In the nature of the theological enterprise, love for God's truth competes in effect with hatred for disagreed-with alternatives: heresy for Christianity, schism for the Torah. Not all music echoes out of Heaven; hell has its orchestra too.

That is why to us, the natural sounds of the yeshiva prove puzzling and alien. For we are not used to rhythmic speech, sung words, sound patterns that bear meaning. Nor are we accustomed to the verbal violence of the yeshiva-song. Sounds natural to us prove ugly to others. Take us Americans, for instance. To foreigners, we Americans slurp and slide and slur our way through our sentences, we talk through our noses; we do not sing. And, for our part, to our American ears, used to our honking through our noses at one another, Swedes and Italians do not really talk with one another so much as they sing. The same is so in the Torah-academy, though the music is of a very different quality.

So in yeshivas bearded men — and today, at long last, young and mature women as well — spend their days shouting at one another, singing to one another, exchanging melodies — not only thoughts but themes — the way duos or trios or quartets take up a melodic line and, player by layer, do with it what they will, the soloists responding one to the next, all of them forming a coherent musical statement. And so it is with the massive noise — the organized noise — of the yeshiva. The contrast between yeshiva-discourse and conventional academic discourse is captured by the comparison between an exchange of information and an argument; between the speech of a play and the recitative of an opera; between prose and poetry. The only moments of silence in the yeshiva come in the solitude of prayer: then you can hear a feather fall off the wing of an angel. That is where Israel responds to God speaking through the oral part of the Torah, which is the Talmud, also expressed in melody.

These then form my theological propositions and the case to be made in their behalf out of the facts of the life of Judaism today. Here, I contend, out of the life of the vital faith, we identify the location and the moment at which Israel meets God: in the synagogue when the written Torah is declaimed, in the yeshiva (and its counterparts in study halls in synagogues) when the oral Torah forms the centerpiece of sustained argument. Music marks the moment. And that fact of the living faith brings us to a simple question: why does God choose the way of song, so that the self-manifestation of God in the Torah takes place only when and where the Torah is sung?

To understand the answer, we turn to that puzzle of the meeting with God, a meeting that takes place in two ways or not at all: I with the you of God, we with the you of God. If "we," Israel meet God in the Torah, but I do not, then God is not a "you" and I am not "Israel." If I meet God, but not within the holy Israel, then what standing do I have, in the setting of the Torah that makes the meeting possible only when Israel comes together? The union of "I" and "we" forms the requirement for the Torah to take place, whether in the synagogue or in the yeshiva. God appears to a "me" — I, Moses, I, Elijah, I Jeremiah, I Isaiah, to name principal cases — but speaks to an "us." God knew Jeremiah in the womb, but calls upon Jeremiah only to speak to Israel all together, the you of Jeremiah shifting over, always, to the you of Israel. No account of how in the Torah we know God can omit the I, and none can conclude with the I. All must speak to the "we" of Israel: God, Torah, and Israel are one. So we come to the question, How is it possible that we are one by one by one, individuals, but at an enchanted number, form Israel, the quorum, the community? And the answer to that question explains the compelling power of the metaphor of music that I offer in explaining (to use secular language) how in Judaism we know God, or, in the language of the Torah, where and when holy Israel encounters the living God.

The answer to the power of song to form community and bring about communion emerges as soon as we ask the question. In the case of Israel, there is no missing the point. But it is not an obvious point. To begin with, music speaks to the imagination, imposing order by reason of rhythm. Or music through melody and its logic or repetition along what otherwise appears to be random sound evokes response in mind. Israel itself forms an act of imagination: here and now related in mind to the ancient Israel of whom and of which the Torah speaks. So sung theology serves especially well to realize and express in words the social order of Israel, a community of the faithful, holy and set apart, that is formed in imagination alone.[4]

Since, to the contrary, perceived reality attests solely to the material, physical reality of Israel — an ethnic group, a people, even a state no less, I have to expand on this matter. Precisely why do I claim to see Israel in the setting of synagogue as a fabricated moment of enchantment and Israel in the setting of the academy as a willful act of transformation? How come I see both then forming an act of vivid imagination, not a mere invocation of simple worldly facts? As a matter of fact, Israel, in the here and now yields only Jews here and there and everywhere, without much in common among themselves except what they declare commonalities. They do not form a community. They do not speak a common language. They do not look alike or talk alike or think alike. No government governs them all, and no one leader speaks for them all, not in politics, not in theology, not in religion. Not only so, but as we move backward through time, to the formation of the Talmud itself, that same inchoate group of people exhibit the same contrasts and yet affirm (then all together in much the same way) the same faith.

For Judaism the categories are Israel, the state, or the Jews, the ethnic group; the Tradition or the culture or the ethnic way of life; and God takes no place at all. For the Torah, "Israel" is a native category of the sacred, not one formed of mere observation of secular facts of politics or demography; the Torah's Israel is an act of imagination. The Torah's God is the commanding voice out of eternity, the sound that sang, "Let there be...," so that there was. And how to say all this? Music (with dance, with drama, with poetry) forms the appropriate medium of re-creation and re-presentation of this imagined Israel. And that is how it should be: the intangible to convey the impalpable. For consider the case of Judaism: here we deal with a religion lacking conventional institutions, without worldly power. The Jewish people (not the Holy Israel of the faith) in the Exile and in the State of Israel is mostly secular most of the time. The Torah's decisions then come about

---

[4] I need hardly elaborate the obvious point that in this world "Israel" stands for "the State of Israel," the Jews for an ethnic group, and Judaism for the ethnic culture of that group. But a moment of reflection will show that in the setting of the Torah, "Israel" forms an act of divine imagination, the Torah (not Judaism) an intervention out of eternity into time, and the God who calls to Israel by singing the Torah the one we know not palpably but in the thin voice of silence, in the adumbrations of a voice calling back to us as we hide in the cave, "The Lord, the Lord...." In this context, only the act of imagination governs.

through consensus; its common patterns of behavior and belief require constant affirmation by individuals, instruments of coercion are few and very local. How does music then serve? It is because it is the way of holding together what is intangible and yet fitting: sound we cannot touch nor yet coerce, yet can hear to resonate on key or off. We cannot coerce music, but music moves us, and not only when we want to be moved.

There is another consideration. It is that where the faith speaks, it is because there the chorus sings together. True, as I claim, "Israel" is an act of mind, and in the everyday, Israel, merely the Jews, form no chorus at all, at least, none that makes music together. And yet, as a matter of fact Judaism also is a religion that in doctrine reaches decision by consensus — or there is no decision, only endless schism. And Judaism stands on vast and vigorous consensus: God is one, the Torah comes from God, Israel is God's first love — and much else.[5] The Torah's then is a religion that, in the world of prose, corresponds in the world of making music to a chorus rightly sung, on key. It is well to sing the theology: set forth the words and the notes, and assign to the chorus of the faithful the task of making them into music, music sung together by all and all at once. Why do I say so? Because, in the nature of the social condition of Judaism, which is to say, the imaginary Israel that hears God sing in the Torah, that is the only way.

Let me recapitulate this point in more secular language: the theology of Judaism — the right ways of thinking, acting, believing, all of which cohere in the consensus of the faithful — takes the form of not creed demanding assent, nor dogma nor doctrine requiring a statement of the faith. All these are necessary, but none suffices. For none, by itself, can attain authority, impose itself upon all; the reason is already in our hands, the simple fact that God speaks to the individual who studies the Torah, and not only to all Israel assembled to hear the Torah. Music is the medium: all can sing, each one by himself or herself, everyone all together: "Hear, Israel, the Lord, our God, is the one God" — that and many other statements of theological fact we sing together, each in the voice God has given; all say the same words, each finds the right pace; all follow roughly the same notes and melody, but who is there to set the key?

The signal that that is how Judaism speaks — in the consensus of shared song — is: we sing just as we pray, one by one yet all together, each one in so very personal a voice, together; we sing one song, in many voices; we sing all together, saying one set of words and following one set of musical notes, forming of the whole nothing so civil as a symphony, but something that nonetheless has its

---

[5] I do not mean to obscure the fact that Reform Judaism and Orthodox Judaism disagree, or that the various segregationist Judaisms, all of them called "Orthodox" but each of them dismissing as heretical all of the others, reject all integrationist Judaisms. But both the vast consensus within Orthodox Judaisms, and the equally long list of propositions to which both Orthodox and other-than-Orthodox Judaisms adhere, testify to, if not unity then, consensus on most of the definitive issues.

distinctive sound. It is right that the Torah should be sung: it is the only way to keep the whole together. The Jews, stubborn individualists, form Israel, one and whole, only because, however diverse belief and behavior, in the end the Torah is sung in one and the same way everywhere. Hear it here, it sounds one way, here it there, another; declaimed in Tel Aviv, the vowels are clipped, the consonants exploded, in New Orleans or Atlanta, the vowels drawled, the consonants slurred, in my native New England, the whole sung from not the diaphragm but the nose. The words are the same, the melody is the same, the Israel is one and the same. God alone fully grasps the harmony, fathoms the counterpoint.

To understand what is at stake when and where we meet God, come with me to the place where Judaism lives, which is, the academy and the synagogue, in the hour of prayer, when God is present. Here is where I construct my theology of the encounter with God in the Torah. In the synagogue we pray individually, but all together. Each one, at the moment of petition, is alone. Silence prevails. Yet all say the same words, if not at the same pace or with the same intent, still, at the same moment. Specifically, observe worship in an academy or a synagogue and you will see, at the most solemn moment of petition, in the recitation of The Prayer itself, the members of the congregation rise together, but pray each person by himself or herself. So speaking to God, all Israel pray by themselves, but pray, too, all together. Then someone repeats it all; but that is the formality, the authentic encounter of prayer, when people talk to God and tell God what they ask and want, has already taken place. All have spoken by themselves, individually; but they have said the same words, whatever other words they may have chosen to add. And that is how it is with the song. Each sings, but all sing together; each voice registers, but the chorus is heard all together.

So it is hardly surprising that a religion that treats prayer at its most public as entirely personal and private should find its voice in a chorus, and make its statement through consensus. Music is the medium of consensus — or cacophony. And God sings one song, and Israel hears that one song. But each hears with his or her own ears. And when they sing, each sings with his or her own voice, but all sing one song together: that is what happens in the synagogue when the Torah is sung, that is what happens in the academy when the study of Torah evokes song.

How does Israel come into being in song? Many voices join in the song; diverse timbers, keys, quality of sound from sweet to hoarse, perfectly pitched to nearly monotone, join in song. This is not in unison — by definition, people with their many varied voices really cannot sing in unison at all — but it is all together. And why should all Israel not sing the same tune, since it is the Torah's melody, in God's key. Now, as a matter of fact, the diverse and motley Jews by definition are not going to sing on the same key, not even on key at all. But the words are the words of the Torah, and the trope the trope of the Torah, and the musical exchanges — the counterpart to the parts to the quartet, changing and trading the melody — are trades of the Torah. Then it is all the same: in unison if not with one another then with God. And in the ears of God, who is to say what is on key and what is off key, except by appeal to the Torah that God sings as we sing. So to state the simple point: just as ballet is physicalized music, so for Judaism, theology is sung thought. That is to say, God's song is truth conveyed through not propositions formed into music, and not through words shaped into works of beauty, feeling, and sensibility, so much as ideas formed rhythmically in their natural sounds, into formations of sense and proposition.

Let us now turn from the facts of the lived faith to the propositions that those facts sustain. What conclusion do I draw from the bed-rock facts of lived theology that we have now surveyed and transformed into propositions? Judaism is a religion that forms a union of individual and community; emotion and attitude, fact and truth, belief and behavior, and therefore seeks a medium for many voices to say many things all at once. Music is that way: words set to music, rhythmic thought, melodized intellect. Music so uniquely suited to serve as the medium for normative theological doctrine requires us to speak, in particular, of a "theological voice" and of a "Talmudic melody." That is because music has the power to allow many voices to speak, each its own line of melody, and all to form a single composition. Only music (with its close friends, poetry, drama, and dance) can do that.

Words speak for this one or for that one, until many adopt them as authoritative: the one, the many, but not both and equally, in the balance, as with music. By contrast, the singular voice that is music has the capacity to sustain this one's voice alongside that one's voice, each enjoying its own integrity, and to form of them all a single chorus. Only music can do that. It is no surprise, then, that the Torah in both its parts, written and oral, should be sung; there is no other way that serves. Music matches the mode of prayer: individuals, reciting their prayers on their own, yet in tandem. So too in song: all sing individually, in chorus. So when I say, God sings, I speak of Israel's response: the theological acts of the Judaic faithful, and I mean that as God speaks in organized, intelligible sound, so does Israel, and so do Israel. One by one and all together, Israel sings this song that God sings. In declaiming the Torah Israel responds to song with song, not in prose but in poetry, not in a monotone of speech, but in the many colors of rhythm and nuanced voice and proper pitch and key, all forming harmony and bearing that ineluctable logic that only organized sound can convey. That is why I refer to the natural sounds of the Torah, its sung theology. God's singing, in the language of religious experience, corresponds, in the language of Israel's holy life, to the giving of the Torah, by which I mean, pressing our metaphor to its limit, the music of the spheres.

Since I have invoked the power of imagination, readers may suppose I treat music as a metaphor, telling us in one set of images how things are in some other realm. But that is not my meaning. To the contrary, when I say God sings and the Torah is God's song, I mean that statement literally: through the music of the Torah, God becomes known to us. And when we sing our learning in the

Torah, God hears our song. The character of music serves because it helps us to define the character of the theology of Judaism, or, in the language I prefer to state matters, *God sings to Israel and the Torah is sung theology*. The norms of belief and behavior fully reveal themselves when we know how to hear the music and how to sing in tune: what makes notes into melodies, sound into music. So to state my thesis in just a few words: speaking only descriptively, alluding to established and entirely familiar facts of the practiced piety of the faithful, I claim that, when Israel hears the Torah sung, Israel hears God's song. This constructive theology may be expressed, then, in a single sentence: since God's voice in the Torah is an active voice, in the Torah God sings to Israel.

What, then, of the theological propositions that, at a later point, take shape in a theological system? I have already stressed how God sings to Israel not only in music but also in very particular words. God sings a specific melody, saying particular words: "the Lord spoke to Moses saying, speak to the children of Israel and say to them...." "You will love the Lord your God with all your heart...." "Love your neighbor as yourself." "Remember the Sabbath day to keep it holy." That is why Moses did not need to see God's face; the behind sufficed, for Moses had already heard God's voice in song. The particularities of God's song for Israel now come to the fore.

The first concerns the time and place of meeting: where and when do we meet God, and what happens in the meeting? Here we take up not only the record of the encounter but its consequences: when we meet God, God gives us the Torah, which tells us who we are and what we are therefore supposed to do. The liturgy of the synagogue itself insists that the synagogue rite of proclaiming the Torah forms a moment of revelation: God giving the Torah. The language of the blessings recited before and after the reading of a Torah-lection says precisely that. The blessing speaks of the here and now, using as it does the present tense: "blessed...who gives the Torah." That refers to what happens here and now, in fact and in effect, just as the blessing for bread, "who brings forth bread to the earth," speaks of what happens in the here and now. Other blessings using the perfect tense, "who has kept us in life, has sustained us, and has brought us to this season," show that the tense represents a matter of choice. Furthermore, even the blessing over the Torah fore and aft mixes tenses: "who has chosen us from all peoples and has given us the Torah...blessed...who gives," and at the end, "who has given us the Torah of truth and planted in our midst eternal life," and, then again, "...who gives." The election took place in the beginning and endures; the Torah marked and marks the election. Through the authentic Torah eternal life has taken root among us. These statements reach far into the distant, governing past: time gone. But they speak to the present, especially to the present: "...who gives...."

The choice of present tense is deliberate, It serves to say that Sinai is not a place nor a merely one-time, past-time historical event. It is a moment of eternity, when the eternal breaks into time and shatters one-time history with timeless truth:

reliable mathematics replicates nature's uncertain processes. It is an hour beyond time marked specifically by what happens whenever in the holy community of the faithful the Torah is removed from the holy ark, danced with and paraded, displayed, read, opened full breadth to the community to inspect, paraded again and reverently returned to its ark. That is what "giving the Torah" and "receiving of the Torah" by God and Israel, respectively, or, in theological language, what "revelation," means. And in the synagogue and academy that is not an act of commemoration or even replication but — once more I stress — of re-presentation. When the Torah is given, then we are, we become, Israel, there we know God.

God is made manifest in the Torah and only there. People think otherwise, finding God in the stars or in ourselves, in the power of the seas or in the silence of the desert. But unless God tells us that there God is, we do not know it. Let me state matters in a simple and logical way: God is not made manifest in nature, outside of the Torah's account of natural creation. Nor is God made known through what happens in history, outside of the Torah's interpretation of events. That is to say, if the Torah did not tell us that the heavens tell the glory of God, how should we know? And if the Torah did not tell us that Assyria was the rod of God's wrath, how might we have come to such a conclusion? Contemporary confusion concerning the meaning to be drawn from our mortal wounds — the proclamation out of hell that God is dead, for example — shows the alternative: every one a theology for himself or herself; none left with personal doubt, but none with a faith susceptible to sharing either. But that is not how things are in the framework of the faith, the Torah ("Judaism"). So without the Torah, nature and history fall dumb — or set forth messages too diverse to command universal assent. And, it goes without saying but has always to be repeated, Israel receives the Torah in community. There is no revelation to Israel that does not take place in the Torah or in entire unity with the Torah. The mountains danced — for Israel at Sinai. The kings heard the roar — of God at Sinai. Nature and politics or history find their sense — through God at Sinai, in this morning's giving of the Torah.

The theological encounter recorded in this morning's proclamation of the Torah takes form in propositions and becomes real in the specific words we hear and say. So while music may take the form of a song without words, the song that God sings has many words. Let me digress to provide an ample explanation of what is critical to the theology of Judaism, which is, an enormous corpus of carefully criticized language. Up to now I have identified only the locus and the medium of God's self manifestation, the Torah, but not explained either the character or the form that the Torah takes. I have therefore to pause and answer some questions about the Torah itself. First, its character: why not a Torah that reveals God's Presence not in words but in silence? Do we not meet God in the heights and in the depths, in joy or suffering when these take place? Why so much talk when God meets Moses, or when in the synagogue the Torah is set forth, why the flood of words, and, in the academy or yeshiva, why the waves and whole oceans of passionate words? Whence insistence upon the passion borne outward on wings of speeches, allegations and points of insistence? Before the power of the song with many words can make itself manifest, we have to explain to ourselves why when God sings to Israel, God sings the words of a song, those specific words, no other words; and no song without words, and that particular song for those specific words.

To answer this question, we have to consult the Torah itself. There we find that the reason (from the perspective of the Torah itself) is that the other way — the way of wordless revelation in nature or in history — did not work, has not worked God's purpose from creation and the dawn of humanity in history. Uninstructed, with only a few perfectly natural responsibilities, the children of Noah missed the lessons of the flood. Nor did the history made, even by the elect family of Abraham and Sarah and their descendents, accomplish the goal. The children of Abraham and Sarah included Ishmael, of Isaac and Rebecca, Esau; Jacob and Leah cannot have boasted about all their sons and daughters, and Jacob's last word — brutal in its honesty about them, shocking in the absence of sentimentality — left no doubt of his view of matters. So genealogy was not enough; the presence, indeed even the blessing, could not suffice. Israel without the Torah knew only that God is, but not what God says.

Revelation required articulation: not only that God is, but what God wants. Humanity is like God in intellectual power, but not God: humanity has to be told what God knows. What makes humanity like God, to be sure, is that, humanity at least can understand when told: can obey, or can sin. But even heirs of the patriarchs, in the elected genealogy, needed to be told what to do: to respond to the presence. That explains (at least from the perspective of the Torah) why, when God proposed to undertake self-revelation to humanity, in the end it was not through mere nature, with its mute testimony (no more floods), nor even through the lessons of consequential events called history (Ishmael and Esau had history, but did not draw the right conclusions from it, as their disappointed parents learned). Not content with nature's or history's ambiguous message, God through the Torah, eloquent and unambiguous, conveyed what God wished and now wishes to say.

Nor would God rely only upon this man and that woman, even Abraham, even Sarah; family by itself could not suffice, for the reason just now given in the names Ishmael and Esau. It would be to an "us" that was made up of not only the children of Abraham and Sarah and their children, but that "all Israel" that made a place for even the hangers on who in the wake of freedom flooded out of Egypt in the flotsam. It was to that enlarged Israel that God would speak. Israel would not suffice only as one extended family; it would have also to be a kingdom — of priests; a people — that was holy. These other social metaphors besides family bore each its own paradigm. And so too, once the Torah came forth at Sinai, it formed the paradigm of revelation with no further misunderstandings: creation could no longer be misread, history misconstrued. Prophecy then would serve as a reminder, until sages uncovered in the Torah rules of rigorous analysis so reliable that even prophecy became redundant. The Torah sets forth what God chose through Moses to tell humanity, which is, God's self-revelation in relationship to humanity: the story of nature's creation, Israel's revelation, humanity's end in redemption. So much for the reason that when God sings to Israel, it is a song of many words.

So much for a Torah made up of not only records of God's appearance, but reports of God's points of insistence. Now to move to the next main point. It concerns the matter of attitude. In the context of music, the importance of attitude is easy enough to understand. What infuses music is our feelings in singing it: the joy of joyful music, the poignancy of the sad — these must come from our own hearts, or the music itself will not convey its message. If we sing, but not to God, it is not worship. If the Torah is sung, but not to convey God's music but a merely secular song, it is not the Torah. Our attitude takes the love songs collected in the Song of Songs (known to Christians as the Song of Solomon) and turns those songs into melodies of the love of God for Holy Israel, and of Israel for God. That transformation — an enchantment, really — underscores the power of attitude, the magic of intentionality. So when we think about meeting God in the song of the Torah, we introduce an element that only we can provide: the heart. That is why the Talmud says, above all, "God wants the heart," and, further, "the commandments" — actions that we carry out in submission to God's will expressed in the Torah — "were given only to purify us."

If we sing with all our heart and soul and might, the music resonates. In meeting God in the Torah, the encounter takes place not in random sound but in music made manifest in circumstance and occasion: intention and attitude above all. The attitude that draws Israel to synagogue worship or yeshiva-learning makes all the difference, then, since the Torah may be read, not sung; cited as fact or studied as data, not at all received with reverence. God's self-manifestation in the Torah requires no footnotes and takes place elsewhere than in scholarly meetings. Nor, just because a Jew opens Scripture, is God present. The giving of the Torah demands the receiving of the Torah and therefore requires holy Israel, assembled in sanctity. The attitude characteristic of authentic synagogue worship and yeshiva study enchants and so transforms the act of learning. That at stake is not merely acquiring information, as in a class room, but reverently receiving revelation, the setting itself reveals. In the synagogue the Torah is taken out of its holy ark with song and dance, psalms and hymns precede, blessings surround the proclamation, then the scroll is displayed and its claim conveyed: "this is the Torah" — this scroll from which we have just now read — "that Moses set before Israel at the command of God" — no ambiguities there.

We cannot imagine that we are sitting in the Library of Congress or in a class room of diverse students, all races and all faiths or none, of the vast and diverse University of South Florida — or the even the Hebrew University of Jerusalem itself, for that matter. In the academy that is the yeshiva, when the Torah is studied through the teaching of the master to the disciples, rules of sanctity govern, and prayer concludes the action. That is why there is no confusing the yeshiva study hall with the university lecture room. We cannot suppose that a sage in a yeshiva is a professor in a university, only with a long beard. In both cases, attitudes concerning what is done, where one is, transform what can be secular into what must be holy: the act of receiving the gift of the Torah.

So for the giving of the Torah — in secular language, revelation — to take place what is required is not place but identification of place, not just persons whom it may concern, but the holy people. The right people, at the right time, with the right attitude receive the Torah and what they do at such a time in such a place furthermore defines what it means for Israel to receive the Torah. In this context "situation" speaks of circumstance, not location: God comes through the Torah to Israel, which is a utopian, not a locative category. And God comes not promiscuously but in measured moments: at the time of finding, when in the Torah God wishes to be found. The circumstance of saying "blessed...who gives the Torah," or reciting at the end, "Magnified and sanctified be the great name in the world that he created in accord with his will," defines the conditions of giving and receiving the Torah, that is, the act and moment of revelation.

This point forms the critical turning in my argument. Now that I have explained how, in Judaism, we know God, I double back to explain where, in Judaism, the meeting takes place. So I raise the following proposition: Where God is to be found, there, the words that are said, and the manner of their enunciation, will tell us whatever we are going to know about the actual encounter with God, or, (once more the secular use) the theological voice of Judaism. Just as I invoke music as not metaphor but the theological medium, so I point to the encounter with God in synagogue and yeshiva not as a this-worldly description but as a statement of the norm of encounter and dialogue. How holy people act tells me what I need to know. My identification of the theological voice of Judaism accords with the implications of common conduct, past and present: the Judaism of real people.

In the nature of things it is especially in the synagogue and in the yeshiva or academy that the meeting with God is constant. "Seek God at the time of finding" speaks of where and when God is made manifest. There is where the Torah is taken out of its holy ark and declaimed; where people gather, in intense concentration, to examine its words and their logic and their structure. In the one place, through proper rite, all Israel embodied in a quorum of ten hears the words of the Torah. In the other, people who devote all their real time to learning in the Torah undertake to be changed by the Torah. So while when even one studies the Torah, God is made manifest in its words, where Israel in community studies the Torah, the Torah comes to full realization in the song that is sung only in chorus: God sings, Israel hears and responds, in the Torah. The Torah is in two parts, however, and each introduces its own kind of meeting. So in stressing throughout the singular encounter with God in synagogue and yeshiva, I should not represent the two meeting places as uniform or obscure that the two components of the Torah afford quite different kinds of meetings with God. God sings in one way here, in the other way there, as Moses and Elijah could have taught one another.

The two public occasions of God's self-manifestation in the Torah not only are alike but they also differ. They differ in the very obvious fact that in the synagogue, the written part of the Torah is displayed and proclaimed, while in the academy, the oral part of the same Torah is set forth. While, furthermore, the synagogue celebrates, the Torah, in the academy in particular the Torah gains its true voice and is heard in all solemnity. That is for two reasons. First, in the synagogue Israel sits and listens; affirms without a more than passive engagement. In most circumstances a rabbi explains what has been read; or no one does; the words speak for themselves. But in the academy Israel takes part in a colloquy of proposition and objection, analysis and argument, an on-going conversation and dialogue with allegations as to truth. In the academy's unique way of receiving the Torah, Israel pays the compliment of utter and total conviction: the tribute of sustained argument as to truth, along paths dictated by public reason and compelling rationality.

The second reason is that, in the academy, in theory and practice, disciples of sages through learning in the Torah are changed in mind and therefore also in character and soul. For the academy through Torah-learning means to form right attitudes, in the language of the Torah itself, to purify the human heart. In the academy or yeshiva, that means, to shape their minds in response to the rules of rigorous inquiry by which the inner order and sense of the Torah are uncovered so that they too may think in the way in which the Torah was thought. The religious experience of encounter and dialogue with God that the Torah affords takes the form of prayer or study; but study is the more immediate, the more intense, the more intimate: there God gets inside our minds. The Talmud says that God wants the heart, and the Talmud says that God gave the Torah only to purify our hearts. All that I said about the centrality of attitude and intentionality means only to bring to the surface the profound insistence upon the why of the encounter with God: what difference meeting God is supposed to make.

What makes the argument of the academy a medium of theological discovery, so that the modes of argument convey the melodies of the Torah? Right thinking in the academy affords access especially to those rules of intellection that governed when the Torah took shape and express what was on God's mind. If God is made manifest in the Torah, then all can see how God forms thoughts, makes sentences, brings about connections (e.g., juxtapositions) and draws conclusions: how God thinks in a way we can understand, in a way we ourselves can think. Disciples of sages not only gain possession of teachings of the Torah but are possessed by the modes of thought that produced those teachings and therefore reformed. The reformation takes place in the heart and mind, where the Torah makes its mark. But even hearing the Torah in the synagogue may change minds and affect the intellect of hearers; properly proclaimed in careful song, the Torah in the synagogue touches the heart and soul.

Observing the difference between the giving of the Torah in the synagogue and the receiving of the Torah in the academy, we now note that synagogue and academy share the implacably public character of their activity. The religious encounter afforded by the Torah takes principal place not for the private person but in public, in a moment of community and of communion: Israel with Israel, Israel with God. In both cases, then, synagogue and yeshiva, the act consists in the shared act and moment of hearing and receiving the gift of the Torah. The gift has to be received, accepted, acknowledged, and, in the nature of the holy life of Israel, that means, by Israel as a whole, as at Sinai. The unacknowledged gift is an insult.

How is this shared acknowledgement, this public engagement with the gift, to be accomplished? The Torah not only reveals that God is, but what God says and wants: propositions. And it follows, the way in which Israel receives the gift of the Torah is through its understanding, its capacity to persuade itself in all rationality to affirm and obey. That is why in the synagogue the Torah is not only displayed but read. That fact further explains why in the academy the Torah is not only read but analyzed. It is in the life of the mind that Israel receives the gift, that Judaism affirms revelation. The rigorous composition of theology then forms the counterpart, in secular language, to the act of rational affirmation, in the language of the Torah: we shall do and we shall obey. And that fact brings us back once again to the center of matters, the public and communal quality of the meeting with God and leads us to understand why we must understand the Torah as God's song. There is nothing so public, and that by definition, as intellect.

Now let us dwell on the requirements of the shared and public receiving of the gift of the Torah. When we have grasped what is required we will more vividly understand the necessity of singing, singing in particular, in the giving and receiving of the Torah.

The first rule of thought is the sharing of thought: to speak intelligibly to the other is to ascertain that what one thinks is intelligent. The contemporary philosophical words, "universalizability" and "generalizability," serve as the model. These refer to what can be shown to others to be true and can be demonstrated to apply to many cases. Where thought cannot be communicated by some protocol of rationality or convention of agreed signals that sustain communication, we deal with what is not asocial but insane. Rationality is always public, by definition. And, given the public character of the giving of the Torah, the propositional character of what is given, and the active and engaged character of the act of receiving the Torah, it is no surprise that the rule for studying the Torah and therefore also the requirement for meeting God is as with Moses and Elijah. God gives the Torah through the prophet to be sure, but always to the "us" of Israel." So "we" meeting the One may be embodied in the "I," the individual of whom Halafta speaks, but "we" always stands for the "we" of Israel. Rationality requires community.

If revelation is public and communal, how in the theology of Judaism does the individual relate to the community? I speak of theology that is shared, public, and communicable, not only solipsistic and personal. While the Torah may be studied in private, it is received and proclaimed only in the public square of shared worship or shared learning: synagogue, yeshiva. One's obligation to hear the Torah read can be fulfilled only in community, in a quorum. That is where we meet God. This is the point of R. Halafta of Kefar Hananiah, in a familiar saying of Torah-learning that explains how we meet God in the Torah:

> "Among ten who sit and work hard on Torah the Presence comes to rest, as it is said, 'God stands in the congregation of God (Ps. 82:1). And how do we know that the same is so even of five? For it is said, 'And he has founded his group upon the earth' (Am. 9:6). And how do we know that this is so even of three? Since it is said, 'And he judges among the judges' (Ps. 82:1). And how do we know that this is so even of two? Because it is said, 'Then they that feared the Lord spoke with one another, and the Lord hearkened and heard' (Mal. 3:16). And how do we know that this is so even of one? Since it is said, 'In every place where I record my name I will come to you and I will bless you' (Ex. 20:24)."

TRACTATE ABOT 3:6

So — Halafta maintains — Israel meets God in the Torah, and that encounter may take place among many or even one on One. But Halafta has spoken of even a single individual, and, it is manifest, Israel is made up of individuals, each of whom is supposed to receive and reverence the Torah and its teachings. How hold the whole together, making place for each along the way? I speak of a theological voice, but in the adventitious accidents of personality, there may be only voices. The answer unfolds in yet another sequence of facts, to be specified and analyzed.

We recall how music serves to hold together individual voices in a single moment of music. We now leave the medium of music behind and identify the facts of the living faith and the propositions those facts convey. The first is that the character of the Torah tells private persons what they are, all together, and it tells Israel, all together, how the families of which Israel is comprised are to conduct themselves.

[1] Israel is made up of individuals in families, of families in communities, of communities in all Israel.

[2] And all Israel takes place when it is all together, all at once.

That assembly takes place on Sabbath after Sabbath when Israel is assembled, as at Sinai, to celebrate the Torah by paying attention to it and so asserting who Israel too is, as the blessing before the Torah states: "Blessed are you, Lord, our God, ruler of the world, who has chosen us from among all the peoples by having given us the Torah. Blessed are you, who gives the Torah." At the end come similar words, referring to us, Israel: "who has given us the Torah that is true and planted within us eternal life." So much for individuals in families assembled in the synagogue: chosen through the Torah. That is not the end of the matter of the public character of the assembly with God, but it carries us far beyond the beginning.

What about God's presence, in secular language, the theological voice itself? The second, and more important aspect already has impressed us: the immediacy of the presence of God in the Torah, despite Halafta's contrary assurance, really does require the presence of the many, for in fact the Torah insists upon Israel's presence, represented by some sort of quorum; Halafta does after all commence with a quorum. In the synagogue the quorum makes possible the public declamation: the reading of the Torah at the climax of the act of worship. Without a quorum Qaddish — the sanctification of God's Name in public — cannot be recited or the Torah read. This quorum by definition invariably marks the present tense; there is no quorum out of the past. Merely because, an hour earlier, ten people were present does not validate the public proclamation of the Torah. And merely because, an hour from now, someone will come to complete the quorum, does not permit us to remove the Torah from its ark and to read it now. God gives the Torah (so the blessing states) here and now, this minute, to these people, in this quorum. And that is where the academy (and its civilian counterparts, groups of Jews assembled for Torah-study wherever they meet) comes into the picture. The Torah speaks in the hear and now when people learn how to listen.

So we come to the critical question concerning the giving and the receiving of the Torah, which is to say, how God is made manifest in Israel, in me, you, him, her: us: how to hold the whole together? The answer once more derives from the facts of the lived theology of Judaism, or, in the native categories of Judaism, from the moment when God gives the Torah: it is to listening Israel in the here and now, all of us, all together.

We form a quorum specifically to listen, which or course means to understand and to respond. Then the whole holds together in our shared act of understanding and responding: reasoning together, hearing at once and thinking along the same lines of rationality. In the ordinary world we understand through reasoning, specifically, through a process of thought that we share with the other, that makes two minds work in one way so that both understand the same thing. In Torah study, properly conducted, we undertake the disciplines of reasoning that show us not only what the Torah says, but how the Torah works: the way in which our minds work in correspondence with, therefore in response to, how the mind of the One who gives the Torah works.

So much for the exposition of the known. Now everything is in place, and I have evoked only entirely familiar, universally acknowledged facts concerning the practice of the faith. Our somewhat slow progress, with an occasional doubling back, through the facts of the giving and receiving of the Torah in the vivid existence of holy Israel yields this conclusion: when Israel meets God, it is

[1]   in a public event, which

[2]   requires a meeting of minds, a shared rationality.

Then the mystery is, how, in what media, through what processes of ratiocination, joined through what shared rationality, do our minds join — and also meet God's mind? How do we form a communion of intellects, and what are the media by which minds are brought into union? Several questions here are melded:

[1]   the question of the giving of the Torah to me through us,

[2]   the question of shared communication,

[3]   the question of the how of revelation.

When we know the solution to that complex of mystery and paradox, we shall hear how the Torah is supposed to speak to us, which is to say, in the categories of the world at large, how to identify Judaism's theological voice. So now I have set the stage for the consideration of the critical issue: how the Torah makes intelligible statements, at once compelling and persuasive, to which we give uncoerced assent, which is to say, through our own rigorous reasoning coming to God's own conclusions.

I do not mean to deal in paradox or mystery. The evidence of faithful humanity tells that God speaks not only in silence but also in the mystery of what comes to us as contradiction. But in the Torah all things lie on the surface. The voice of Sinai was heard by the uneducated slave girl as much as by the sages of the day, and, when she heard, she heard more, and with more nuance and also more conviction, than sages later on with their acute logic, working with the mere memory of Sinai. Even the infants and babes in their mothers' wombs joined in the Song at the Sea:

> "Then [Moses and the people of Israel sang this song to the Lord, saying, 'I will sing to the Lord, for he has triumphed gloriously; the horse and his rider he has thrown into the sea" (Exodus 15:1):
>
> R. Meir says, "Even embryos in their mothers' wombs opening up their mouths and recited the song song before the Omnipresent: 'Bless God in full assemblies, even the Lord, you who are from the fountain of Israel' (Ps. 68:27).
>
> "And it was not Israel alone that recited the song before the Omnipresent.
>
> "Even the ministering angels did so: 'O Lord, our Lord, how glorious is your name in all the earth, whose majesty is rehearsed above the heavens' (Ps. 8:2)."
>
> Mekhilta XXVI:I.17 = Shirata Chapter One

So there are no mysteries before God, though from the world that God has made come many to us. So how are we do accord uncoerced assent to propositions that God has already reached and revealed? The critical point lies in the character of God's self-manifestation, which defines the conditions for communion of minds, ours with one another, ours with God's. The fact, as we have already observed, is that God's self-manifestation proves in the Torah to make a highly propositional statement, which forms facts into truth and means to persuade us, to compel through a process of thinking and feeling. So the medium by which minds are formed into a communion affects intellect but also emotion, attitude and also feeling, deed and also intentionality: how we are and what we may become in the whole of our being.

Let me spell this claim out with some care, so that the final solution to the mystery of the giving and receiving of the Torah will prove commensurate to the problem: what medium serves, or, to adumbrate my goal at the end: why song in particular? And, to signal what is coming, my answer will be, it had to be music, and only music. That claim paraphrases what the Talmud itself states in so many words:

> Said R. Shephataiah said R. Yohanan, "Whoever recites from the Torah without melody or repeats Mishnah-traditions without song — concerning him Scripture states, 'Moreover I gave them statutes that were not good and ordinances by which they could not have life' (Ezekiel 20:25)"
>
> BAVLI MEGILLAH 32A

Essential to learning Torah-traditions and not forgetting them is song:

> R. Joshua b. Qorhah says, "Whoever studies the Torah and does not review it is like a man who sows seed but does not harvest it."
> R. Joshua says, "Whoever learns the Torah and forgets it is like a woman who bears and buries."
> R. Aqiba says, "A song is in me, a song always"
>
> TOSEFTA AHILOT 6:8H-I=BAVLI SANHEDRIN 99A-B

So my insistence on the centrality of song in receiving the Torah once more is shown merely to paraphrase what our sages of blessed memory themselves maintained. But the point of relevance to the argument here is different. Why song in particular? The reason is that song uniquely bears the power to unite one person to the next, and also form the union of feeling and intellect, proposition and sentiment. When we sing, we sing words but we may also smile or laugh or cry; and pray, and also study — especially study: "an ignorant person cannot be truly pious."

Am I right to insist upon a medium for theological expression that unites feeling and thought? To respond, let me give a single compelling case of the union of the public and the private, the intellectual and the affective, the propositional and the emotional, conviction, attitude, and conscience. The Torah contains the words that say not only that God is one and unique ("Hear O Israel, the Lord is our God, the one God"), but also how we are supposed to feel and what we are supposed to think in that very context of the pronouncement of the doctrine concerning the one unique God: presence. The next words state, "And" (meaning, therefore) "you shall love the Lord your God with all your heart, with all your soul, and with all your might." Now love is a gift, not a given, and cannot be coerced by mere commandment. There is always, after all, the possibility of hypocrisy, or duplicity, or mere obedience; and coerced love is not love, nor are the formalities of love love.

Love then is the space in the heart left open for our own volition, the gift that, by definition, is never a given but must be presented and unless an offense is intended must also be acknowledged and received. The commandment of loving God speaks of soul: then what does the soul have to do in the transaction of the commandment to love? The soul, the being or person of each one, is formed of conscience and consciousness, which are the work of reason and persuasion, and it is in the soul that information is turned into truth, knowledge into conviction. Love flows from the union of mind and soul and fills the heart. So heart and soul form mind: where God meets humanity through, or in, the Torah.

IV

Is God Male or Female?

How does Scripture propose to settle the question of God's gender? Israel achieves its authentic relationship to God when Israel is feminine to God's masculine role; its proper virtue when it conforms to those traits of emotion and attitude that the system assigns to women. In Chapter Seven I raised the question of gender, and in the years since, I have learned more about the subject as worked out in the canonical writings of Judaism. The main point that I have found out is simple: the Torah in fact portrays God as androgynous. Because our traits correspond to Gods, God too turns out to share in and value the gender-traits of both sexes.

Why does the issue matter? The reason is that, even now, presentations of the Scriptures as well as of the liturgy of Judaism and Christianity struggle with the gender-language appropriate for use in referring to God. Just now, Oxford University Press, for example, has tried to make the Bible "gender-inclusive," by speaking of the Father-Mother and by avoiding "he" and "him" when speaking of God. So too, the United Church of Christ, the Methodists, and the Presbyterians, Reform and now Conservative Judaism, and other religious communities and organizations, have struggled with the problem. It is natural to turn back to the Torah — the written Torah as mediated by the oral Torah — in this dialogue of ours. When a rabbi and a priest read Scripture together, they will want to share the challenges of contemporary sensibility as well. For the issue of language contains within itself very profound questions about God's gender and relationship to gender.

The Torah as our sages present its teaching holds that God wants holy Israel now to embody traits defined as feminine. Specifically, holy Israel plays the role of woman to the nations' ravishing man, so that, in the world that is coming, Israel may find itself transformed into man — but man still with woman's virtues. That is why any account of the feminine in the Torah must represent its account of God as profoundly androgynous in its fundamental structure and system. The unity of the Torah comes to expression in its portrayal of the profound complementarity and mutual dependency of the two sexes, each prior in its realm and exemplary in its virtue. The unity of the two parts of the Torah in a profound sense finds its corporal counterpart in the unity of man and woman.

Not only so, but the androgyneity was made to stand, in the life of human relationships between the sexes, for the condition of Israel among the nations: feminine Israel, masculine nations — for now. That remarkable sense for the proportion, balance, and deep harmony of the feminine and the masculine, realized in the here and now of normative behavior and belief, action and attitude alike, accounts for the success of Judaism through the ages in governing that specific "Israel" that it aspired to define. The Judaism of the dual Torah is neither masculine nor feminine, but something else: [1] a perfect union of the two, [2] according to the masculine priority in setting the forms, the feminine the status of the exemplary in determining the substance in all matters that count.

Let me spell out some of the sources that portray a serially-feminine, then masculine, Israel, and a God that values the virtues of both genders but the feminine ones more. How, specifically, does Israel's androgeneity come to expression? It turns out to be serial: now feminine, in the end of days, masculine. The relationship of Israel to God is the same as the relationship of a wife to the husband, and this is explicit in the following:

Song of Songs Rabbah to Song 7:10

7:10 I am my beloved's, and his desire is for me.

XCIX:i.1 A. "I am my beloved's, and his desire is for me:"
B. There are three yearnings:
C. The yearning of Israel is only for their Father who is in heaven, as it is said, "I am my beloved's, and his desire is for me."
D. The yearning of a woman is only for her husband: "And your desire shall be for your husband" (Gen. 3:16).
E. The yearning of the Evil Impulse is only for Cain and his ilk: "To you is its desire" (Gen. 4:7).
F. R. Joshua in the name of R. Aha: "The yearning of rain is only for the earth: 'You have remembered the earth and made her desired, greatly enriching her' (Ps. 65:10).
G. "If you have merit, the rains will enrich it, but if not, they will tithe it [the words for enrich and tithe differ by a single letter], for it will produce for you one part for ten of seed."

Here, therefore, we find that gender-relationships are explicitly characterized, and, with them, the traits associated with the genders as well.

The passage permits us to identify the traits the sages associate with feminine Israel and masculine God, respectively. These traits of submission, loyalty, and perfect devotion do not exhaust the feminine virtues. But they take priority, because they set forth the correct attitude that feminine Israel must take in regard to the masculine nations, not only in relation to the masculine God.

Song of Songs Rabbah to Song 2:7, 3:5, 5:8, 8:4

Song 2:7: "I adjure you, O daughters of Jerusalem"

Song 3:5, "I adjure you, O daughters of Jerusalem, by the gazelles or the hinds of the field"

Song 5:8, "I adjure you, O daughters of Jerusalem, if you find my beloved, that you tell him I am sick with love"

Song 8:4, "I adjure you, O daughters of Jerusalem, that you not stir up nor awaken love until it please"

XXIV:ii.1. A.   R. Yosé b. R. Hanina said, "The two oaths [Song 2:7: 'I adjure you, O daughters of Jerusalem,' and Song 3:5, 'I adjure you, O daughters of Jerusalem, by the gazelles or the hinds of the field'] apply, one to Israel, the other to the nations of the world.

     B.   "The oath is imposed upon Israel that they not rebel against the yoke of the kingdoms.

     C.   "And the oath is imposed upon the kingdoms that they not make the yoke too hard for Israel.

     D.   "For if they make the yoke too hard on Israel, they will force the end to come before its appointed time."

  .4 A.   R. Helbo says, "There are four oaths that are mentioned here [Song 2:7, 'I adjure you, O daughters of Jerusalem,' Song 3:5, 'I adjure you, O daughters of Jerusalem, by the gazelles or the hinds of the field,' Song 5:8, 'I adjure you, O daughters of Jerusalem, if you find my beloved, that you tell him I am sick with love,' Song 8:4, 'I adjure you, O daughters of Jerusalem, that you not stir up nor awaken love until it please'], specifically,

     B.   "he imposed an oath on Israel not to rebel against the kingdoms and not to force the end [before its time[, not to reveal its mysteries to the nations of the world, and not to go up from the exile [Simon:] by force.

     C.   "For if so [that they go up from the exile by force], then why should the royal messiah come to gather together the exiles of Israel?"

The point is unmistakable and critical. Israel is subject to an oath to wait patiently for God's redemption, not to rebel against the nations on its own; that is the concrete social politics meant to derive from the analogy of Israel's relationship to God to the wife's relationship to the husband: perfect submission, and also perfect trust. Rebellion against the nations stands for arrogance on Israel's part, an act of lack of trust and therefore lack of faithfulness. Implicit in this representation of the right relationship, of course, is the promise that feminine Israel will evoke from the masculine God the response of commitment and intervention: God will intervene to save Israel, when Israel makes herself into the perfect wife of God.

The upshot is, Israel must fulfil the vocation of a woman, turn itself into a woman, serve God as a wife serves a husband. The question then follows: is it possible that the Torah asks men to turn themselves into women? And the answer is, that demand is stated in so many words. Here we find a full statement of the feminization of the masculine. The two brothers, Moses and Aaron, are compared to Israel's breasts, a reversal of gender-classifications that can hardly be more extreme or dramatic:

SONG OF SONGS RABBAH TO SONG 4:5

4:5 Your two breasts are like two fawns, twins of a gazelle, that feed among the lilies.

XLIX:i.1 A. "Your two breasts are like two fawns:"

B. this refers to Moses and Aaron.

C. Just as a woman's breasts are her glory and her ornament,

D. so Moses and Aaron are the glory and the ornament of Israel.

E. Just as a woman's breasts are her charm, so Moses and Aaron are the charm of Israel.

F. Just as a woman's breasts are her honor and her praise, so Moses and Aaron are the honor and praise of Israel.

G. Just as a woman's breasts are full of milk, so Moses and Aaron are full of Torah.

H. Just as whatever a woman eats the infant eats and sucks, so all the Torah that our lord, Moses, learned he taught to Aaron: "And Moses told Aaron all the words of the Lord" (Ex. 4:28).

I. And rabbis say, "He actually revealed the Ineffable Name of God to him."

J. Just as one breast is not larger than the other, so Moses and Aaron were the same: "These are Moses and Aaron" (Ex. 6:27), "These are Aaron and Moses" (Ex. 6:26), so that in knowledge of the Torah Moses was not greater than Aaron, and Aaron was not greater than Moses.

.6 A. Happy are these two brothers, who were created only for the glory of Israel.

B. That is what Samuel said, "It is the Lord that made Moses and Aaron and brought your fathers up" (1 Sam. 12:6).

.7 A. Thus "Your two breasts are like two fawns:"

B. this refers to Moses and Aaron.

So too, principal documents of the Torah, and the actors within the uniquely-male bastion, the house of study, are set forth through the same process of metaphorical feminization, all being women:

.2 A. R. Isaac interpreted the verse to speak of components of the Torah: "'There are sixty queens:' this refers to the sixty tractates of laws [in the Mishnah].

B. "'and eighty concubines:' this refers to the lections of the book of Leviticus.

C. "'and maidens without number:' there is no end to the Supplements.

D. "'My dove, my perfect one, is only one:' They differ from one another, even though all of them derive support for their conflicting views from a single proof-text, a single law, a single argument by analogy, a single argument a fortiori."

.3 A. R. Yudan b. R. Ilai interpreted the verse to speak of the tree of life and the garden of Eden:

B. "'There are sixty queens:' this refers to the sixty fellowships of righteous persons who are in session in the Garden of Eden under the tree of life, engaged in study of the Torah."

.5 A. [Continuing 3.B:] "'and eighty concubines:' this refers to the eighty fellowships of mediocre students who are in session and study the Torah beyond the tree of life.

B. "'and maidens without number:' there is no limit to the number of disciples.

C. "Might one suppose that they dispute with one another? Scripture says, 'My dove, my perfect one, is only one:' all of them derive support for their unanimous opinion from a single proof-text, a single law, a single argument by analogy, a single argument a fortiori."

.6 A. Rabbis interpret the verse to speak of those who escaped from Egypt:

B. "'There are sixty queens:' this refers to the sixty myriads aged twenty and above who went forth from Egypt.

    C.   "'and eighty concubines:' this refers to the eighty myriads from the age of twenty and lower among the Israelites who went forth from Egypt.

    D.   "'and maidens without number:' there was no limit nor number to the proselytes."

It is not surprising, therefore, that, having reviewed the main components of the faith, the framer should revert at the end to feminine Israel:

  .10 A.   Another explanation: "My dove, my perfect one, is only one:" this speaks of the community of Israel, "And who is like your people, like Israel, a nation that is singular in the earth" (2 Sam. 7:23).

    B.   "the darling of her mother:" "Attend to me, O my people, and give ear to me, O my nation" (Is. 51:4), with the word for "my nation" spelled to be read "my mother."

    C.   "flawless to her that bore her:" R. Jacob translated in the presence of R. Isaac, "Beside her, there is no child belonging to the one who bore her."

    D.   "The maidens saw her and called her happy:" "And all the nations shall call you happy" (Mal. 3:12).

    E.   "the queens and concubines also, and they praised her:" "And kings shall be your foster-fathers" (Is. 59:23).

So the three points of application of our base-verse to the feminine gender of the faith's principal parts are, first, Israel vis a vis the nations of the world, then the genealogy of the family of Abraham, Isaac, Jacob, then Torah, and finally, Israel. I cannot imagine a more satisfying repertoire of meanings identified with the social components of the system, nor a clear message than the one that is given: in the here and now, Israel is feminine, in the age to come, it will be masculine. But femininity and its virtues — submission, loyalty, trust — are to be cherished, because these represent the media of Israel's future salvation — and, not at all incidentally, its return to whole masculinity.

    The androgeneity of Israel and, in context, also of God, yields a doctrine of virtue that unites the traits of both genders. Specifically, the Torah is presented by our sages as teaching that the Israelite was to exhibit the moral virtues of subservience, patience, endurance, and hope. These would translate into the emotional traits of humility and forbearance. And they would yield to social virtues of passivity and conciliation. The hero was one who overcame impulses, and the truly virtuous person, the one who reconciled others by giving way before the opinions of others. All of these acts of self-abnegation and self-denial, accommodation rather than rebellion, required to begin with the right attitudes, sentiments, emotions, and impulses, and the single most dominant motif of the Rabbinic writings, start to finish, is its stress on the right attitude's leading to the right action, the correct intentionality's producing the besought decision, above all, accommodating in one's heart to what could not be changed by one's action. And that meant, the world as it was. Sages' prepared Israel for the long centuries of subordination and alienation by inculcating attitudes that best suited people who could govern little more than how they felt about things.

The feminine traits, according to Song of Songs Rabbah, are patience, submission, deep trusting; conciliation and accommodation; Israel is represented as feminine, therefore accepting and enduring. What, in concrete terms, does it mean for androgynous Israel to feel the feelings of a woman — and how do we know which emotion is feminine, which masculine? Israel is to cultivate the virtues of submission, accommodation, reconciliation, and self-sacrifice — the virtues we have now seen are classified as feminine ones. But, later on, in time to come, having realized the reward for these virtues, Israel will resume the masculine virtues — again, in accord with the classification just now set forth — of aggression and domination.

An epitome of the oral Torah's sages' treatment of emotions yields a simple result. Early, middle, and late, a single doctrine and program dictated what people had to say on how Israel should tame its heart. And it is not difficult to see why. In this world, Israel was a vanquished nation, possessed of a broken spirit. Sages' Judaism for a defeated people prepared the nation for a long future. The vanquished people, the broken-hearted nation that had lost its city and its temple, had, moreover, produced another nation from its midst to take over its Scripture and much else. That defeated people, in its intellectuals, as represented in the Rabbinic sources, found refuge in a mode of thought that trained vision to see other things otherwise than as the eyes perceived them. And that general way of seeing things accounts also for the specific matter of the feminization of Israel: Israel now was to endure as a woman, so that, in the age to come, it would resume its masculine position among the nations: dominant and determinative. Among the diverse ways by which the weak and subordinated accommodate to their circumstance, the one of iron-willed pretense in life is most likely to yield the mode of thought at hand: things never are, because they cannot be, what they seem. The uniform tradition on emotions persisted intact because the social realities of Israel's life proved permanent, until, in our own time, they changed. The upshot was that Rabbinic Judaism's Israel was instructed on how to tame its heart and govern its wild emotions, to accept with resignation, to endure with patience, above all, to value the attitudes and emotions that made acceptance and reconciliation into matters of honor and dignity, and, therefore, also made endurance plausible.

What have feminine virtues to do with God's traits? The reason that emotions form so critical a focus of concern in Judaism that God and the human being share traits of attitude and emotion. They want the same thing, respond in the same way to the same events, share not only ownership of the Land but also viewpoint on the value of its produce. For example, in the law of tithing, the produce becomes liable to tithing — that is, giving to God's surrogate God's share of the crop of the Holy Land — when the farmer deems the crop to be desirable. Why is that so? When the farmer wants the crop, so too does God. When the householder takes the view that the crop is worthwhile, God responds to the attitude of the farmer by forming the same opinion. The theological anthropology that brings God and the householder into the same continuum prepares the way for understanding what makes the entire Mishnaic system work.

Israel must be like God: as God is humble, long-suffering and patient, so Israel must be humble and avoid arrogance. That counsel leaves no doubt that the doctrine of emotions, feminine in classification by the documents' own characterization, encompasses man as much as woman, God as much as Israel. The upshot is clear: Israel must be like God, and the way in which it must imitate God finds definition in virtue. And the definition of virtue comes to feminine Israel from its relationship with God. In the definition of a religious system, whole and entire, it would be difficult to identify a more complete, a more closed circle; androgynous Judaism encompasses God, the Torah, and Israel, all together and all at once.

How are the masculine and feminine reconciled and made one? Through the feminization of Israel in virtue, attitude, and emotion, Israel will attain that unearned grace (the Hebrew word is zekhut) to which God will respond by the sending of the Messiah. Keeping the commandments as a mark of submission, loyalty, humility before God is the rabbinic system of salvation. These are explicitly labeled feminine virtues. So Israel does not "save itself." Israel never controls its own destiny, either on earth or in heaven. The only choice is whether to case one's fate into the hands of cruel, deceitful men, or to trust in the living God of mercy and love. The stress that Israel's arrogance alienates God, Israel's humility and submission win God's favor, cannot surprise us; this is the very point of the doctrine of emotions that defines Rabbinic Judaism's ethics.

Emotions classified by the sages as masculine ones — arrogance, impatience — produce disaster, feminine ones, redemption. This is spelled out in so many words. The failed Messiah of the second century, Bar Kokhba, above all, exemplifies arrogance against God. He lost the war because of that arrogance. His emotions, attitudes, sentiments, and feelings form the model of how the virtuous Israelite is not to conceive of matters. In particular, he ignored the authority of sages:

YERUSHALMI TAANIT 4:5

[X J] Said R. Yohanan, "Upon orders of Caesar Hadrian, they killed eight hundred thousand in Betar."

[K]   Said R. Yohanan, "There were eighty thousand pairs of trumpeters surrounding Betar. Each one was in charge of a number of troops. Ben Kozeba was there and he had two hundred thousand troops who, as a sign of loyalty, had cut off their little fingers.

[L]   "Sages sent word to him, 'How long are you going to turn Israel into a maimed people.

[M]   "He said to them, 'How otherwise is it possible to test them?'

[N]   "They replied to him, 'Whoever cannot uproot a cedar of Lebanon while riding on his horse will not be inscribed on your military rolls.'

[O]   "So there were two hundred thousand who qualified in one way, and another two hundred thousand who qualified in another way."

[P]   When he would go forth to battle, he would say, "Lord of the world! Do not help and do not hinder us! 'Hast thou not rejected us, O God? Thou dost not go forth, O God, with our armies'"[Ps. 60:10].

Bar Kokhba treats heaven with arrogance, asking God merely to keep out of the way. Israel had to choose between wars, either the war fought by Bar Kokhba or the "war for Torah."

What then is called for? These are the feminine virtues it is to exhibit: negotiation, conciliation, not dominance, not assertiveness. The paradox must be crystal clear: Israel acts to redeem itself through the opposite of self-determination, namely, by subjugating itself to God. Israel's power lies in its negation of power. Its destiny lies in giving up all pretense at deciding its own destiny. So weakness is the ultimate strength, forbearance the final act of self-assertion, passive resignation the sure step toward liberation. Israel's freedom is engraved on the tablets of the commandments of God: to be free is freely to obey — or disobey. That is not the meaning associated with these words in the minds of others who, like the sages of the rabbinical canon, declared their view of what Israel must do to secure the coming of the Messiah. The passage, praising Israel for its humility, completes the circle begun with the description of Bar Kokhba as arrogant and boastful. Gentile kings are boastful; Israelite kings are humble.

Reconciliation with a circumstance of weakness bears within itself enormous strength; power lies in turning the enemy into a friend; power lies in overcoming one's own natural impulses. But then, the entire history of humanity will respond to Israel's will, to what happens in Israel's heart and soul. With the Temple in ruins, repentance can take place only within the heart and mind. Self-abnegation, forbearance, and the other feminine virtues turn out to define the condition for the redemption of Israel. Israel can free itself of control by other nations only by humbly agreeing to accept God's rule. The nations — Rome, in the present instance — rest on one side of the balance, while God rests on the other. Israel must then choose between them. There is no such thing for Israel as freedom from both God and the nations, total autonomy and independence. There is only a choice of masters, a ruler on earth or a ruler in heaven.

This Judaic system explicitly held that humility and forbearance were feminine virtues and at the same time articulately declared its social entity, its "Israel," to be feminine in relationship to God. And that Israel dominated among the Jews, so that from late antiquity to our own day, the feminine virtues were normative; even in the academies, or especially there, robustness gave way to refinement, gentile masculinity to Israelite masculinity. So let us not at the end lose sight of the remarkable power of this religion of humility, for, after all, it is a religion that endures not in long-ago books of a far-away time and place, but in the lives of nearly everybody who today practices a Judaism. It is a religion of mind and heart, but also family and community, one that asks entire devotion to God, not only the parts of life God can command, the life of the people together in community, but especially the secret places of existence not subject to God's will but only one's own.

Men must feel like women, women must act like (true, authentic, Israelite) men. But they can act like men, because the authentic Israelite man exhibits virtues that, for women, come quite naturally. What was asked of the women was no more than the men themselves accepted at the hand of the nations. What was demanded of the men was no more than the relationship that their wives endured with them, which was identical to that that Israel affirmed with God. The circle then is closed: God is to Israel as the nations are to Israel as man is to woman — for now. But, of course, as we have seen, that is only now; then matters will right themselves. By its femininity now, Israel will regain its masculinity. To turn survival into endurance, pariah-status into an exercise in Godly living, the sages' affective program served full well. Israel's hero saw power in submission, wealth in the gift to be grateful, wisdom in the confession of ignorance. Like the cross, ultimate degradation was made to stand for ultimate power. Like Jesus on the cross, so Israel in exile served God through suffering. True, the cross would represent a scandal to the nations and foolishness to (some) Jews. But Israel's own version of the doctrine at hand endured and defined the nation's singular and astonishing resilience. For Israel did endure and endures today.

V

A Rabbi Talks with Jesus

Introducing a Book

In my A Rabbi Talks with Jesus. An Intermillennial, Interfaith Exchange. N.Y., 1993: Doubleday, I explain in a very straight-forward and unapologetic way why, if I had been in the Land of Israel in the first century, I would not have joined the circle of Jesus's disciples. I would have dissented, I hope courteously, I am sure with solid reason and argument and fact. If I heard what he said in the Sermon on the Mount, for good and substantive reasons I would not have become one of his disciples. That is hard for people to imagine, since it is hard to think of words more deeply etched into our civilization and its deepest affirmations than the teachings of the Sermon on the Mount and other teachings that of Jesus. But, then, it also is hard to imagine hearing those words for the first time, as something surprising and demanding, not as mere clichés of culture. That is precisely what I propose to do here: listen and argue.

I wrote that book to shed some light on why, while Christians believe in Jesus Christ and the good news of his rule in the kingdom of Heaven, Jews believe in the Torah of Moses and form on earth and in their own flesh God's kingdom of priests and the holy people. And that belief requires faithful Jews to enter a dissent at the teachings of Jesus, on the grounds that those teachings at important points contradict the Torah. Where Jesus diverges from the revelation by God to Moses at Mount Sinai that is the Torah, he is wrong, and Moses is right. In setting forth the grounds to this unapologetic dissent, I mean to foster religious dialogue among believers, Christian and Jewish alike. For a long time, Jews have praised Jesus as a rabbi, a Jew like us really; but to Christian faith in Jesus Christ, that affirmation is monumentally irrelevant. And for their part, Jews have praised Judaism as the religion from which Jesus came, and to us, that is hardly a vivid compliment.

We have avoided meeting head on the points of substantial difference between us, not only in response to the person and claims of Jesus, but also, and in these pages especially, in addressing his teachings. He claimed to reform and to improve, "You have heard it said...but I say...." We maintain, and I argue here, that the Torah was and is perfect and beyond improvement, and the Judaism built upon the Torah and the prophets and writings, the originally-oral parts of the Torah written down in the Mishnah, Talmuds, and Midrash — that Judaism was and remains God's will for humanity. By that criterion I propose to set forth a Jewish dissent to some important teachings of Jesus. It is a gesture of respect for Christians and honor for their faith. For we can argue only if we take one another seriously. But we can enter into dialogue only if we honor both ourselves and the other. I treat Jesus with respect, but I also mean to argue with him about things he says.

What's at stake? If I succeed, Christians will find renewal for their faith in Jesus Christ — but also respect Judaism. I mean to explain to Christians why I believe in Judaism, and that ought to help Christians identify the critical convictions that bring them to Church every Sunday. Jews will strengthen their commitment to the Torah of Moses — but also respect Christianity. I want Jews to understand why Judaism demands assent — "the All-Merciful seeks the heart," "the Torah was given only to purify the human heart." Both Jews and Christians should find reason to affirm, because each party will locate here the very points on which the difference between Judaism and Christianity rests.

What makes me so certain of that outcome? Because I believe, when each side understands in the same way the issues that divide the two, and both with solid reason affirm their respective truths, then all may love and worship God in peace — knowing that it really is the one and the same God whom together they serve — in difference. So what I wrote is a religious book about religious difference: an argument about God.

My goal is to help Christians become better Christians, because they may come in these pages to a clearer account of what they affirm in their faith, and to help Jews become better Jews, because they will realize here — so I hope — that the God's Torah is the way (not only our way, but the way) to love and serve the one God, creator of heaven and earth, who called us to serve and sanctify God's Name. My point is simple. By the truth of the Torah, much that Jesus said is wrong. By the criterion of the Torah, Israel's religion in the time of Jesus was authentic and faithful, not requiring reform or renewal, demanding only faith and loyalty to God and the sanctification of life through carrying out God's will.

Do I then propose that, after they have read my book, Christians reexamine their convictions about Christianity? Not at all. Christian faith finds a legion of reasons for believing in Jesus Christ (not merely that Jesus was and is Christ); all I argue is, maybe so, but not because he fulfilled the Torah or sustained the Torah or conformed to the Torah; not because he improved on the Torah. By that criterion, I should not have followed him then, and I should not counsel anyone to follow him now. But, of course, Christian faith has never found troubling the fact of its own autonomy: not a mere continuation and reform of the prior faith, Judaism (always represented as corrupt and venal and hopeless anyhow), but a new beginning. So this argument — set forth on a level playing field — should not trouble the faithful. And I don't mean it to. But if Christians take seriously the claim that the criterion of Matthew is valid — not to destroy but to fulfill — then I do think Christians may well have to reconsider the Torah ("Judaism" in secular language): Sinai calls, the Torah tells us how God wants us to be,.

Do I mean, then, to set forth an argument of Jewish apologetics that consists in the rather tired claim, yes to the historical Jesus, no to the Christ of Christianity? For not a few apologetists for Judaism (including Christian apologists for Judaism) distinguish between the Jesus who lived and taught, whom they honor and revere, from the Christ whom the Church (so they say) invented. They will maintain that the apostle, Paul, invented Christianity; Jesus, for his part, taught only truth, which, as believers in Judaism, we can affirm. I take a different path altogether. I am not interested in what happened later on; I want to know, how, if I were there, that very day, standing at the foot of the mountain where Jesus said the words that came to be called "the Sermon on the Mount," I would have responded.

So my argument dissent is entered not against "Christianity" in all its forms and versions, nor is it against the apostle, St. Paul, nor even against that complex and enormous "body of Christ" that the Church was and would become. And I mean to offer no apology for a "Judaism" that focuses upon that negative, "why not Christ?" Judaism does not have always to explain "why not," when the message of the Torah is always, Why...because... Judaism in all its complex forms constitutes something other than merely Christianity without Christ (the Old Testament without the New, in terms of revealed writings). Judaism is simply another religion, not merely not-Christianity; and at issue here is not Judaism as against Christianity, all the more so, Jesus as against Christ (in that formulation in narrowly biographical-historical terms, which I find irrelevant to argument).

It is not a book about scholarship. I address only one picture of what Jesus said, that of the Gospel according to Matthew. For reasons spelled out in the after-word, I have chosen that Gospel as particularly appropriate for the dialogue with the Torah, or Judaism. The Jesus with whom I compose my argument is not the historical Jesus of a scholar's studious imagination, and that is for a simple reason: those fabricated historical figures are too many and diverse for an argument. Moreover, I don't see how religious people can differ about what confronts them only in scholarly works. When Jews open the New Testament, they assume they are hearing from the Jesus Christ of Christianity, and when Christians open the same book, they surely take the same view. That is not to say the historical Jesus is not a presence within and behind the Gospels; it is only to affirm that the Gospels as we read them portray Jesus to most of us who propose to know him. I write for believing Christians and faithful Jews; for them, Jesus is known through the Gospels. I address one of those Gospels. Now let me give a sample of the larger work, so that readers in Italy may have some sense of what I have offered as my version of a conversation with Jesus in his role as a sage in Israel. Here is Chapter Five, the center and climax of my book.

You Shall Be Holy,
for I the Lord your God am Holy
vs.
If you would be perfect,
go, sell all you have and Come,
Follow Me

> And behold, one came up to him saying, "Teacher, what good deed must I do to have eternal life?"
>
> And he said to him, "Why do you ask me about what is good? One there is who is good. If you would enter life, keep the commandments."
>
> He said to him, "Which?"
>
> And Jesus said, "'You shall not kill. You shall not commit adultery. You shall not steal. You shall not bear false witness. Honor your father and mother' (Ex. 20:12-16), and, 'You shall love your neighbor as yourself' (Lev. 19:18)."
>
> The young man said to him, "All these I have observed, what do I still lack?"
>
> Jesus said to him, "If you would be perfect, go, sell all you have and give to the poor, and you will have treasure in heaven, and come, follow me."
>
> When the young man heard this, he went away sorrowful, for he had great possessions."
>
> Mt. 19:16-22

Details of the Ten Commandments, honoring parents or following Christ, observing the Sabbath as holy or acknowledging the son of man as lord of the Sabbath — these really are the side show. All of them are important, but they merely illustrate the fundamental issue that Jesus comes to address. But what about what really counts, the main event is: what does God want of me? And how can I make myself into what God wants me to be, made me to be? Is there an argument to be constructed about that most fundamental issue? And if I were there, what should I have heard, and how might I have responded to the heart of Jesus's teaching?

Well, imagine that one day I was nearby when I witnessed this wonderful exchange: what must I do to have eternal life? I would have come close to the master to hear his every word: here is the center of matters, what will happen to me when I die, which is another way of asking, what does God really want me to do and to be in this life?

Jesus, among all us Jews, would take for granted that the Torah answers that question, and, all of us together would have understood that what I do in this life helps decide what happens to me in eternity. The young man's question is a mature and proper one, and what he really wants the master to tell us all is, when all is said and done, what really counts?

That question, standard and urgent for those Israelites who believe in life after death and the world to come, takes for granted that what I do matters to God, and that God will reward or will punish me for what I do in this life. The young man who asked the question, Jesus and his disciples, and all of us together share this faith. Not only is it a natural question for all of us: what do I have to do to merit eternal life? but the answer Jesus gives too is true to the Torah: keep the Ten Commandments and the Great Commandment, Lev. 19:18.

Here we have a response wholly in accord with the teaching of the Torah. Had the story ended here, I would have gladly tagged along to hear more from this authentic master of the Torah. For a great master is not one who says what is new, but one who says what is true, and the master I seek is one who speaks to me, who wants to be found by me — so that I too may learn what God through the Torah has asked of me.

But the conversation didn't stop. The young man found the answer wanting. As I watched his face, I could see the disappointment. He wanted more than a standard answer — he and I could well have argued about that, for, I would have told him, what the Torah gives is all you get, and all you should want. But he was talking with Jesus, not with me.

The young man: "Is that all? What do I lack?"

Jesus: "Well, if it's perfection you have in mind...."

The rapid exchange startled me. Jesus shifts the discussion from "what do I have to do to have eternal life" to "if you would be perfect." Here is a profound turn. Jesus has grasped the question the young man really wanted to ask, which was not merely about eternal life but about "perfection" — something else altogether.

This young man wants to be more than mortal, for who aspires to be perfect, accepting what we human beings are? All of us, after all, know the story of Adam and Eve. We remember the sad tale of the Ten Generations from Adam and Eve to Abraham, the descent of humanity to the Flood. Perfection indeed! Let me at least do what God, understanding my frailty, asks: at least (some of) the Ten Commandments, at least "love your neighbor as yourself".

Perfection? Who ever mentioned it, who thought of it? (Mere) eternal life is for mortals, and God understands what and who we are: "The Lord saw that the wickedness of man was great in the earth, and that every imagination of the thoughts of his heart was only evil continually...and the Lord was sorry that he had made man on the earth and it grieved him in his heart" (Gen. 6:5-6). Given the frailty of humanity, none can expect perfection as the price for eternal life.

To understand what is at stake in this exchange, we do well to turn the clock forward for a couple of hundred years and listen to what other masters of the Torah, besides Jesus, found in response to the issue of what I have to do to gain eternal life or the world to come or life after death or the kingdom of heaven, a mixture of different ways of speaking of the same matter, so it seems to me. They defined matters in a much less restrictive way than did Matthew's Jesus, asking not even for perfect obedience to the Ten Commandments or the Golden Rule of Lev. 19:18. All they asked for was faith and loyalty to God; a merciful and forgiving God will do the rest.

Indeed, these masters' yoke was easy, their burden light, when they stated very simply: everybody who believes in life after death will merit life after death, with exceptions of a rare sort:

> All Israelites have a share in the world to come, as it is said, "your people also shall be all righteous, they shall inherit the land forever; the branch of my planting, the work of my hands, that I may be glorified" (Is. 60:21).
>
> And these are the ones who have no portion in the world to come:
>
> He who says, the resurrection of the dead is a teaching which does not derive from the Torah, and the Torah does not come from Heaven; and an Epicurean.
>
> Rabbi Aqiba says, "Also: He who reads in heretical books, and he who whispers over a wound and says, 'I will put none of the diseases upon you which I have put on the Egyptians, for I am the Lord who heals you' (Ex. 15:26)."
>
> Abba Saul says, "Also: He who pronounces the divine Name as it is spelled out."
>
> Mishnah-tractate Sanhedrin 11:1

The contrast between the encompassing definition before us — everybody except a few very rank sinners, heretics mainly, as against only those who keep the principal commandments, on the one side, or, still fewer, only the perfect — is stunning. Reading the same Torah as Jesus read, these sages, for reasons we shall see very soon, simply said all the saints — that is, holy people — are saved, and all Israel is holy. So their very doctrine of who, and what, is eternal Israel also instructed them on who shares the world to come, and the Torah defined Israel very simply: "You shall be holy, for I the Lord your God am holy."

But these thoughts of mine have distracted my attention from the conversation between Jesus and his young interlocutor. Not only so, but I would like to ask the master, "Sir, so few?"

But that is not what I really want to ask, and, emboldened by the patience of the teacher, I press forward, stand near to hand, and speak up. I rely on his patience, and remembering God's patience with Abraham at Sodom and even Israel through time, trust Jesus that, in asking what I think is a tough question, I shan't be disappointed by an impatient reply.

"Sir, you seem to me to have answered a question the young man didn't ask, and maybe he asked a question you didn't answer. What he wanted to know is what good deed he had to do. He didn't aspire to perfection.

"But in telling him how to be perfect, you have disrupted the very life you promise: 'If you would enter life, keep the commandments.' But if he listens to you, what will become of him? He gives up home and family, cuts his ties to everything and everyone but you: get rid of everything and follow me."

So we find ourselves back among the details: honor parents or serve the master? Remember the Sabbath or acknowledge the master? Is this really a fair framing of the question?

Again moving the clock forward, I can define matters in a way the master will approve: the choice of wealth as against the Torah is a choice, so why not the choice of wealth as against Christ? So the master, perspicacious and knowing, points me toward a passage in which other sages of this same Torah of Moses at Sinai in time to come would give the same advice — sort of. Jesus in his wisdom looks toward Aqiba, coming along a few decades hence. In time to come, he tells me, there will be a master of the Torah who will tell his disciple to sell all he has — in order to study the Torah.

So, he might fairly claim, "My advice is not so very different from that of the master that is coming along in time ahead:"

Rabbi Tarfon gave to Rabbi Aqiba six silver centenarii, saying to him, "Go, buy us a piece of land, so we can get a living from it and labor in the study of Torah together."

He took the money and handed it over to scribes, Mishnah-teachers, and those who study Torah.

After some time Rabbi Tarfon met him and said to him, "Did you buy the land that I mentioned to you?"

He said to him, "Yes."

He said to him, "Is it any good?"

He said to him, "Yes."

He said to him, "And do you not want to show it to me?"

He took him and showed him the scribes, Mishnah teachers, and people who were studying Torah, and the Torah that they had acquired.

He said to him, "Is there anyone who works for nothing? Where is the deed covering the field?"

He said to him, "It is with King David, concerning whom it is written, 'He has scattered, he has given to the poor, his righteousness endures forever' (Ps. 112:9)."

Leviticus Rabbah XXXIV:XVI

What has Aqiba done, if not the same thing that Jesus demanded in a different context: get rid of worldly possessions, devote all things of value to the Torah. The advice is the same, only the context shifts. We have dwelt long enough on Jesus's teachings to find familiar the counterpart: sell all you have, give the money away to the poor, and follow me: the equation is the same, but Christ replaces Torah.

And yet, my sense is that matters have come to a radical reduction, moving as we do from perfection to "follow me." Is that the whole message of the master? Of course not, far from it. Once more conversation — it really isn't an argument any more — shifts from the detail to the main point. But the afternoon is fading, and we have to part.

Later on, a few days having passed, I had the good fortune to hear Jesus taking up this same question, now in straight and simple terms: what in fact does the Torah want from me? No longer an issue of what do I have to do to get what I want, it is framed in a more sincere and innocent, holy way: just what does God want of me? And Jesus here responded and taught a message of the Torah, telling people what Israel's sages found in the Torah, what the Torah required them to say:

> "Teacher, which is the great commandment in the law?"
> And he said to him, "You shall love the Lord your God with all your heart and with all your soul and with all your mind. This is the great and first commandment. And a second is like it: you shall love your neighbor as yourself. On these two commandments depend the whole Torah and the prophets."
>
> Mt. 22:36-40

Here we have what is familiar and authentic: to love God, as the *Shema*, the prayer proclaiming God's unity and Israel's submission to God's rule, demands; and to love your neighbor as yourself. No sage could take exception to these teachings. But in how they are elaborated, there is room for argument and exception.

To understand why, we have first of all to examine the context in which the second of the two commandments is set:

> And the Lord said to Moses, "Say to all the congregation of the people of Israel, You shall be holy, for I the Lord your God am holy..."
>
> Lev. 19:1-2
>
> "You shall not hate your brother in your heart, but you shall reason with your neighbor, lest you bear sin because of him. You shall not take vengeance or bear any grudge against the sons of your own people, but you shall love your neighbor as yourself: I am the Lord."
>
> Lev. 19:17-18

If I had to point to one of those "great commandments" of the Torah, I would have said: "Master, there is a third that is like it: 'You shall be holy, for I the Lord your God am holy.'" Here, after all, is a commandment that addresses not me personally and how I love God, or not me in relationship to someone else, but to all of us, all Israel together. Once more, therefore, I am struck by the dimensions of the world that Matthew's Jesus addresses: the individual in search of salvation, the private person in quest of God. And all due honor for the Torah-teachings that he cites, but the Torah says something about a dimension of human existence that, in these sayings, Jesus does not discern: the community as a whole, all of us together, what in today's language we should call the social order.

So the silence bears a message too. And the silence bypasses not only the life of us all together, the family, not only the daughter or son; the community, not only the private home. Why no message about that third dimension of human existence, besides the life of the human being in relationship to himself or herself, besides the life of one person to another — what about our relationship to God?

Is love of God all there is? Is there no relationship of us all before God? I can love God and my neighbor and yet live in Sodom. But God destroyed Sodom. So God surely cares about more than humanity, one by one by one. God cares about humanity, all at once and all together. And that is — so the Torah teaches — the reason that God called Abraham and Sarah, Isaac and Rebecca, Jacob and Leah and Rachel — and loved their children enough to give them the Torah at Sinai.

That is why, in my mind, what Jesus has not said takes on profound weight: he has spoken to me, but not to us: there is no dimension of holy and eternal Israel in his reading of the Torah's fundamental teaching. He has said that I should sell all I have, give to the poor, and follow him; Aqiba in context told Tarfon no less. But he has not said that we — not I, but we, Israel — are to be: how are we, eternal Israel, to strive to be like God. After all, "loving your neighbor as yourself," Lev. 19:18, comes at the end of the very passage that commences with, "You shall be holy because I am holy." Since Jesus knows the Torah at least as well as anybody else, he has made his choices, selecting what counts and silently bypassing what does not. That, after all, is to be expected from a master so original in his teachings about the fence around the Torah: "you have heard it said...but I say to you...." Here, the thought passes my mind, he might have said, "You have heard it said...but I don't say that to you...."

So in bypassing the foundation-statement at Lev. 19:2-3, of which the concluding statement comes as a climax at Lev. 19:18, Jesus has — so it seems to me — left the main point out of his message. Why should I love my neighbor as myself? Because — so Moses has taught us — "you shall be holy, for I the Lord your God am holy." And that is part of what it means to be like God, to strive for holiness like God's. All the rest of that chapter of the Torah, reaching its climax with the second of the two great commandments, forms a commentary on the commandment of holiness; and that commandment Jesus has not mentioned.

In all fairness to the master, I owe him my criticism. What kind of respect would I show, if I just dismissed him in my mind and gave him no chance to respond?

"Sir," I ask, "how about 'You shall be holy'? What does the Torah want me to be, when it tells me to be holy?"

He motions me to continue.

"In fact, my lord, our sages of blessed memory find in the commandment to be holy all of the Ten Commandments, and to be holy means to keep those commandments. So our sages teach." And, again relying upon the perspicacity of a master to foresee the lessons later sages would derive from the Torah he knew so well, I would have pointed into the future for the exposition.

"Sir," I say to him, "in time to come, sages will read the Torah and show how this very passage that we study together — Leviticus Chapter Nineteen, which teaches Israel to be Holy — goes over the Ten Commandments. They will demonstrate, and I'll show you how, that in the commandments of Leviticus Nineteen are the Ten Commandments of Exodus Twenty. So there is a good reason for me to keep the Ten Commandments, and that is, so that I shall be holy, because God is holy. I want to be like God, and the Ten Commandments, restated in Leviticus Nineteen, teach me how to be like God.

"Sir, will you have the patience to hear out the way in which, in a time to come, a rabbi will spell all this out for us?" He nods, and I proceed:

> Rabbi Hiyya taught, "[The statement, 'Say to all the congregation of the people of Israel' (Lev. 19:2)] teaches that the entire passage was stated on the occasion of the gathering [of the entire assembly.]
>
> "And what is the reason that it was stated on the occasion of the gathering [of the entire assembly]? Because the majority of the principles of the Torah depend upon [what is stated in this chapter of the Torah]."
>
> Rabbi Levi said, "It is because the Ten Commandments are encompassed within its [teachings].
>
> "'I am the Lord your God' [Ex. 20:2], and here it is written, 'I am the Lord your God' [Lev. 19:2].
>
> "'You shall have no [other gods]' [Ex. 20:3], and here it is written, 'You shall not make for yourselves molten gods' [Lev. 19:4].
>
> "'You shall not take [the name of the Lord your God in vain]' [Ex. 20:7], and here it is written, 'You shall not take a lying oath by my name' [Lev. 19:12].
>
> "'Remember the Sabbath day' [Ex. 20:8], and here it is written, 'You will keep my Sabbaths' [Lev. 19:3].
>
> "'Honor your father and your mother' [Ex. 20:12], and here it is written, 'Each person shall fear his mother and his father' [Lev. 19:3].
>
> "'You shall not murder' [Ex. 20:13], and here it is written, 'You shall not stand idly by the blood of your neighbor' [Lev. 19:16].

"'You shall not commit adultery' [Ex. 20:13], and here it is written, 'Do not profane your daughter by making her a harlot' [Lev. 19:29].

"'You shall not steal' [Ex. 20:13], and here it is written, 'You shall not steal and you shall not deal falsely' [Lev. 19:11].

"'You shall not bear false witness [against your neighbor]' [Ex. 20:13], and here it is written, 'You shall not go about as a talebearer among your people' [Lev. 19:16].

"You shall not covet" [Ex. 20:14], and here it is written, 'And you shall love your neighbor as yourself'" (Lev. 19:18).

Leviticus Rabbah 24:5

There is a moment of silence. The conversation pauses. The young man, the master, and I reflect for a moment on what has passed among us. "You shall be holy...love your neighbor as yourself..." — these form nothing more than a recapitulation of the Ten Commandments! How then can someone say, "I've done it all, what more is there?"

Then I speak up again: "When the young man asked what he had to do to 'enter life,' you told him to keep the commandments. Well and good. And when I heard what you said, I thought of why I am taught by the Torah to keep those commandments, and that is, because I want to be holy, because God is holy."

A voice in the crowd: "Holier than thou?"

"No, — just holy, because God is holy."

I go on: "Now when God speaking through Moses tells me how to keep the Ten Commandments, he says it is so that I may be holy like God. Isn't that enough?"

The crowd comes closer. Who said it wasn't enough?

I remind him, "The young man asked that very question: 'All these I have observed, what do I still lack?' And you answered him quite clearly. He still lacks something. 'If you would be perfect, go, sell all you have and give to the poor, and you will have treasure in heaven, and come, follow me.' So there we have it again, sir.

"What I hear you saying is, the Ten Commandments are not enough, the Great Commandment, the Golden Rule — these too are not enough. Perfection consists in poverty and obedience to Christ."

So — to return to our own day — Matthew's Jesus, having addressed Exodus 20 and Leviticus 19, clearly has maintained.

Well, precisely what do I offer as a counter? Jesus contrasts Christ and wealth, as Aqiba later on would contrast Torah and wealth. I have no argument with him on that score. But a more troubling issue persists. Jesus wants me to follow him and be like him. Have I heard such a commandment in the Torah? Of course I have: "You shall be holy, for I the Lord your God am holy." I am called upon by the Torah to try to be like God: holy. (I'll have more to say about that in my argument with Jesus about the Pharisees, which is coming in the next chapter.)

But we have come a long way and reached our goal: the possibility of an argument about the main point.

For here we stand at the center of matters. And at this point, we find grounds for an argument, in which both parties talk about the same things and in the same terms, as I have already shown. Sell all I have and —

— study the Torah

— follow Christ

— Which?

Surely we can now argue about the same matter in the same terms, namely, what is the truly highest value in life? For what should I give my life? That is what is at stake, and well does Jesus answer by saying, follow me; and well does the Torah answer by saying, ""be holy, for I am holy."

For what difference does it make to the Christian or the Jew if, in either case, we hold "all that we have" to be worth what we most value, which is Christ or the Torah, respectively? No difference at all: the structure is the same. The argument can commence. About what? About the main chance: what is life about? what makes life worth living? Christ and the Torah concur that God answers that question, Christ and the Torah agree that to be perfect, I must strive to be holy like God, or I must give up everything for Christ.

So which? What, then, does the Torah teach me, am I supposed to do in order to imitate God, to be like God? And what then does Matthew's Jesus teach me, am I supposed to do in order to follow Christ? And how are we to choose between these two matched counterparts: two answers to one question, two readings of one Torah?

Here I cannot argue with Matthew's Jesus. For an honest and fair answer in behalf of Matthew's Jesus would require us to move far beyond the limits of our argument. I said we should argue only with Jesus's teachings, not calling into doubt any detail of Matthew's "good news" about what Jesus did, the miracles he wrought, the messages he gave to his disciples, what was done to him, and how he triumphed over death.

But to accomplish an argument between Christ and Torah, the entire picture of Christ (in Christian language) demands its place at center-stage, and not Matthew's Christ alone, but Mark's and Luke's and John's, and Paul's — and above all, the Christ of the Church and the faithful Christians from then to now. That testimony about what it means to sell all you have and follow me cannot be reduced to a few simple propositions about love for neighbor.

We should, indeed, have to retell the entire Gospel of Matthew in order to answer the question, how shall I try to follow Christ? What does it mean to do so? For not in the teachings of Jesus alone, with which we concern ourselves, is the answer to that question to be found, but in everything he did, and in his submission to God's will in everything that was done to him; and not only so, but also, and especially, in his days in hell and rise from the grave: everything all together, all at once. It would be presumptuous on my part to propose to answer only on the basis of the handful of sayings I find susceptible of argument the question: what must I do when I come to follow him?

And the same is so for the Torah. To set into juxtaposition — and conflict — the account that the Torah provides of what it means to strive to be holy, like God, I should hardly do justice to the matter by merely quoting a few verses of the Torah. I should have to call to give testimony all of the masters of the Torah from then to now, all those who have studied the Torah with learning and wisdom and, each one in order, set forth for here and now what it means to be holy, like God. For we have come to the heart of matters, and the conflict is a very real one.

Limiting ourselves to Matthew's representation of Jesus, on the one side, and the Torah, on the other,* we find ourselves unworthy of the task. And that is how it should be. For who in the end has the perspective upon things to compare and contrast Christ and the Torah, eternal Israel and the Church — who but God? And God is not party to this argument, except that it concerns the Torah, God gave to eternal Israel, on the one side, and, the Torah Christ made over, in his time and in his way and through his Church, to Christianity, on the other side.

But, leaving the final say to God, perhaps even in the here and now, we may point to the outlines of the argument: where do we differ, and where do we, eternal Israel, register our dissent? Meaning, I repeat, not to give offense but sincerely to take issue, what have I to say?

If we examine what our sages teach we must do in order to be holy, like God, the beginnings of a fair exchange may be discerned. If I had to point to the single difference between the message of the Torah, at least as our sages mediate that message, and the message of Jesus as Matthew quotes and portrays that message, it is in one simple fact.

The message of the Torah always concerns eternal Israel. The message of Jesus Christ always concerns those who follow him.

---

* I have made reference, also, to documents that, in Judaism, are regarded as part of the Torah, but are not in the Hebrew Scriptures or "Old Testament." These are the Mishnah, defined earlier, the two Talmuds (the Talmud of the Land of Israel, ca. A.D. 400, and the Talmud of Babylonia, ca. A. D. 600), which form extensions and amplifications of the Mishnah, and various compilations of interpretations of Scripture, called Midrash-compilations, which form extensions and amplifications of the (written part of the) Torah. For the sake of argument, we need not quibble; for Judaism these all are part of the one whole Torah given by God to Moses at Mount Sinai. It is the fact that none of these writings had come to closure by the time of Jesus, but only many centuries later. But in an argument between religions, just as for the purposes of argument I invoke Matthew's Jesus as Christianity has affirmed that gospel of Jesus (among others) so I represent "the Torah" as Judaism defines the Torah. Religions don't argue about historical facts but about God's truth, and that is what I mean to do.

The Torah always speaks to the community and concerns itself with the formation of a social order worthy of God who called Israel into being. Jesus Christ in Matthew's account speaks of everything but the social order of the here and now; here he speaks of himself and his circle; then, in time to come, he speaks of the kingdom of heaven.

Lost in between the man and the coming kingdom is the everyday of the common life. But it is that everyday, common life that the Torah commands Israel to sanctify. And at stake in that life of a social order aimed at sanctification is nothing less than the sanctification of God on high.

So I turn once more to the master, imposing on his patience to be sure, with this insistence of mine: "We matter not only one by one by one, but all together, all at once. Holiness is not for thee and me, but for all of us: we all, all together all at once, are the ones to whom God spoke when, using the plural "you," God said, "You shall be holy, for I the Lord your God am holy." God uses the plural you nearly always, and in these critical, emblematic sayings of yours " — I speak now to Matthew's Jesus, — "the 'you' is — well, a young man. What about all Israel — that 'you' of 'you shall be holy, for I....'"

"Let me spell out, sir, what is at stake, as our sages in time to come would explain matters. When Israel forms a social world that conveys the sanctity of life, then Israel sanctifies God." Then, taking license with time, I point to this statement:

> "You shall be holy, for I the Lord your God am holy:"
>
> That is to say, "if you sanctify yourselves, I shall credit it to you as though you had sanctified me, and if you do not sanctify yourselves, I shall hold that it is as if you have not sanctified me."
>
> Or perhaps the sense is this: "If you sanctify me, then lo, I shall be sanctified, and if not, I shall not be sanctified"?
>
> Scripture says, "For I...am holy," meaning, I remain in my state of sanctification, whether or not you sanctify me.
>
> Abba Saul says, "The king has a retinue, and what is the task thereof? It is to imitate the king."
>
> Sifra CXCV:I.2-3

To this the disciples of Christ must surely respond, "That indeed is our faith: to imitate Christ." To that we devote our lives. So wherein do we differ, and how come you take exception? Why the great dissent?

My answer comes to me from our sages' exposition of the details of imitating God, of being like God, of being holy like God. In our times the accusation that one is "holier than thou," which no one wants to admit but many would like to be, gives a bad name to sanctification. So we do well to hear what Israel's sages make of this commandment to be like God.

Here is how our sages of blessed memory read some of the critical verses before us:

"You shall not take vengeance [or bear any grudge]:"

To what extent is the force of vengeance?

If one says to him, "Lend me your sickle," and the other did not do so.

On the next day, the other says to him, "Lend me your spade."

The one then replies, "I am not going to lend it to, because you didn't lend me your sickle."

In that context, it is said, "You shall not take vengeance."

"or bear any grudge:"

To what extent is the force of a grudge?

If one says to him, "Lend me your spade," but he did not do so.

The next day the other one says to him, "Lend me your sickle,"

and the other replies, "I am not like you, for your didn't lend me your spade [but here, take the sickle]!"

In that context, it is said, "or bear any grudge."

"but you shall love your neighbor as yourself: [I am the Lord]:"

Rabbi Aqiba says, "This is the encompassing principle of the Torah."

Sifra CC:III.4, 5, 7

Being holy like God means not taking vengeance in any form, even in words; not pointing out to the other that I have not acted in the nasty way he did. In many ways, we find ourselves at home. This counsel recalls, after all, the message that if the Torah says not to murder, then we must not even risk becoming angry. Loving God means going the extra mile. Aqiba has the climax and conclusion "love your neighbor as yourself" as the great commandment, the encompassing principle, of the entire Torah.

And that brings us to the next question. Precisely what then does it mean to be "like God"? Here is one answer:

Abba Saul says, "O try to be like him:

"Just as he is gracious and merciful," you too be gracious and merciful"

[add: for it is said, ""The Lord, God, merciful and gracious" (Ex. 34:6)]."

Mekhilta Attributed to Rabbi Ishmael XVIII:II.3

To be like God means to imitate the grace and mercy of God: these are what make God God, and these are what can make us like God. So to be like God is to be very human. But to be human in a very special way: it is, after all, the grace of God that in the end accords to us the strength to be merciful and gracious — the grace, but also, the example. Not a few followers of Jesus will point to him in this way, just as we point to God in this way.

And here is another along the same lines. In what follows a sage asks how we can follow God or be like God, that is, what does it mean to be holy, like God? And the answer is, it means to imitate God, to do the things that God does, as the Torah portrays God's deeds:

And Rabbi Hama ben Rabbi Hanina said, "What is the meaning of the following verse of Scripture: 'You shall walk after the Lord your God' (Deut. 13:5).

"Now is it possible for a person to walk after the Presence of God? And has it not been said, 'For the Lord your God is a consuming fire' (Deut. 4:24)?"

"But the meaning is that one must walk after the traits of the Holy One, blessed be he.

"Just as he clothes the naked, as it is written, 'And the Lord God made for Adam and for his wife coats of skin and clothed them' (Gen. 3:21), so should you clothe the naked.

"[Just as] the Holy One, blessed be he, visited the sick, as it is written, 'And the Lord appeared to him by the oaks of Mamre' (Gen. 18:1), so should you visit the sick.

"[Just as] the Holy One, blessed be he, comforted the mourners, as it is written, 'And it came to pass after the death of Abraham that God blessed Isaac his son' (Gen. 25:11), so should you comfort the mourners.

"[Just as] the Holy One, blessed be he, buried the dead, as it is written, 'And he buried him in the valley' (Deut. 34:6), so should you bury the dead."

Babylonian Talmud tractate Sotah 14A=M. 1:8.LXXXVIA-G

So to be holy like God, I must clothe the naked, visit the sick, comfort the mourner, bury the dead — "love my neighbor as myself." These again are very human traits, loving traits. It is not for nothing that, in the Torah, we are told that we are made in God's image, after God's likeness: "So God created man in his own image, in the image of God he created him; male and female he created them" (Gen. 1:27). No wonder, then, that the Torah's sages would find the holiness of God in clothing the naked, visiting the sick, comforting the mourner, burying the dead — maybe even teaching Torah to prisoners.

At this point, Jesus will surely have wanted to say, "Well, what in the world do you think I've been telling you all this time?"

I nod: "Yes. I know. But...."

Then, with infinite tact and courtesy, he nods and goes on his way; we part friends. No ifs, ands, or buts: just friends.

He has, indeed, said no less; but he has said much more. So while we part friends, he goes his way, the young man who brought us together turns sadly homeward — and I find the nearest synagogue.

For it nears dark, and I have my prayers to recite — and the responsibility, also, of studying a little of the Torah. Joining the assembled Israel of that town, I turn to recite the prayers for dusk, beginning: "Happy are those who dwell in your house, they will once more praise you. Happy the people to whom such blessings fall, happy the people whose God is the Lord" (Ps. 144:15).

After we complete the prayer for dusk, we gather around our master in the darkening room. In the Torah-study session that evening, he says, "Tell me what's on your mind? Ask me something, and I'll see if I can answer."

So I ask the master what it's all about: the Torah has so much in it. The master, Jesus, after all, has explained what the important commandments are. He can put it altogether in a few simple words, and much that he says makes sense in line with the teaching of the Torah. Can you tell me what the Torah is all about? Are all the commandments the same, or is one more important than another? And what does it mean, when you come down to it, "to be holy, because God is holy"?

So I lay out what has been on my mind all day long: "Teacher, what good deed must I do to have eternal life?"

The sun has set, darkness covering the village beyond. In the lamplight, the master points out that the Torah itself answers that same question that the master, Jesus, has been asked, the question: what does it all add up to? Indeed, from Moses onward, great prophets told us what counts: David, Isaiah, Micah, Amos, Habakkuk. And here (as a later master put their teachings together) is what they said:

Rabbi Simelai expounded, "Six hundred and thirteen commandments were given to Moses, three hundred and sixty-five negative ones, corresponding to the number of the days of the solar year, and two hundred forty-eight positive commandments, corresponding to the parts of man's body."

"David came and reduced them to eleven: 'A Psalm of David: Lord, who shall sojourn in thy tabernacle, and who shall dwell in thy holy mountain? (i) He who walks uprightly and (ii) works righteousness and (iii) speaks truth in his heart and (iv) has no slander on his tongue and (v) does no evil to his fellow and (vi) does not take up a reproach against his neighbor, (vii) in whose eyes a vile person is despised but (viii) honors those who fear the Lord. (ix) He swears to his own hurt and changes not. (x) He does not lend on interest. (xi) He does not take a bribe against the innocent' (Psalm 15)."

"Isaiah came and reduced them to six: '(i) He who walks righteously and (ii) speaks uprightly, (iii) he who despises the gain of oppressions, (iv) shakes his hand from holding bribes, (v) stops his ear from hearing of blood (vi) and shuts his eyes from looking upon evil, he shall dwell on high' (Isaiah 33:25-26)."

"Micah came and reduced them to three: 'It has been told you, man, what is good, and what the Lord demands from you, (i) only to do justly and (ii) to love mercy, and (iii) to walk humbly before God' (Micah 6:8)."

"Isaiah again came and reduced them to two : 'Thus says the Lord, (i) Keep justice and (ii) do righteousness' (Isaiah 56:1).

"Amos came and reduced them to a single one, as it is said, 'For thus says the Lord to the house of Israel. Seek Me and live.'"

"Habakkuk further came and based them on one, as it is said, 'But the righteous shall live by his faith' (Habakkuk 2:4)."

Babylonian Talmud Makkot 24A-B

"So," the master said, "is this what the sage, Jesus, had to say?"

I: "Not exactly, but close."

He: "What did he leave out?"

I: "Nothing."

He: "Then what did he add?"

I: "Himself."

He: "Oh."

I: "'But the righteous shall live by his faith.' And what is that? 'It has been told you, man, what is good, and what the Lord demands from you, only to do justly and to love mercy, and to walk humbly before God.'"

He: "Would Jesus agree?"

I: "I think so."

He: "Well, why so troubled this evening?"

I: "Because I really believe there is a difference between 'You shall be holy, for I the Lord your God am holy and 'If you would be perfect, go, sell all you have and come, follow me.'"

He: "I guess then it really depends on who the 'me' is."

I: "Yes, it depends."

He: "And now it's time for the evening prayer: you lead us."

I open with the lines with which the evening prayer commences, which speak of how God loves us: "'And he, being merciful, forgives iniquity and does not destroy, abundantly turns his anger away and does not engage all his wrath: O Lord, save us, King, answer us when we call.'

I proceed to the call to prayer: "'Bless the Lord who is to be blessed....

With all my heart and with all my soul, I recite the Shema: "'Hear, Israel, the Lord our God is the one God. And you shall love the Lord your God with all your heart, with all your soul, and with all your might.'"

So then, as always, we offered our evening prayers to the living God. And, in some village across the valley, so did Jesus, and his disciples, and all of eternal Israel, the holy people, living in the holy land, greeting nightfall. They did that then, and we, eternal Israel, do that even now, bowing our knee as we speak to the blessed one, God of Abraham and Sarah, Isaac and Rebecca, Jacob and Leah and Rachel, all of us: the Abrahams and Isaacs and Jacobs and Sarahs and Rebeccas and Leahs and Rachels who were then and are now eternal Israel.

It is now dark. The sun has set, the stars come out. Our prayers end. And we end now as we did then, with words that Jesus used too:

Let the holy name of God be sanctified and made great in the world that God created in accord with God's will. And may God's kingdom come to rule, in your lifetime, and in the lifetime of all Israel, and say, Amen.

Our father who is in heaven, may your name be sanctified. Your will be done, your kingdom come, on earth as it is in heaven...

So we prayed that night, so we pray through time; so he prayed that night, so his disciples would pray through time. Yes, we argue and contend: but we pray to the same God. And that in the end is why we shall always contend and argue, but serve God by loving one another, as God loves us.

But how does God show that love for us?

The next morning was a Thursday, when the holy Torah is removed from the ark and displayed to eternal Israel and read aloud. Being of the priesthood, I am called to the Torah first. And I say the blessing that we say before reading the words of the Torah:

Blessed are you, Lord, our God, ruler of the world, who has chosen us from among all peoples and give us the Torah. Blessed are you...who gives the Torah.

Gives — here, now, every day.

And afterward:

Blessed are you, Lord, our God, ruler of the world, who has given us a true Torah, and so planted in us life forever. Blessed are you...who gives the Torah.

That is how God shows that love for us. I left the synagogue services and looked to the far horizon. And I was glad to be who I was, and where I was, and what I was — along with all Israel then and now and forever.

PART THREE

DEBATES WITH OTHER SCHOLARS

VI

German Scholarship on Rabbinic Judaism: The Goldberg-Schäfer School

Debates on the future of Judaic studies in Germany do well to survey not only the past, but also the present state of that field here. For while acknowledging the definitive role of German scholars of Judaic learning (Wissenschaft des Judenthums) in founding the field within the framework of the academy, parties to the discussion do well to consider the concrete facts of scholarship in our own times. And, when they do, they will come to recognize the parlous and flimsy foundations for future scientific work. For, as we shall see with reference to the study, in Germany, of the classics of Judaism, the field proves not only small but idiosyncratic and asymetrical to world scholarship. The dominant German school of Rabbinic Judaism today, the Goldberg-Schäfer School, shows the price paid when a tiny, isolated group pursues a subject in an essentially subjective manner.

That school takes as its gravamen the importance of critical editions of the classics, which is surely a common truth, but then imagines that no one but that school appreciates the importance of diverse versions of a single document. The study of the Rabbinic classics — Mishnah, Talmud, Midrash-compilations — in contemporary Germany focuses upon the mechanical distribution of variant readings among the manuscript and earliest printed testimonies to those documents. That, of course, forms a familiar and unexceptional field of learning. From the beginnings of the formation of the Rabbinic literature at the closure of the Mishnah, "our sages of blessed memory" and their heirs and continuators recognized the fluid state of the textual tradition, both mnemonic for the Mishnah, and in writing or in notes for other components of the canon, redacted as documents and redacted in documents alike. The pages of the Talmud present rich evidence of the variety of readings and versions that sages possessed, and some of the most adventurous — and successful — analytical-dialectical compositions propose to interpret textual variations by appeal to conflicting legal theories — a standard hermeneutics in the great tradition of Rabbinic exegesis of Rabbinic documents. Not only so, but in modern times, a landmark study of the text of the Mishnah, which sits on the shelf of every active scholar of the field, came forth in Y. N. Epstein, *Mebo lenusah hammishnah* (1954). Not only so but the diversity of the readings finds its match in the paucity of manuscript evidence. And, finally, modern scholarship, under academic and theological auspices alike, has yet to produce critical texts for the various documents, or even reached a consensus on what we can mean by a critical text. It follows that admonitions to the scholarly world to take account of the parlous textual tradition for the Rabbinic documents repeat the obvious.

Two centers of the study of Judaism today take as their critical standpoint that obvious fact, Jerusalem and Germany. The two schools are scarcely comparable, the former comprised by many active scholars, the latter by scarcely a handful. The more important difference between them is that the former treats the fact as important but not determinative, while the latter finds itself fixated on the problem of manuscript variants. While the Jerusalem school distinguishes itself in its meticulous concern for variant readings, the entire scholarly community takes full cognizance of the problem. I cannot point to a single scholar who builds tall structures upon the shifting sands of ignoring printed editions and variant readings.

That fact has not prevented the German school, in the persons of the late Arnold Maria Goldberg of Frankfurt and Peter Schaefer of Berlin, from insisting that, by reason of the broad variation in readings of this or that manuscript or passage, no substantive historical work can be carried on in the study of Rabbinic Judaism. In the context of the profoundly historistic universe in which that judgment is set forth, such a position removes from the realm of active culture and contemporary discourse the entire presence of Judaism, embodied as it is in its classical, Rabbinic documents. It is, therefore, a nihilistic position, which reduces scholarship to computerization of manuscript variations and the consequent reproduction thereof — without judgment, indeed, without palpable purpose.

Having devoted forty years to research into the history of the formative age of Judaism, that is, the first six centuries A.D., I took an interest in the German school's position on this matter; but it was a special interest, since I have been focus of that school's negative criticism. In the Goldberg-Schaefer school, no historical work, no history of ideas, no investigation of the context for the text, can take place, for we have no text. My own work explicitly dismissed because, in Schaefer's view, I posit a text that can be studied historically, I found it necessary to take an interest in his criticism, to see what is to be learned from it.

The one thing no one had to learn from Schaefer was that the various documents come to us in diverse versions. Along with everybody else, I was taught to take account of variants, large and small. That is why, from the very beginning of the documentary method,[1] I took account of the problem of determining that on

---

[1] Spelled out in *Introduction to Rabbinic Literature*. N.Y., 1994: Doubleday. The Doubleday Anchor Reference Library, and see also *The Documentary Foundation of Rabbinic Culture. Mopping Up after Debates with Gerald L. Bruns, S. J. D. Cohen, Arnold Maria Goldberg,*

which I was working, taking full account of the uncertainty of the text tradition for any given passage or even for documents as a whole. Indeed, the uncertainty of readings in any one passage provoked the search for recurrent and large-scale formal uniformities. For the case of the Mishnah, for example, the method focused upon the characteristics that recur throughout a document, not on the details that appear only here or there. Not episodic but fixed traits of form therefore dictated the analytical procedures: recurrent patterns in rhetoric, definitive traits in the principles of logical coherence in holding together compositions in composites, composites in a whole and complete statement.

At no point does the description of a document rest upon a specific reading or unique traits that occur in some one place. On the contrary, the very essence of the documentary method is to describe the whole, and that means, traits that are uniform throughout. By definition, these traits of the documnent as a whole also will characterize the diverse manuscript evidence of the bits and pieces of the part, and no one who has examined the problem of the text of the Mishnah can fail to recognize that simple fact! That focus on the permanent, the recurrent, and the characteristic and definitive takes full account of variations of detail. It goes without saying that no thesis on the history or the religion set forth in a given document can rest securely on the foundations of one reading as against some other, any more than we can rely for facts on attributions of sayings to specific named sages, on the one side, or narratives of events involving them, on the other. Other data have to be identified, described, analyzed, and interpreted, for the study of history and the history of the religion, Judaism.

Now, when we ask which text tradition, or which version, of a document we subject to documentary description, analysis, and interpretation, we therefore take up a question that by definition simply does not apply. For, as a matter of fact, every Rabbinic document we possess from the formative age, however diverse or fluid the text tradition on which we work, exhibits throughout its textual testimonies precisely those uniformities of rhetorical, topical, and logical traits that come under description in the documentary method. I cannot point to a single judgment of a documentary character set forth in any of my accounts that relies upon one reading, rather than another. Where we have critical editions, it goes without saying I translate and analyze those versions, e.g., Theodor-Albeck for Genesis Rabbah, Finkelstein for Sifra and Sifré to Deuteronomy; where we do not, I work on the standard printed edition.

And this brings us back to the German school of Rabbinic Judaism. The only major players in that school, Goldberg and his student, Peter Schäfer, have found themselves so impressed by the obstacles put forth by a fluid and sparse text

---

Susan Handelman, Christine Hayes, James Kugel, Peter Schäfer, Eliezer Segal, E. P. Sanders, and Lawrence H. Schiffman. Atlanta, 1995: Scholars Press for South Florida Studies in the History of Judaism.

tradition as to claim we have no documents at all, only variant readings. That nihilistic position — first set forth in the pages of this journal a decade ago — then defines the task of learning as the assembly of variant readings and the publication, with virtually no critical judgment, of a mass of this and that. Work of a historical and cultural character simply loses its bearings, if we have no documents at all.

That is the rather odd position of Arnold Maria Goldberg, "Der Diskurs im babylonischen Talmud. Anregungen für eine Diskursanalyse," in *Frankfurter Judaistische Beiträge* 1983, 11:1-45: "Once it has been written, every text is exclusively synchronic, all the textual units exist simultaneously, and the only diachronic relation consists in the reception of the text as a sequence of textual units whose 'first' and 'then' become 'beforehand' and 'afterwards' in the reception of the text...The synchronicity of a text is...the simultaneous juxtaposition of various units, independent of when the units originated."[2]

Schäfer proceeds, "This emphasis on a fundamental synchronicity of the texts of rabbinic literature is completely consistent with Goldberg's methodological approach. The text as it stands is exclusively synchronic and, since we cannot go back beyond this state, there remains only the classifying description of that which is there...A historical differentiation is deliberately excluded, because in effect the texts do not permit it. Whilst analysis of the forms and functions of a text makes its system of rules transparent, 'the comprehension of rabbinic texts through habituation and insight could be superseded by a comprehension of the rules of this discourse as competence....'"[3]

Goldberg's dogmatic definition of matters notwithstanding, a sustained examination of the various documents leaves no doubt whatsoever that we can identify not only "beforehand" but "first," showing that the formation of composites out of fully-articulated compositions took place prior to the definition of a document's distinctive traits. Had Goldberg read my *The Formation of the Jewish Intellect. Making Connections and Drawing Conclusions in the Traditional System of Judaism.* Atlanta, 1988: Scholars Press for Brown Judaic Studies, he would have found ample grounds, based on the logics of coherent discourse alone, to reconsider his position.

But now data that prove the exact opposite of Goldberg's premised position emerge fully and completely, for the Talmud, in my *The Talmud of Babylonia. An Academic Commentary.* Atlanta, 1994-5: Scholars Press for *USF Academic Commentary Series,* and in its companion, *The Talmud of Babylonia. A Complete Outline.* Atlanta, 1994-1995: Scholars Press for *USF Academic Commentary Series.*

---

[2] Cited in Peter Schäfer, "Research into Rabbinic Literature," *Journal of Jewish Studies* 1986, 37:145.
[3] *ibid., ad loc.*

Not only so, but I have devoted *Initial Phases* to just this problem. [4] Why Goldberg takes the position that he does I cannot say, since they contradict the facts of the characteristics of the documents that he purportedly discusses. The facts that are set forth in *Academic Commentary, Complete Outline,* and *Initial Phases,* indicate that Goldberg certainly cannot have known through his own, first-hand analysis, a great deal about the literary traits of the Rabbinic literature as exemplified by the Bavli. For he seems to have confused a kind of abstract philosophizing with the concrete acts of detailed learning that scholarship requires. That explains why he left no imposing legacy of scholarship to sustain his opinion, which is at once doctrinaire, ignorant, and eccentric. Goldberg's nihilism has no continuators,[5] except for his student, Peter Schäfer, and I do not see much basis on which to contend with his obscure and solipsistic legacy. We shall deal with Schäfer's own, equally nihilistic, position in due course.

I do not share Goldberg's position, because I have shown, on the exactly same basis of phenomenology on which he lays out his view, that the contrary is the fact. Having completed the work on the Talmud of Babylonia, I only now begin the equivalent academic commentary and complete outline for the Yerushalmi, and comparison of the outlines of the Bavli and the Yerushalmi,[6] with the plan of proceeding to the score of Midrash-compilations, so I cannot say what I shall find in continuing a uniform analysis. But the naked eye suggests that Goldberg's position will not find in the other documents any support at all. The documents as we know them certainly encompass not only materials that serve the clearly-manifest

---

[4] *The Initial Phases of the Talmud's Judaism.* Atlanta, 1995: Scholars Press for South Florida Studies in the History of Judaism. I. *Exegesis of Scripture.*

The Initial Phases of the Talmud's Judaism. Atlanta, 1995: Scholars Press for South Florida Studies in the History of Judaism. II. *Exemplary Virtue.*

The Initial Phases of the Talmud's Judaism. Atlanta, 1995: Scholars Press for South Florida Studies in the History of Judaism. III. *Social Ethicse.*

The Initial Phases of the Talmud's Judaism. Atlanta, 1995: Scholars Press for South Florida Studies in the History of Judaism. IV. *Theology.*

[5] When in late April, 1991, just after Goldberg died, I came to Goldberg's University, the University of Frankfurt, as Martin Buber Visiting Professor of Judaic Studies, for the Summer Semester, I was saddened to find that had left as his legacy strict instructions to his students, not only not to study with me or but not even to meet me. That fact does not represent the standards of German scholarship, which maintains a high standard of intellectual professionalism. In no other country did I encounter such a "boycott."

[6] *The Two Talmuds Compared.* Atlanta, 1995-7: Scholars Press for South Florida Studies in the History of Judaism.

I.A *Tractate Berakhot and the Division of Appointed Times in the Talmud of the Land of Israel and the Talmud of Babylonia. Tractates Berakhot and Shabbat.*

I.B *Tractate Berakhot and the Division of Appointed Times in the Talmud of the Land of Israel and the Talmud of Babylonia. Tractates Erubin and Yoma.*

I.C *Tractate Berakhot and the Division of Appointed Times in the Talmud of the Land of Israel and the Talmud of Babylonia. Tractates Pesahim, Sukkah, and Besa.*

program of the framers or compilers of the documents, but also the self-evident interests of authors of compositions and framers of composites who had other plans than those realized in the documents as we have them. But the question is, how do we identify components of a composition, or of a composite, that took shape outside of the documentary framework and prior to the definition of the documentary traits of a given compilation? Unless we take at face value the attributions of sayings to specific, named authorities at determinate times and places, we must work by paying close attention to the material traits of the compositions and composites. That requires, as I said, moving from the end-product backward and inward — and in no other way. Two intellectually lazy ways have led nowhere, Goldberg's denial that it is a question, and the Israelis' insistence that attributions eo ipse equal facts. Finding no promise in such labor-saving devices — settling questions by decree — I have resorted to sifting the facts, and that is what I have done and now do.

This brings us, finally, to the explicit statement of Peter Schäfer that we have no documents, just variant readings.[7] Schaefer's statement of matters proves murky and obscure, so exact citation of his language is required, lest I be thought to caricature or exaggerate the full confusion that envelopes his position. Let me cite his exact language, beginning with his critique of Goldberg and pronouncement of a still more extreme position; I number those paragraphs that I shall discuss below.

1.   The question that arises here is obviously what is meant by 'texts.' What is the text 'once it has been written' — the Babylonian Talmud, the Midrash, a definite Midrash, all Midrashim, or even the whole of rabbinic literature as

---

I.D   *Tractate Berakhot and the Division of Appointed Times in the Talmud of the Land of Israel and the Talmud of Babylonia. Tractates Taanite, Megillah, Rosh Hashanah, Hagigah, and Moed Qatan.*

II.A*The Division of Women in the Talmud of the Land of Israel and the Talmud of Babylonia. Tractates Yebamot and Ketubot.*

II.B *The Division of Women in the Talmud of the Land of Israel and the Talmud of Babylonia. Tractates Nedarim, Nazir, and Sotah.*

II.C *The Division of Women in the Talmud of the Land of Israel and the Talmud of Babylonia. Tractates Qiddushin and Gittin.*

III.A*The Division of Damages and Tractate Niddah in the Talmud of the Land of Israel and the Talmud of Babylonia. Tractates Baba Qamma, Baba Mesia, and Baba Batra.*

III.B*The Division of Damages and Tractate Niddah in the Talmud of the Land of Israel and the Talmud of Babylonia. Tractates Sanhedrin and Makkot*

III.C*The Division of Damages and Tractate Niddah in the Talmud of the Land of Israel and the Talmud of Babylonia. Tractates Shebuot, Abodah Zarah, Horayot, and Niddah*

[7] "Research into Rabbinic Literature," *Journal of Jewish Studies* 1986, 37:145ff.

a synchronic textual continuum whose inherent system of rules it is necessary to describe? Indeed, in such a description, neither the concrete text concerned, nor the form a particular textual tradition takes, needs to be important. Every text is as good — or rather as bad — as every other, the 'best" being presumably the one representing the latest redactional stage.

2.   But this is precisely where the problem begins. Goldberg himself must finally decide on one text, and, in doing so...must decide against or or several other texts. Whether he wants to or not, he inevitably faces historical questions. This problem can be elucidated by the second line of research within the 'literary' approach.

3.   This second line of research...is that of the interpretation immanent in the work. Complete literary works are analyzed as a whole, as literary systems so to speak, and are examined for their characteristic arguments...Neusner has ...sent to press such analyses...The plane on which this research approach moves...is the final redaction of the respective work...Two closely related problems arise from this.

4.   The approach inevitably disregards the manuscript traditions of the work in question. But especially in the case of rabbinic literature, this is essential. Thus, to give an example, both Vatican manuscripts of the Bereshit Rabba...represent texts which are quite different from that of the London manuscript...The variations are sometimes so great that the redactional identity of the work is debatable. Is it meaningful to speak of one work at all, or rather of various recensions of a work? But then how do these recensions relate to one another? Are they different versions of one and the same text...or are they autonomous to a certain extent, and is Bereshit Rabba' merely an ideal or a fictitious entity? What then constitutes the identity of the work 'Bereshit Rabbah'? Any preserved manuscript or the modern 'critical' edition by Theodor-Albeck...

5.   The problem becomes more acute when the question of the boundaries of works is taken into consideration. To remain with the example of Bereshit Rabba, the problem of what relation Bereshit Rabba and the Yerushalmi bear to one another has been discussed since the time of Frankel...How are Bereshit Rabba and Yerushalmi related to one another...? Does Bereshit Rabba quote Yerushalmi, i.e., can we regard Bereshit Rabba and Yerushalmi at the time of the redaction of Bereshit Rabba as two clearly distinguishable works, one of which being completed? Did the redactor of Bereshit Rabbah therefore 'know' with what he was dealing and from what he was 'quoting'? With regard to the Yerushalmi, this conclusion is obviously unreasonable, for we immediately have to ask how the Yerushalmi of the Bereshit Rabba is related to the Yerushalmi existent today. The Yerushalmi cannot have been 'complete' at the time of the redaction of Bereshit Rabba since it is not identical to the one we use today.[8]

---

[8] Schäfer, pp, 146-147.

6.   A brief reference to Hekhalot literature will constitute a last example. This is without doubt the prototype of a literature where the boundaries between the works are fluid. Every 'work' in this literary genre that I have investigated more closely proves to be astonishingly unstable, falls into smaller and smaller editorial units, and cannot be precisely defined and delimited, either as it is or with reference to related literature. This finding is of course valid with regard to the works of Hekhalot literature to a varying degree, but can be generalized as a striking characteristic feature of the whole literary genre....[9]

7.   The questioning of the redactional identity of the individual works of rabbinic literature inevitably also disavows the research approach to the work at the level of the final redaction. The terms with which we usually work — text, "Urtext," recension, tradition, citation, redaction, final redaction, work — prove to be fragile and hasty definitions that must be subsequently questioned. What is a "text" in rabbinic literature? Are there texts that can be defined and clearly delimited, or are there only basically "open" texts which elude temporal and redactional fixation? Have there ever been "Urtexte" of certain works with a development that could be traced and described? How do different recension of a "text" relate to one another with respect to the redactional identity of the text? How should the individual tradition, the smallest literary unit, be assessed in relation to the macroform of the "work" in which it appears? What is the meaning of the presence of parts of one "work" in another more or less delimitable "work"? Is this then a quotation in work X from work Y?

8.   And finally what is redaction or final redaction? Are there several redactions of a "work" — in chronological order — but only one final redaction? What distinguishes redaction from final redaction? What lends authority to the redaction? Or is the final redaction merely the more or less incidental discontinuation of the manuscript tradition?[10]

Enough of Schäfer's presentation has now been quoted to permit a simple statement in response.

It is simply put forth: the "text" loses its quotation-marks when we describe, analyze, and interpret recurrent formal properties that occur in one document, but not in some other, or, in the particular congeries at hand, not in any other. To state matters as required in the present context, we simply reverse the predicate and the subject, thus: a writing that exhibits definitive traits of rhetoric, logic, and topic, that occur in no other writing constitutes a text.

That simple definition permits us to respond to the long list of questions and to sort out the confusion that characterizes Schäfer's conception of matters. Let me systematically respond to Schäfer's unsystematic formulation of his position,

---

[9] *ibid., ad loc.,* p. 149.
[10] *ibid., ad loc.,* pp. 149-150

which, as we see at the end, rests heavily on his observations of an odd and unrepresentative writing, which may or may not originate in the Rabbinic canon at all.

[1] I shall stipulate that my "document" corresponds to Schäfer's "text." The rest of this paragraph is unintelligible to me. I do not grasp the distinctions that Schäfer thinks make a difference, e.g., between "a definite Midrash, all Midrashim, or even the whole of rabbinic literature...." Here Schäefer seems to me to shade over into sheer chaos. How the several following sentences relate to one another I cannot discern. I am baffled by the sense of his allegation, "Every text is as good — or rather as bad — as every other, the 'best" being presumably the one representing the latest redactional stage." It is not clear to me whether this is his view or one he imputes to someone else, and, as is clear, apart from Goldberg, I know no one to whom these words even pertain.

[2] Goldberg's comments leave no doubt on his meaning; he denies all possibility of historical or cultural research. This he says in so many words. As I said, in the context of German academic culture, such a result condemns the Rabbinic classics to the dustbin.

[3] Schäfer's characterization of my description ("for their characteristic arguments") proves uncomprehending. I define a document by appeal to the standard indicative traits of classic literary analysis: rhetoric, logic, topic. Rhetoric covers the forms of expression; logic the principles of coherent discourse; topic pertains to the prevailing program, hermeneutics, or even proposition of a given piece of writing. (Not all compilations can sustain such documentary analysis, Mekihilta — dubiously assigned to late antiquity to begin with — standing apart from all the other items in the Rabbinic canon, for instance.) Still, Schäfer is correct in his main point: I do focus on what in his terms is "the final redaction of the work," and, in my terms, the definitive congeries of traits distinctive to this complex of composites and no other.

[4] Here Schäfer spells out what he means by disregarding manuscript traditions, and he gives as his example the diverse versions of Genesis Rabbah. But he would do well to address more directly the question of the occurrence of a single pericope in two or more documents. When we find such a case, are we able to identify the document to the definitive traits of which the pericope conforms? If we are, then we can safely describe the pericope within the framework of one document and not the other(s) in which it appears.

When Schäfer made these statements, they formed a set of fair and pertinent questions. But they have been answered, and whether or not Schäfer has found the answers persuasive (or has even understood them) I cannot say, since so far as I know, he has not followed up on this point at all. Indeed, his astonishing silence on this matter since he printed the paper at hand suggests that Schäfer appears quite oblivious to work that raised precisely the question he asks — and answered it. I refer in particular to *From Tradition to Imitation. The Plan and Program of*

Pesiqta deRab Kahana and Pesiqta Rabbati. Atlanta, 1987: Scholars Press for Brown Judaic Studies. I raised that question when I reflected on Schäfer's problem and systematically addressed the challenge he set forth; that is why it is so disappointing to seek evidence of his serious response to the answer. There I am able to show that pericope common to both compilations conform to the definitive traits that characterize Pesiqta deRab Kahana and do not conform to those that characterize those pericopes of Pesiqta Rabbati that do not occur, also, in Pesiqta deRab Kahana. It is not clear that Schäfer follows the scholarly literature on the very matters on which he passes his opinion.

[5] Here Schäfer wanders a bit, and his problem with "boundaries of works" suggests he cannot hold to a single subject. For the problem of the peripatetic pericope has nothing to do with that of the shared pericope. The entire range of questions he raises here reveals an underlying confusion, which can be overcome by detailed work, an examination of the specifics of matters; this Schäfer has never done for the matter at hand. But, at any rate, for reasons already stated, his questions have nothing to do with the documentary method.

[6] Schäfer here talks about that on which he is expert. His allegation about generalizing from the document he knows to those on which he has not worked therefore hardly demands serious consideration. He can be shown to be wrong in treating the one as in any way analogous, or even comparable, to the other. What he does not know and cannot show, he here simply assumes as fact.

[7] This is the most egregious break in the strain of coherent argument, for here Schäfer confuses the pre-history of documents with the documents as we now know them. What I have said about the phenomenological inquiry into the pre-history of documents suffices to answer the questions that he raises. His questions are probably meant, in his mind, to form arguments in behalf of his fundamental proposition. In fact they are susceptible to clear answers; his labor-saving device of sending up obscure clouds of rhetorical questions accomplishes no good purpose. But for his instruction, let me take up his questions and address those that pertain to the documentary method.

[A] What is a "text" in rabbinic literature? A text in Rabbinic literature is a writing that conforms to a distinctive set of definitive traits of rhetoric, topic, and logic.

[B] Are there texts that can be defined and clearly delimited, or are there only basically "open" texts which elude temporal and redactional fixation? The Rabbinic canon (with only a few exceptions) contains texts that can be defined and clearly delimited (from one another) by reference to the distinctive congeries of rhetoric, topic, and logic, characteristic of one but not the other, or, as I said, characteristic solely of the one. We can establish sequence and order among these documents, determining what is primary to a given document because it conforms to the unique, definitive traits of that document. What Schäfer means by "open" texts I cannot say, so I do not know the answer to his "or"-question, but what I do grasp suggests he is reworking Goldberg's position.

[C] Have there ever been "Urtexte" of certain works with a development that could be traced and described? The answer to this question remains to be investigated, text by text (in my language: document by document).

I do not know the answer for most of the documents. I have done the work to state the answer for some of them. The Mishnah, it is clear, proves uniform through all but two of its tractates, Eduyyot and Abot. All the others conform to the single program of formulary traits, logical characteristics, modes of exposition and argument. That does not suggest within the Mishnah are not already-completed compositions, utilized without much change; the contrary can be demonstrated on formal grounds alone. Forming compositions by appeal to the name of a single authority, as in Mishnah-tractate Kelim, or by utilization of a single formulary pattern, as in Mishnah-tractate Arakhin and Megillah, or by illustration through diverse topics of a single abstract principle, — all these other-than-standard modes of composition and composite-making do occur. But these ready-made items take up a tiny proportion of the whole and do not suggest the characteristics of an Urtext that would have held together numerous compositions and even composites of such an order. We may then posit (and many have posited) the existence of documents like the Mishnah but in competition with it, formed on other rhetorical, logical, and even topical bases than the Mishnah. But these do not stand in historical relationship with the Mishnah, e.g., forming a continuous, incremental tradition from some remote starting point onward to the Mishnah as we know it.

[D] How do different recensions of a "text" relate to one another with respect to the redactional identity of the text? This repeats Schäfer's earlier question, e.g., concerning Yerushalmi and Genesis Rabbah. Here by text he seems to me, a given saying or story that circulates from one document to another. Part of Schäfer's problem is imprecision in the use of terms, e.g., employing the same word when he means different things.

[E] How should the individual tradition, the smallest literary unit, be assessed in relation to the macroform of the "work" in which it appears? The answer to this question is both clear and not yet fully investigated. It is obvious that we move from the whole to the parts, so the individual composition (Schäfer's "tradition," whatever he can mean by that word) finds its place within the framework of the document's definitive characteristics. But the investigation of the traits of compositions and composites that stand autonomous of the documents in which they occur has only just begin, and only with the continuation and completion of my Academic Commentary will the data have been collected that permit us to deal with this question document by document. For the Bavli we have a set of viable answers; for no other document do I claim to know the answer. For the Mishnah, as I said, I do not think that this is an urgent question, though it is a marginally relevant one.

[F] What is the meaning of the presence of parts of one "work" in another more or less delimitable "work"? Is this then a quotation in work X from work Y? The question of the composition or even composite that moves hither and yon is a variation of the question just now considered. My preliminary probe is in *The Peripatetic Saying: The Problem of the Thrice-Told Tale in Talmudic Literature.* Chico, 1985: Scholars Press for Brown Judaic Studies. Reprise and reworking of materials in *Development of a Legend; Rabbinic Traditions about the Pharisees before 70* I-III. Schäfer does not appear to know that work, which appeared long before the article under discussion here. Here again, he sets obstacles in the path of scholarly progress when he ignores work already in print at the time of his presentation.

[G]   And finally what is redaction or final redaction? Are there several redactions of a "work" — in chronological order — but only one final redaction? What distinguishes redaction from final redaction? What lends authority to the redaction? Or is the final redaction merely the more or less incidental discontinuation of the manuscript tradition? These questions suggest only more confusion in Schäfer's mind, and since I cannot fathom what he wants to know, or why he frames matters as he does, I also cannot presume to respond. If Schäfer spelled out with patience and care precisely what he wishes to know, others could follow his line of thought, e.g., what he means by "authority...redaction?" Schäfer makes such remarkable statements as the following: And finally what is redaction or final redaction? What distinguishes redaction from final redaction? What can he possibly mean by this set of questions? When we look at such unintelligible sentences as this, we wonder, indeed, whether Schäfer is not simply saying the same thing over and over again.

My best sense is that Schäfer has not reflected very deeply on the premises and arguments of the work he wishes to criticize; if he had, he would have grasped the monumental irrelevance of his critique. The formulation of his thought suggests to me not so much confusion as disengagement; the wordiness conceals imprecision, for we naturally assumed that each sentence bears its own thought and are not disposed to conclude that he is simply repeating himself. But one judgment surely pertains: in the end, Schäfer simply has not understood that in taking account of precisely the considerations that he raises, I formulated the form-analytical problem in such a way address the issue of the definition of a text. As I reflect his machine-gun bursts of questions and slowly examine each in turn, I find not so much a close engagement with issues as utter disengagement, an offhand contentiousness rather than a considered critique — in all, more silliness than sense. But Schäfer's inattention to how others have responded to precisely the problems he highlights finds its match in the case that comes next, which draws our attention to a failure even to grasp the sorts of data that yield the results of form-analysis. This is not to suggest that the study of Rabbinic Judaism on the contemporary German academic scene promises no important results, only to state that, to date, the results prove at best mechanical and witless.[11]

---

[11] I am sad to have to report that when I sent a copy of this chapter for comment to Professor Schäfer in Berlin, he returned it to me unopened, and without comment.

VII

Schorsch on Historicism in Judaism

From Text to Context: The Turn to History in Modern Judaism. By Ismar Schorsch. Hanover, NH: University Press of New England. Tauber Institute for the Study of European Jewry Series. 403 pp. $39.95.

In this collection of twenty-one free-standing essays, Ismar Schorsch, Chancellor of the Jewish Theological Seminary of America and principal institutional voice of U.S. Conservative Judaism, treats topics connected with the advent of historical study as a medium of Judaic theological discourse, or, in his language, "historical consciousness in Modern Judaism." He credits the main figures, Leopold Zunz and Heinrich Graetz, with creating "a historical consciousness that could serve as a base for a voluntaristic and secular Jewish community." Reform and what we now know as Conservative Judaism founded their theological systems on the primacy of historical data. Schorsch describes matters in the following epitome of the whole:

> The emergence of historical consciousness in modern Judaism...comprises a fundamental change in mentality and epitomizes the dialectic process of Westernization that transformed medieval Ashkenazic Judaism...historical thinking facilitated the urgent and agonizing effort to rethink the nature of Judaism. It quickly became the primary vehicle for translating the ideas, institutions, and values of an ancient oriental religion into equivalent or related Western categories...

That Schorsch recognizes the fundamentally theological character of the enterprise emerges in his description, as first-rate apologetics, of historical study:

> ...the heady recovery of the Jewish past filled Jews with pride and self-confidence. Their growing appreciation for the pathos of Jewish history, for the power of Jewish values and ideas, and for the persistence of the Jewish

people countered the blandishments of assimilation. To unfurl the antiquity
of Judaism created new grounds for a sense of sacred obligation.

These represent theological, not academic and historical, judgments. We stand at
the end of the period of historicism in the theology of Judaism, marked by the loss
of self-evidence once enjoyed by the conceptions set forth by the theologian-
historians of reformist Judaisms, Reform, Conservative, and Modern Orthodoxy
alike. For the same ideas that Schorsch argues provided an apologetics for being
Jewish (for the secular Jews) or for acknowledging a "sacred obligation" imposed
by history (for the religious ones, the Judaists) no longer serve. Those ideas have
lost plausibility for the Jews, and they are many, who through marriage or sheer
inactivity opt out of that organized community, secular, eleemosynary, and
voluntaristic, that in the USA stands for all but segregationist Orthodox Judaism.
Schorsch here tells the story of the beginnings of what in our own day comes to an
end.

He himself adduces ample evidence of that fact, when he presents as
"evidence for the formative role of Jewish history in the shaping of the multiple
identifies of modern Jews" such data as "the role of the Maccabees, Masada, and
archaeology in Israeli culture, or the grip of the Holocaust on the contemporary
American Jewish scene." The same argument would point to the celebration of the
Torah in synagogue worship as an act of historical consciousness of Sinai, or of the
celebration of the Lord's Supper as an act of mere mimesis. But for the Israelis the
mythopoeic power of Masada derives not from the study of history but the utilization
of history for political myth, and the Holocaust forms a principal component for
secular Jewish ideology for quite other than narrowly-academic, historical
considerations. In both cases the past serves because it contributes events ripped
out of context, not because the past imposes a philosophy of history, a proportionate
and cogent statement of beginnings, middles, and endings, such as would validate
the claim that historicism has triumphed. Events out of the past serve theological
or ideological purposes without attesting to the presence of historical consciousness
at all.

While time and again stressing what was novel, Schorsch goes still further,
when he alleges that "historical consciousness was always the substratum of Jewish
identity." That defines the theme of the twenty-one collected essays that comprise
the book: historical scholarship and the scholars that produced it. That allegation,
critical to the book as a whole, will have surprised the sages of Judaism from the
formative age to the nineteenth century, and the vast majority of those sages in the
world today, who speak not of "Judaism" but of "the Torah," and for whom "the
Torah" stands in judgment upon history. That is because the Torah — a.k.a.,
"Judaism" — speaks out of eternity into time. To its statements, one-time, historical
facts prove monumentally irrelevant, and historians' allegations as to what "really"
happened or did not happen — and that is what Schorsch celebrates as historicism

— bear no consequences whatsoever for the Torah. The issue concerns the place of historical fact in the formulation of theological truth. Many of the scholars cited by Schorsch take for granted that "Judaism" is a "historical religion" and rests on an interpretation of historical fact. Their position takes shape in their reading of Scripture. Specifically, the Hebrew Scriptures of ancient Israel ("the written Torah," to Judaism and "the Old Testament" to Christianity), all scholarship concurs, set forth Israel's life as history, with a beginning, middle, and end; a purpose and a coherence; a teleological system. All accounts agree that Scriptures distinguished past from present, present from future and composed a sustained narrative, made up of one-time, irreversible events. All maintain that, in Scripture's historical portrait, Israel's present condition appealed for explanation to Israel's past, perceived as a coherent sequence of weighty events, each unique, all formed into a great chain of meaning. That historicist reading violates the position of the Torah, oral and written, which at no point submits questions of theological truth to the judgment of historical fact. "Judaism" may be "a historical religion," but for those who live life within the Torah, ours is a world framed by other-than-historical boundaries.

Reading Schorsch's essays themselves amply demonstrates that the idea of history, with its rigid distinction between past and present and its careful sifting of connections from the one to the other, came quite late onto the scene of intellectual life — specifically at the beginning of Reform Judaism, born in the midst of the historical-romantic age of the early nineteenth century. To the contrary, both Judaism and Christianity for most of their histories have read the Hebrew Scriptures in an other-than-historical framework. They found in Scripture's words paradigms of an enduring present, by which all things must take their measure; they possessed no conception whatsoever of the pastness of the past. For our sages of blessed memory of Judaism, as for the saints and sages of Christianity, the past took place in the acutely present tense of today, but the present found its locus in the presence of the ages as well. And that is something historical thinking cannot abide. Not only so, but it contradicts the most fundamental patterns of explanation that we ordinarily take for granted in contemporary cultural life. Historicism for two hundred years has governed.

In fact, historicism forms a barrier between us and the understanding of time that defined the Judaic and the Christian encounter with God through the Scriptures of ancient Israel. The givenness of the barrier between time now and time then yields for us banalities about anachronism, on the one side, and imposes upon us the requirement of mediating between historical fact and religious truth, on the other. Receiving those Scriptures and systematically reviewing them, the Judaism of the dual Torah represented by the canonical writings of rabbis from the Mishnah, ca. 200, through the Talmud of Babylonia, ca. 600, recast this corpus of historical thinking, substituting paradigm or pattern for narrative sequence, by redefining the received notion of time altogether. That transformation of ancient Israel's Scripture from history to paradigm defines the conception of history of

Rabbinic Judaism — calling into question the notion that that Judaism possessed a conception of history at all.

In the Judaism set forth by principal documents that record the oral part of the dual Torah, particularly those that reached closure from ca. 200 to ca. 600 C.E., both documents of law such as the Mishnah and Tosefta, and documents of Scriptural exegesis, such as Sifré to Deuteronomy, Genesis Rabbah, Leviticus Rabbah, and Song of Songs Rabbah, concepts of history, coming to expression in the categories of time and change, along with distinctions between past, present, and future utterly give way to a conception of recording and explaining the social order different from that of history. It is one that sets aside time and change in favor of enduring paradigms recapitulated in age succeeding age. The modernization of Judaism repudiated the paradigmatic thinking of the received tradition.

In that tradition the concept of history as we know it, and as Scripture (not read within the Torah, as part of the whole Torah) knows it, surrenders to an altogether different way of conceiving time and change as well as the course of noteworthy, even memorable social events. The past takes place in the present. The present embodies the past. And there is no indeterminate future over the horizon, only a clear and present path to be chosen if people will it. With distinctions between past, present and future time found to make no difference, and in their stead, different categories of meaning and social order deemed self-evident, the Judaism of the dual Torah transforms ancient Israel's history into the categorical structure of eternal Israel's society, so that past, present, and future meet in the here and now.

In that construction of thought, as the Reformers recognized, history finds no place, time, change, the movement of events toward a purposive goal have no purchase, and a different exegesis of happenings supplants the conception of history. No place in Rabbinic thought, portrayed in successive documents examined severally and jointly, accommodates the notions of change and time, unique events and history, particular lives and biography. All things are transformed by this other way of thinking, besides the historical one that Scripture's Official History and the Reformers' critical history use to organize the facts of social existence of Israel.

Alas, it is in the nature of a collection of essays to leave us wanting more in one spot, less in another. For Schorsch's book skirts these urgent issues; only one essay among the score, "The Emergence of Historical Consciousness in Modern Judaism," actually addresses the "turn to history." The others, being reprinted journal articles, treat conventional historical subjects, but not historical consciousness, e.g., "the emergence of the modern Rabbinate," "Jewish academics at Prussian universities," "art as social history: Moritz Oppenheim and the German Jewish Vision of Emancipation," "breakthrough into the past: the Verein für Cultur und Wissenschaft der Juden," "From Wolfenbüttel to Wissenschaft: the divergent paths of Isaak Markus Jost and Leopold Zunz," "Jewish Studies from 1818 to

1919," and the like. These are standard academic essays, and in few of them do the great themes introduced in the preface and treated in the cited essay play any part at all. So the book does not hold together very well or work on a single problem or argue in behalf of a cogent proposition. But, I hasten to add, Schorsch presents his ideas in a well-documented way, with first-rate footnotes and clear evidence of substantial erudition. The writing is academic in a less felicitous sense; every verb requires its adverb, every noun its adjective, so the prolixity of topics finds its match in a somewhat uneconomical prose. But overall, for the study of the intellectual modernization of Judaism, Schorsch has raised important questions and provided valuable data for investigating them.

VIII

Liberles on Salo Baron

Salo Wittmayer Baron. Architect of Jewish History. By Robert Liberles. NY, 1995: New York University Press. Modern Jewish Masters Series, edited by Steven T. Katz.

This is an absolutely first-rate book about a first rate academic politician who was burdened, alas, with merely a second-rate intellect, a pretentious windbag. Liberles has written a thorough, literate, enlightened, and unfailingly intelligent and critical account of the subject, taking up not only the man's accomplishments but also his failures of learning, judgment, and scholarship, balancing an account of personal activities with an honest and unsparing reading of Baron's intellectual oeuvre. He deserves a prize in the area of biography, and I hope he gets one. I cannot point to a superior example of the genre — biographies of scholars — but I can think of many inferior ones, Leo Schwarz's hagiographical and intellectually opaque book on Harry A. Wolfson being the outstanding failure in this context. I cannot point to any important omission, any act of mere sycophancy, any element of special pleading, beginning to end. The intellectual issues are addressed, the critics given a sound hearing, and the man shown for what he was. That is because Liberles brings to the task unfailing honesty and candor. In this work he marks himself as a major player in the writing of the contemporary intellectual history of the Jews.

Liberles reviews the context out of which Baron emerged and in which he did his work, the response to Baron's scholarly enterprise, which, over time, became increasingly negative, and accomplishes with elegance both a personal and an intellectual biography. Occasionally the story lags, but that is not Liberles's fault; in the main, he provides a rich picture of Baron's public career — in his day, he was the *Gauleiter* of Jewish studies in US universities — and an adequate and appropriate account of his intellectual life as well. Baron's ungenerous epitaph of his predecessor, Isaac Jost, in the writing of linear histories of "the Jews" (not differentiated histories of coherent Jewish communities at diverse times and places), serves for Baron himself: "Although not a great spirit, he was certainly a pioneer. Although not a man of genius and high aspirations, he was a solid, quiet worker who tried to lay solid reliable foundations for the development of Jewish historical knowledge, and succeeded in doing so to a large extent" (Liberles, p. 110). In the areas where Baron worked on primary sources, his *Social and Religious History of the Jews* finished in three volumes in his earliest forties and then redone in an endless and mindless expansion for the rest of his career indeed contributes to learning. In the numerous areas where Baron simply copied and paraphrased the ideas of specialists but did not important research of his own, Baron's presentation proves not only undistinguished but boring and uncomprehending.

Liberles's subtitle signals what went wrong with Baron's scholarship (as with all scholarship in "Jewish history." It is the very conception of "Jewish history" as Baron and everyone else in his time conceived the topic. That conception fabricates a unitary, linear history for all Jews at all times and in all places. Most Jews affirm, for secular or religious reasons, that the Jews constitute "a people, one people" (secular) or, all together, the "Israel" of which Scripture speaks (religious). But do the data present such a social entity? Yes, but only if they are so composed as to yield it.

For his part, Baron confused ideology with learning. That is why he set off in quest of facts to demonstrate a theological or ideological proposition. Specifically, he treated as fact what he actually had to demonstrate in order to accomplish his goal of a *Social and Religious History of the Jews,* treated as a single people with a single history what he treated as his premise. That is, that the Jews constitute a single, continuing political and social entity, throughout all time, in all parts of the world. The confusion between the Jews as a set of groups, each with (diverse) traits that, in its context, are deemed indicative and definitive of "being Jewish," and Judaism, a religious system which, in its normative definition, appeals to God's revelation to Moses at Sinai of the Torah revealed, formulated, and transmitted in two media, oral and written, yields conceptual chaos. People identify Jews' attitudes with teachings of Judaism.

Or they impute to Jews here, there, and everywhere, ideas that they find in some book of Judaism, wherever and whenever written, and without regard to the context in which the book makes its statement. Since the Talmud says thus and so, Jews therefore believe, and also act upon that belief, in this way, not in that. The confusion between behavior of diverse persons and belief of a religious system, moreover, affects not only the uninformed, but also scholars. The romantic and racist view of the Jews as a single continuing people with innate characteristics which scientific scholarship can identify and explain has stands behind Baron's entire enterprise and accounts for the massive failure that, in its wake, discredits the entire field of "Jewish history" when conducted "from Abraham to...," as it is in most Jewish-sponsored schools but only in a few universities. That is, specifically, where Jews pay for the chairs (or use political influence to start them); when universities establish Judaic studies on their own funds, it is in the discipline of religious studies.

Can I offer a cogent instance of the intellectual blunder represented by the unitary, linear conception of Jewish history? I turn to my own area of study and take for my example Baron's notion that the Jews have had an economic history, which is part of his notion of the Jews' have had a single history as "a people, one people," in the slogan of Theodore Herzl, founder of Zionism, in 1897. That unitary conception of the Jews as a single, distinctive, on-going historical entity, a social group forming also a cogent unit of economic action, is surely romantic. If the Jews do not form a distinct economy, then how can we speak of the Jews in particular in an account of economic history? If, moreover, the Jews do not form a distinct component of a larger economy, then what do we learn about economics when we know that (some) Jews do this, others, that? And if Jews, in a given place and circumstance, constitute a distinct economic unit within a larger economy, then how study Jews' economic action out of the larger economic context which they help define and of which they form a component? The upshot of these question is simple: how shall we address those questions concerning rational action with regard to scarcity that do, after all, draw our attention when we contemplate, among other entities, the social entities that Jews have formed, and now form, in the world?

People assemble pictures of traits held to have proved common to Jews in whatever circumstances in which they conduct their economic activities are adduced in justification of the description not merely of diverse Jews' economic action, but of "*the* Jews' economic history." The appeal is to a principal distinctive trait, allegedly indicative of Jews and not of others and therefore demonstrative of Jews' forming an economic entity, namely, Jews' "marginality." Whether or not that characterization has received precise definition need not detain us. The impressionistic character of the category, its relative and subjective applicability — these matters need not detain us. Now Baron claims to know about economic trends among Jews in the second, third, and fourth centuries, and I focus on volume II of the second version of his *Social and Religious History* because that covers the only area I claim to know. As evidence of his position Baron cites and exploits episodic statements of rabbis, as in the following:

> In those days R. Simon ben Laqish coined that portentous homily which, for generations after, was to be quoted in endless variations: "'You shall not cut yourselves,' this means you shall not divide yourselves into separate groups...." Before the battle for ethnic-religious survival, the inner class struggle receded.
>
> Age-old antagonisms, to be sure, did not disappear overnight. The conflict between the scholarly class and "the people of the land" continued for several generations...

Class differences as such likewise receded into the background as the extremes of wealth and poverty were leveled down by the unrelenting pressure of Roman exploitation. Rarely do we now hear descriptions of such reckless display of wealth as characterized the generation of Martha, daughter of Boethos, before the fall of Jerusalem. Even the consciously exaggerated reports of the wealth of the patriarchal house in the days of Judah I fell far short of what we know about the conspicuous consumption of the Herodian court and aristocracy....

Baron's naive conception that whatever the sources say was so really was so can be bypassed for the moment. In fact, his volume on "talmudic history" is a mere curiosity, in the main exhibition hall of the museum of scholarly gullibility. But it would be difficult to find a better example of overinterpretation of evidence than Baron's concluding sentence of the opening paragraph of this abstract. Not having shown that there was an inner class struggle or even spelled out what he means by "class struggle," how he knows the category applies, let alone the evidence for social stratification on which such judgments rest, Baron leaps into his explanation for why the class struggle receded. That is not the only evidence of what can only be regarded as indifference to critical issues characteristic of writing on Jews' economies, but it is probative. The rest of the passage shows how on the basis of no sustained argument whatsoever, Baron invokes a variety of categories of economic history and analysis of his time, e.g., conspicuous consumption, class struggle ("inner" presumably different from "outer"), and on and on.

When discussing economic policies, which draw us closer to the subject of this book, Baron presents a discussion some may deem fatuous. Precisely how he frames the issues of economic theory will show why:

Economic Policies: Here too we may observe the tremendous influence of talmudic legislation upon Jewish economy.

The premise that there was (a) Jewish economy (as distinct from Jews' economic behavior), and also (b) that talmudic legislation affected economic action, is simply unsubstantiated. How Baron knows that people did what rabbis said they should, or that Jews formed an economy in which people could make decisions *in accord with sages' instructions* — that is, to say, in accord with Judaism! — he does not say. The premise of all that follows, then, is vacant. More to the point of our interest in matters of economic theory in relationship to Judaism, we turn to Baron's program of discourse on what he has called "policies:"

The rabbis constantly tried to maintain interclass equilibrium. They did not denounce riches, as some early Christians did, but they emphasized the merely relative value of great fortunes....The persistent accentuation of collective economic responsibility made the Jewish system of public welfare highly effective. While there was much poverty among the Jews, the community, through its numerous charitable institutions, took more or less adequate care of the needy.

Man's right, as well as duty, to earn a living and his freedom of disposing of property were safeguarded by rabbinic law and ethics only in so far as they did not conflict with the common weal....

Private ownership, too, was hedged with many legal restrictions and moral injunctions in favor of over-all communal control....

Rabbinic law also extended unusual protection to neighbors....

Nor did the individual enjoy complete mastery over testamentary dispositions....

Apart from favoring discriminatory treatment of apostates, who were supposed to be dead to their families, the rabbis evinced great concern for the claims of minor children to support from their fathers' estate....

In a period of economic scarcity social interest demanded also communal control over wasteful practices even with one's own possessions....

How this *Gemisch* of this and that and the other thing — somethings akin to economic policy, some odd observations on public priority over private interest that sounds suspiciously contemporary (to 1952 liberal Democratic politics in NYC), counsel about not throwing away bread crumbs — adds up to "economic policies" I cannot say. But the data deserves a still closer scrutiny, since Baron represents the state of economic analysis of both Jews' economic behavior and also Judaism and so exemplifies precisely the problem I propose to solve in a different way. Here is his "man's right" paragraph, complete:

> Man's right, as well as duty, to earn a living and his freedom of disposing of property were safeguarded by rabbinic law and ethics only in so far as they did not conflict with the common weal. Extremists like R. Simon ben Yohai insisted that the biblical injunction, "This book of the law shall not depart out of thy mouth, but thou shalt meditate therein day and night," postulated wholehearted devotion to the study of Torah at the expense of all economic endeavors. But R. Ishmael effectively countered by quoting the equally scriptural blessing, "That thou mayest gather in thy corn and thy wine and thine oil." Two centuries later, the Babylonian Abbaye, who had started as a poor man and through hard labor and night work in the fields had amassed some wealth, observed tersely, "Many have followed the way of R. Ishmael and succeeded; others did as R. Simeon ben Yohai and failed." Sheer romanticism induced their compeer, R. Judah bar Ila'i, to contend that in olden times people had made the study of the law a full-time occupation, and devoted only little effort to earning a living, and hence had proved successful in both.... R. Simeon ben Yohai himself conceded, however, that day and night meditation had been possible only to a generation living on Mannah or to priestly recipients of heave-offerings.... In practice the rabbis could at best

secure, as we shall see, certain economic privileges for a minority of students, relying upon the overwhelming majority of the population to supply society's needs to economically productive work.

This, I submit, is little more than flatulent gibberish, windy prose about sweeping aimlessly across the page. From the right to earn a living being limited by the common weal, we jump to study of the Torah as the alternative to productive labor. That move of Baron's I cannot myself claim to interpret. I see no connection between the balance between "freedom of disposing of property" and "conflict with the common weal," on the one side, and " the issue of work as against study, on the other. The rest of the discussion concerns only that latter matter, and the paragraph falls to pieces by the end in a sequence of unconnected sayings joined by a pseudo-narrative ("two centuries later...") and an equally-meretricious pretense of sustained argument "...himself conceded"), all resting on the belief that the sayings assigned to various sages really were said by them.

To his credit, Liberles on his own addresses these and other, equally remarkable failures of Baron's scholarship. It is difficult to imagine a better treatment of the subject, and easy to see why Liberles has written a definitive account of matters. Even though Baron's legacy proves insubstantial and dull, he is not wrong to devote a book to Baron, because of the man's prominence in his time. But in the end one has to find a subject worthy of effort and emulation. So now, I hope, he will turn to the substance of scholarship, addressing the intellectual challenges, rather than lives of principal but long-past politicians of the field. This book represents a waste of a highly-talented intellect on the life and works of a mediocre one.

IX

Cohn-Sherbok on *The Future of Judaism*

The Future of Judaism. By Dan Cohn-Sherbok. Edinburgh, 1994: T&T Clark Ltd. 227 pp. L 12.50.

Cohn-Sherbok, a Reform rabbi who teaches at University of Kent, here presents a theology for a Judaism in the coming millennium. He articulates a theological problem in the following language: "If Jews are so divided among themselves that they cannot agree on basic questions of belief, practice, and identity, is there a future for Judaism as a religious system?" To answer this question, he reviews what he represents as the history of Judaism. He maintains that "until the beginning of the nineteenth century the Jewish religious tradition was essentially uniform in character." He finds the uniformity in belief in one God and the like, and minimizes differences among various groups, maintaining that in general all remained loyal to Scripture. From the Enlightenment forward, what he calls "the Jewish tradition" fragmented, with Reform, Conservative, Reconstructionist, Humanistic, Polydox, Modern Orthodox, and other "religious groupings" taking shape, resulting in "the dissolution of the Jewish faith." That is why he wishes to propose "the formulation of a new philosophy of Judaism, which could provide a basis for Jewish living in the twenty-first century." What he has in mind is "a theological framework consonant with a contemporary understanding of Divine Reality...Within this framework the Jewish understanding of God cannot be viewed as definitive and final. Instead it should be perceived as only one among may ways in which human beings have attempted to make sense of Ultimate Reality." This philosophy is based on personal autonomy as a fundamental principle of Jewish life...and conforms to the realities of everyday Jewish existence. In modern society Jews across the religious spectrum determine for themselves which features of the Jewish heritage they find spiritually significant. Open Judaism...acknowledges and celebrates this aspect of contemporary Jewish life." The shank of the book then spells out these allegations and propositions.

As a history of Judaism, the work fails because it ignores a variety of problems scholarship has addressed in the past several decades. At some points I wondered where the author has spent his time, he seems to have read nothing of contemporary study of Judaism within the disciplines of the history of religion. The basic problem is captured in the references to "the Jewish faith," "the Jewish religious tradition," and the like, treating the Jewish-ethnic and the Judaic-religious as one and the same thing. But everybody knows that the Jews as an ethnic group practice a variety of religions — Judaisms in the main but not alone — and also no religion at all. So too what he can possibly mean by "the Jewish tradition" hardly emerges, since he defines nothing and assumes everything. Perhaps his most serious error, never telling us what he means by "Judaism" or addressing the problem of definition to begin with, best accounts for the intellectual fiasco that he has produced: not history, not philosophy, not theology, not even religion, just confusion.

Cohn-Sherbok ignores fundamental works on every period he treats, so the presentation is superficial and often simply impressionistic. But a number of intellectual problems demand more substantial attention. First, Cohn-Sherbok confuses a religion with an ethnic group, thus "Judaism" for him appears to be what all Jews affirm. Second, he portrays the history of the people, Israel, as the history of Judaism, going so far as to paraphrase the biblical tales to compose his history of the faith. Third, he seems to imagine that this (pseudo-)historical narrative takes the place of serious theological inquiry. Fourth, on the historical side, he insists that there has been, and should be again, a single Judaism, ignoring the strong case for the recognition of multiple Judaisms over time, not only in modern and contemporary times. He explains away the real differences that distinguish one Judaism from another and lays heavy emphasis only on trivialities and platitudes that he maintains everyone accepted. Fifth, the work further confuses theology with philosophy of religion, in much of the book dealing with the former, but in his constructive chapters presenting the latter. Sixth, errors small and large (small: he has Louis Ginzberg as president of the Jewish Theological Seminary, which he never was; large: he sees the Mishnah as just a set of picayune rules, missing its essential philosophical character altogether) abound throughout; the presentation of Rabbinic Judaism is wooden and uncomprehending.

But what of the stated purpose, to present a new Judaism, which everybody can accept? This author honestly believes people get religion from a book, or, in more academic language, he confuses the system with the canon. But the canon recapitulates the system, the system never recapitulates the canon. As to the constructive and systematic "theology" he wishes to present, we have to wonder whether his "Open Judaism," consisting as it does of various propositions of philosophical interest to whom it may concern, but no purchase on Judaic religious sensibility, has not once more confused allegations of a theological philosophy with the realities of a religious community. The errors of special interest here concern Cohn-Sherbok's infirm grasp of the simple fact that religions take shape within community; they form a public, corporate, communal statement, not simply a set of personal opinions, beyond all social verification, about this and that. It must follow, he cannot found a Judaism by writing a book, and his lowest-common-denominator Judaism — what all Jews can accept at once — proves risible. I cannot think of a single important error in theology and in history of religion in the case of Judaism that Cohn-Sherbok does not commit. This is a lightweight and silly book, confusing history with theology, religion with ethnicity, personal and individual philosophy with a public and shared, practiced faith — and rather shoddy philosophy of religion with any Judaism.

X

Lewis on *Cultures in Conflict*

Bernard Lewis. *Cultures in Conflict. Christians, Muslims, and Jews, in the Age of Discovery.* New York, 1995. Oxford University Press

A slight, charming but not very deep, and only formally coherent set of lectures, Lewis's three talks at the University of Wisconsin cover three topics, using 1492 as the gravamen for some murky philosophizing on a variety of subjects only marginally related to one another. The formal program treats conquest, expulsion, and discovery. Of the three, the first is treated most coherently, an account of how the Christians moving southwestward through Spain and northeastward from Moscow forced back the Muslims, out of lands held by Islam for many centuries. Christianity and Islam differed from all other religions because of their powerful missionary zeal, expressed in each case in attacks and counterattacks. Here Lewis puts the reconquest of Spain into its larger context, that of Christian-Muslim competition for world-domination. The expulsion of the Jews from Spain expressed Christian uneasiness with a weak people professing a powerful, attractive religion. The Muslims were forced out as a matter of power politics. The second lecture covers familiar ground.

The third lecture is incoherent, for it treats a variety of topics; "discovery" focusing upon the Christian counterattack, following the fall of Constantinople; the spice trade and other economic interests leading Christian Europe to leapfrog over the Muslim middlemen in the trade with India and China; the diverse pictures of world geography, the division of the Old World by through the European imagination; the diversity of Africa and Asia and the cultural coherence of Europe; how the Muslims divided the world; how Muslims and Christians perceived one another; the adoption of the European scheme of things; and, finally, out of the blue, multi-culturalism. How a book that starts with the European encounter with five great civilizations, two in the New World and as well as India, China, and Islam, reaches its concluding lines with these words I cannot say: "It may be that

Western culture will indeed go: The lack of conviction of many of those who should be its defenders and the passionate intensity of its accusers may well join to complete its destruction. But if it does go, the men and women of all the continents will thereby be impoverished and endangered." Lewis has written weightier books than this one — and better constructed ones.

PART FOUR

DEBATES ON CONTEMPORARY JUDAISM

AND THE JEWISH CONDITION

XI

Christmas and Israel: How Secularism Turns Religion into Culture

[Prepared for the conference, CHRISTIANITY AND CULTURE IN THE CROSSFIRE, Hope College and Calvin College, Grand Rapids, April 27-29, 1995]

Responding to the question of the conference prospectus: what place do race and ethnicity have in a community shaped by Christian values, translated into, "the place of race and ethnicity in the community of Judaism"

The religion, Judaism, affords no recognition whatsoever to the secular categories of race and ethnicity, any more than the mystical body of Christ can take account of ethnic difference among Christians; Christ is represented in every color. True, people think otherwise, deeming Christmas secular, and identifying "Israel" with the State of Israel, or the Land of Israel. But as a matter of long-established fact Christmas in Christianity forms a religious celebration; "Israel" in Judaism refers to a supernatural social entity, God's people. But the Supreme Court declared Christmas sufficiently secular to take its place in the public square, and a great part of the Jews in the world have for two hundred years treated "Israel" as not a supernatural but a wholly this-worldly, secular and ethnic entity, first "the Jewish People," now, "[the State of] Israel." And "state" means not moral condition but political entity. In both cases, what we find is that the secular enemies of the religions, Christianity and Judaism, have taken over from within. How are we to understand the processes by which secularism turns religion into culture?

The process penetrates into the deepest layers of category-formation, challenging not doctrine but the structural foundations of the faith. Let me explain by pointing out that the great monotheist traditions insist upon the triviality of culture and ethnicity, forming trans-national, or transethnic transcendental communities. The "Israel" of the Judaism of the dual Torah (that is, the Judaism definitive for two thousand years) makes no distinction between "children of the promise and children of the flesh," such as Paul does, but defines "all Israel, to receive a portion in the world to come," by appeal to conviction, for instance, that the Torah comes from God. All, then, who affirm what such definitions of the faith proclaim and who practice what those definitions set forth come within Israel. Within the Torah the gentile finds no recognition; the gentile is fully Israel. The recognition of the Jews as an ethnic group, as distinct from holy Israel of the Torah, awaited the secular age, when post-Judaic Jews wished to retain the culture without the faith. But the culture was contingent, notional, episodic, and occasional, not universal, not encompassing. There is no one Jewish culture, so far as cuisine, accent and language, sentiment and attitude, and politics, are concerned; but there is one Torah, so far as the Torah is concerned. When a secular Jew became possible and remained within the categorical-formation, "Israel," then Judaism confronted that process of inner secularization that has nearly obliterated the possibilities of faith within the category, "Israel," meaning, God's people.

Let me now generalize on this matter. Post-modernism affirms cultural diversity. Judaism, Christianity, and Islam mean to overcome diversity in the name of a single, commanding God, who bears a single message for a humanity that is one in Heaven's sight. In the theology of the Torah, "Israel" stands for a supernatural entity, defined by appeal to valid faith; "the Church" overcomes difference; "Islam" finds place for both genders and all races in perfect equality within the divine imperatives. To state matters in more this-worldly terms, the categories of race and ethnicity, critical in post-modernist discourse, represent secular and profoundly anti-theological notions. Judaism, Christianity, and Islam all find exceedingly difficult the recognition that the social and cultural categories of ethnicity and race have bearing upon the authentic imperatives of the sacred community, whether the "Israel" of Judaism, or "the mystical body of Christ," or "the Nation of Islam." So far as the Torah addresses undifferentiated humanity and forms thereof its supernatural Israel, so far as Christ speaks to Greek and Jew, and so far as Islam forms the imperative for all races and both genders, no monotheist religion can afford recognition, or accord legitimacy, to the socially-constructed categories, race or ethnicity. Not only so, but when Judaism, Christianity, or Islam concede entry to those categories, it is at a cost of self-secularization, the self-transformation of a religious system into a contingent, cultural entity bearing principally this-worldly and social valence. When we take up the matter of ethnicity in the context of Judaism, we encounter the effects of self-secularization, as a religious community redefines itself and in the process treats the uncontingent and imperative as instrumental and merely useful, commandments becoming matters of custom and ceremony, divine imperatives turning into mere folk-traditions.

Two distinct categories therefore come together, ethnicity (inclusive of race) and secularization, for, as I shall try to show, the ethnicization of a religious community comes about within the secularization of religion, its transformation into culture. To a conference on the theme, "Christianity and Culture in the Crossfire," the condition of contemporary Judaism makes a singular contribution. It is, specifically, to underscore the profound challenge to Judaic, Muslim, and Christian convictions that secularism presents in a benign form, as I shall explain. The challenge takes shape, in the case of Judaism, in such a way as to offer to Christianity (and I think, Islam in time to come) the chance to peer over into the future. For most, though not all, of the Judaisms ("Judaic religious systems") that take center stage today show what happens when religion is transmuted into culture, the holy community into a secular social entity, and the religious calling into an essentially secular loyalty to the group. The power to disenchant the religious life and transform into something merely instrumental what for the faithful represents God's purpose derives, in particular, from the decision for essentially secular reasons to strengthen and make use of religion to work out problems of a merely social character and venue, political or sociological or psychological ones, for example.

To make this point clear and unambiguous: do I mean to say that when Abraham Heschel marched with Martin Luther King, Jr., in Montgomery, he engaged in a secular act? Quite to the contrary, he understood his commitment, along with that of the hundreds of American rabbis and other Jews, as an act in sanctification of God's name. A case can be made for a Judaic position on matters of public policy — a Judaic, not merely a Jewish-ethnic position. That case is presented, to give one instance, by Michael Lerner (on the left) in his writings in *Tikkun*; by Daniel Lappin (on the conservative side) in *Toward Tradition*; by David Saperstein, writing in the *Washington Jewish Week* (January 26, 1995), when he maintains that "in Jewish thought and history, the public sector plays a key role in ensuring justice, fairness, and equity." Saperstein turns to the Rabbinic canon to find justification for his secular politics. With these efforts, right and left, I have no quarrel, since I do not know how to distinguish proof-texts from pretexts. But where the state of Jewish public opinion is offered as the position of "Judaism," without reference to the canonical and authoritative writings and doctrines of Judaism, then I find the subversion of religion — in this case, Judaism. When we are told, for example, that "Judaism is pro-choice," meaning, abortion on demand, I contemplate the explicit and authoritative texts of the Torah that state the contrary and conclude, Judaism has been made to adopt some, perhaps many, Jews' opinion as the norm; and that opinion speaks not for God in the Torah but for quite ordinary people altogether indifferent to religion but claiming the moral authority of religion.

To understand what I identify as secularism with a friendly face, let me point to how the civil religion of America proposes to sort out the issues of the place of religion in the public square. That is to accept religion on the condition of its secularization. The policy finds its concrete expression in the Supreme Court's declaration that Christmas may be accepted in its secular dimensions, Jingle Bells but not Silent Night, Santa Claus but not the Magi. A second example derives from the conception that in a non-sectarian formulation, an act of prayer appropriate to the deepest convictions concerning that most solemn and difficult religious gesture may take place, thus prayer from no one in particular to whom it may concern: a you without personality or specificity. Yet a third instance well-known to Christians is the secularization and de-sectarianianization of chaplaincies, in hospitals and in the military for example, so that ministers, priests, and rabbis are interchangeable, without regard to race, creed or color.

Now raising the issue of the transformation of religion into culture and the religious community into a secular, ethnic group, the secularization of the other-worldly in the interests of this world may legitimately appear to cross the bounds of the post-modernist debate, moving backward into a world passed by. Harvey Cox's *Secular City,* after all, found its audience three decades ago, and issues of the secularization of religion and the "death of God" no longer provoke vivid debate. And yet, upon reflection, some may recognize points of continuity between the "cultur-ization" of religion, on the one side, and the shifting of the debate over religion to mostly this-worldly terms and issues, on the other. When, for example, truth becomes relative, revelation reduced to historical facts (as in "the historical Jesus" debates), and knowledge treated as a expression of consensus, beyond all objective testing, then the conditions of the uncompromising faith of the ages — truth about God comes from God, through God's own self-manifestation (in Christ Incarnate, in the Torah, to the Prophet, to take the pertinent cases of Christianity, Judaism, and Islam) no longer pertain.

And that is by reason of an assessment of truth-claims that precludes the very foundations of the religious affirmation of truth breaking from eternity into time. Even when critical movements that undertake a critique of secular theories and methodologies appear to align themselves with religious positions, the appearance deceives, since, in the end, the criteria of plausibility (not truth) find their definition within the secular and this-worldly framework of those critical movements. Rejection of "authoritarianism" extends to God's authority (however mediated), the very notion of commandment and divine imperative falling victim to the rejection of the notion of authority altogether. In these and other ways, post-modernism has carried to an extreme limit the initial premises and points of insistence of the secularizing movement in culture and politics. The "culture war" against religion did not begin this morning, it began with the formation of culture not only apart from, but superior to, religion that encompassed, also, the epiphenomena of culture.

True, some argue, in practical terms of this country's everyday politics the secularization of politics requires precisely the compromises evident in the re-presentation of artifacts of faith as instruments of culture. If Christmas is to establish any presence at all, better Santa Claus than nothing; so too with civil chaplaincies, so too with public prayer. Now in these compromises worked out for the sake of social harmony, Christianity loses its soul, conceding Christmas to be secular, the priesthood and ministry to be a mere this-worldly profession and not a supernatural calling, and accepting prayer that does not take place through Jesus Christ (to speak within the Christian idiom). In the academy, moreover, a parallel culture war against the specificity and authenticity of distinctive religious traditions, resting on revelation and a claim to unique possession of the truth, goes forward on another front. It is the homogenization of religions into religion, not for purposes of analysis and generalization, but in order to dismiss as essentially irrelevant to learning the specific traits and convictions of living faiths. Religions are presented as a shared quest, all equal; they are portrayed as essentially saying the same thing; their distinct messages are homogenized and strained into a single spread, with a uniform flavor. Here too the concrete and particular truth of theology, whether theology of Judaism or of Protestant Christianity, is set aside in favor of an abstract and general affirmation of what are essentially this-worldly commonplaces.

While, therefore, I realize that these concerns of mine, which I shall translate into the contemporary situation of Judaism, derive more from the modern than from the post-modern intellectual circumstance, I consider that the post-modernist challenge to the autonomy of religious truth stands in an unbroken line that extends back to the sustained war against religion ("superstition") undertaken by the Enlightenment. But, as I shall try to explain, in the case of Judaism, we see a striking example of the war against religion in the name of religion. I point toward an attack upon religion from within, rather than from without; an effort to treat religion as trivial and marginal, rather than to overthrow religion through a violent attack upon, e.g., its insufficiency in response to the feminist aspiration, or its ambiguous record in matters of race. Indeed, even invoking the category, secularization, may strike some as an effort to reach back to the issues of a prior generation, when the advent of religion in the secular world came to be celebrated by important theological voices of the day.

But the secularization of religion from within falls well within the framework of thought that treats all truth as relative and notional and episodic, all learning as negotiable, and all morality as instrumental. In the name of cultural diversity religious communities are asked to give up the right to make judgments of their own; in the name of a particular brand of feminism, religious institutions are asked to abandon arrangements of an ancient and enduring order; and so far as culture can be everything and its opposite, religions do find themselves compelled to take up opposition and to say, we make judgments, resting on revelation and reason, in favor of one thing and against some other. It is, I maintain, when the secular attitudes that favor relativism, negotiability, and instrumentalism, pervade the inner world of religion that religion finds itself under the most severe attack, when, for the wrong reason, people find themselves doing the right thing.

Now to the case of Judaism as we know it today, let me begin with an acutely contemporary moment, the discovery of religion as the solution to a problem of sociology and politics. To understand the phenomenon at hand, which is, the secularization of Judaism, a.k.a. the Torah, for this-worldly, essentially political purposes, let me explain that, as everyone knows, Jews remain Jewish even while not practicing Judaism, the religion; they may define a personal religion, speaking in the oxymoron, "my Judaism," as though a religion could ever submit to utter personalization and individuation. They may affirm their "Jewishness," denying the religion, Judaism. They may define a relationship to the Jewish community in other than religious terms altogether, that is, through philanthropy or through political support for the State of Israel. In these ways, secular Jews present a confusing picture for Christians and Muslims, who understand the distinction between the ethnic or national and the religious, even while forming this-worldly communities that express the transcendent faith.

The difference is, in the West Jews believed in the promises of the Enlightenment, affirming an undifferentiated humanity, in which even Jews might find a legitimate place, a community of humanity shaped by reason. Apart from a handful of intellectuals, the Jews stood apart from the rest of Western humanity in this perfect faith of theirs in the possibility of a transnational and cosmopolitan culture; the rest of the European peoples and their diaspora took a different route. They affirmed blood and iron, defining nationality as not territorial but ethnic, assigning distinctive traits to this race or that ethnic group, denying in word and (alas) in deed the premises of the Enlightenment concerning not the unity but the uniformity of humanity. Western Jews, in France, Britain, and especially Germany, by contrast, formed the notion of a secular Jewishness, infused with the values of international culture (art, music, philosophy, for instance). The ticket of admission to European civilization, they supposed, would be purchased at the price of not religious affirmation (as Jews universally conceived before the nineteenth century) but cultural assimilation. That Jews founded the Universities of Frankfurt and Hamburg and London conveys the policy and program of this newly-framed secular Jewishness.

One more set of facts will permit us to return to our own time. That concerns the response to the conception of a secular entity, the Jews, as distinct from the supernatural entity, "Israel," that Christianity had long recognized, along with Islam, as a transcendent social reality. The Judaism of the dual Torah set forth an "Israel" that found its definition in matters of faith. "All Israel has a portion in the world to come, except those who deny that the Torah comes from God" forms a definition of Israel in wholly supernatural terms, for example. For the entire history of Western civilization until the nineteenth century, "Israel" stood for that entity that various Christianities knew as "the Church," that is, not a this-worldly ethnic group but a supernatural society projected into time by a purposeful God. For Christians, "Israel" in Judaism can be understood only by comparison to "the mystical body of Christ;" while Christians understood that the churches in the here and now represent in this worldly terms that mystical body, they also saw their churches as God's stake on earth. And so did holy Israel — and so do important sectors of the Jewish people today.

But at the very moment that "the Jews" took on social form outside the framework of supernatural Israel, the twin-conceptions of ethnicity and race were taking shape, so that a general theory stood ready to make sense of what "the Jews" were saying to themselves about themselves. That theory divided humanity by allegedly-intrinsic or innate, genetically-transmitted this-worldly categories. Nations replaced multi-cultural empires, and races, once defined, took on innate characteristics. Ethnic groups formed territorial claims, with catastrophic results for the ethnic mosaic that covered nearly the whole of Europe. New nationalities had to be invented to take account of the result, Great Britain holding together the Welsh, Scots, Irish, Manx, and many other groups within the English-dominated framework, to take the oldest but least striking instance. And in that mix, "holy Israel" gave way to the Jews, who were given a social identity that, outside of the faith, had formerly found slight validation in shared traits of culture. Anti-Semitism as a political doctrine, with its match in Zionism as a politicization of "Israel," ultimately yielding the State of Israel as the sole point to which "Israel" would make reference, come together in two points. First, both concurred that the Jews formed a people, one people (in the language of Herzl). Second, both agreed that a single Jewish grand-parent suffices to classify a person as "Israel," as the Nuremburg Laws stated in 1935 and the State of Israel's Law of Return affirmed some fifteen years later. Both stood for the radical secularization of what had for the entire history of Western civilization stood for a supernatural category and a theological position.

These facts out of modern history bear upon the post-modernist circumstance, because they help us to understand why, in the name of the Torah, a.k.a., Judaism, one must insist upon the utter exclusion of all considerations of race and ethnicity from the community of Judaism, and, I would expect, of Christianity as well. Religions such as ours, which affirm the unity of the genders and the peoples in Christ Jesus, or the perfect equality and orderly integration of the genders and persons of diverse origin within the Torah, in the end can accord to the accident of birth no governing standing or even autonomous value. True, a child born to a Jewish mother is on that account classified as "Israel." But that fact rests upon the theological conviction, deep within the written and oral parts of the Torah alike, that the seed of the patriarchs is holy, the unearned grace of the patriarchs forms the inheritance of their children, for Israel forms an extended family. But children of Abraham and Sarah form a supernatural community, not to be confused with a this-worldly family.

Not only so, but the same fact — transmission of the condition of holy Israel through birth — competes with the superficially-contradictory one, that a convert to Judaism enjoys exactly the same status, within holy Israel, as the child born to a Jewish mother; and as a result, the theological sense of the first of the two facts — indelibility of "being Israel" from birth — has to be discovered in dialogue with the second. But Christianity, Judaism, and Islam present in the end the denial that ethnicity and race and even gender bear within themselves definitive or indicative traits, and that theological fact forms the foundation for the religious struggle against secular ethnicity, on the one side, and biological or genetic racism, on the other, that secular politics today fosters. And all three great traditions of monotheism find great difficulty in mediating between culture and race and territorial nationalism and the claims of the supernatural community of Israel, the body of Christ, and the Nation of Islam.

It must follow that when the monotheist religions accord recognition to gender, race, and ethnicity as autonomous social categories, classifications bearing their own intrinsic traits over against the traits accorded to all members of the faith-community equally, they prove complicit in their own secularization; they admit worldly-categories within the sanctum of faith. The result for Judaism proves so striking that the faithful of the companion-religions will learn an easy lesson. To understand the case, we have to move from theology to the sociology of the Jewish communities in Western Europe and its overseas diaspora in the South Pacific (Australia and New Zealand), South Africa, South America, the USA and Canada. In all of these communities young Jews have grown up within a secular Jewish culture framed by remembering the Holocaust, on the one side, and looking for meaning in Jewish existence to the State of Israel, on the other; this is a Judaism I have called, "the Judaism of Holocaust and Redemption," or, on the gloomier mornings, the Judaism of blood and iron.

For three decades now the answer to the questions of why and how to be Jewish emerged from the two mythopoeic moments: be Jewish so you won't join "them," that is, the gentiles, who hate us and will never accept us and ultimately destroyed a third of us; and be Jewish because of the State of Israel. Now, as a matter of fact, both reasons neglected the condition — as distinct from the state — of Israel, bearing no message for the critical moments of human existence: death, for instance; or for the chronic issues of a life: how to live a good life, for example; or for the enduring questions confronting any social group: who are we on our own, not in relationship to others? That is to say, the Judaism of blood and iron addressed a public and corporate community, but ignored the family, the home, and the everyday community of the here and now to which the Torah addresses its imperatives. The Judaism of Holocaust and Redemption was formed in the model of the nineteenth century's nationalisms, treating historical events as media of divine revelation, and the nation as the successor to the supernatural social entity, whether holy community (the historical communities of Israel always called themselves, in their local and corporate being, kehillah kedoshah), or church.

What secular Jews have learned after these three decades of a public Judaism quite neglectful of the private life is, alas, that the coming generations found no self-evident truth in the Judaism of blood and iron — at least none with bearing upon the home, family, and everyday community. Consequently, at the critical point of continuity — marriage and the formation of a family in Israel, the holy people — the new generations in West Europe and its overseas diaspora have opted out. The imperatives of the Judaism of Holocaust and Redemption — build Holocaust Museums, support the State of Israel — pertain without distinction to whom it may concern; one did not have to be Jewish to build or visit a Holocaust Museum (though if one was not Jewish, one would not likely pay a second visit to such a place); and if support for the State of Israel marked the measure of the good Jew, then successive U. S. presidents, from Lyndon Johnson onward, and Congresses for nearly half a century must claim the status of saints within the faith.

So the secular Jews, organized in philanthropic and political bodies and labeling themselves "the organized Jewish community" have today taken the measure of the received tradition of Holocaust and Redemption and found it wanting. Discerning the indications of an unraveling community, they turn to — of all things — Judaism. That is to say, they have formed in the USA and in Britain organizations to utilize the religion, Judaism, for the purpose of sustaining the organized Jewish community and persuading the next generation to continue to be Jewish, hence the name, "continuity," used in Britain, and its counterparts here as well. Now to me it is self-evident that when secular groups wish to exploit religion for secular purposes, they are in for some surprises. The reason is that in the end religion bears its own autonomy; it is uncontingent; it is an independent variable; it uses, but it cannot be used. I would claim that theology best accounts for this unpredictable character of religion — to state matters simply, God in the end surprises us. But remaining in a this-worldly framework, it suffices to observe that when Jewish organizations discover Judaism as the solution to all their problems, the Enlightenment has run its course, and the formation of a secular Jewish identity, alongside of, and in competition with, the identity of Israel, the holy community of the God of Sinai, has come to its last path. The final solution to the Jews' problem turns out to be that Torah that knows not "the Jews" but only "Israel," as in, "The one who keeps Israel slumbers not, nor sleeps," a reference not to the Israel Defense Force's radar, not at all.

This brings us back to matters of race and ethnicity within the community of Israel, the holy people. The alternative to the received definition of holy Israel was the Jewish people. But the end of the Jewish people need not lead inexorably to the rebirth of Holy Israel as the Jews' governing social metaphor. True, I have argued that the secular reading of "Israel" as "the Jewish people" has lost plausibility. But the demise of secularism does not carry in its wake the renewal of religiosity. For understood theologically, Holy Israel derives not from the sociology of synagogue life but from the theology of the Torah. So far as the Jews wish to make use of the Torah ("Judaism") as the medium for maintaining the Jewish group, the Torah cannot help them accomplish their goals. The reason is that, for Judaism as for all other religions, religion is not a means to an end but an end in itself. It is not, in the language I used earlier, a dependent variable, a contributory factor. Religion is an independent variable, one that explains other things but is not explained by other things. What that means is simple: religion uses, but it does not use, the facts of this world.

If people do not find self-evidently valid the affirmations of faith, self-evidently compelling the requirements of faith, then faith cannot come to realization for those people. If we have learned anything through two hundred years of militant secularization of the Jews, it is that, when originally-religious attitudes and actions are taken over for worldly purposes, they lose their power; commandments presented as customs and ceremonies no longer compel. Truths set forth as preferences, convictions transformed into merely-secular facts (as in "Jewish history proves" in place of "the Torah says" and "God spoke to Moses saying, speak to the children of Israel and say unto them") lose all power of persuasion. The power of religion defines its pathos, its strength yields its weakness. What compels when believed does not even influence when not believed. Kosher when applied to food means, this is how God wants us to eat, or what God wants us not to eat; kosher when used to indicate a style of cooking that appeals to an ethnic group does not compete on a menu that lists, also, French or Italian or Chinese or Mexican dishes, and that is why kosher-style sells only pickles.

It follows that if people appeal to Judaism as the foundation for "Jewish continuity," as the self-styled "organized Jewish community" in the form of united Jewish charities contends should be the ideology of the hour, none will respond to that appeal for very long. Such an appeal — our "ideology" for being Jewish is now to be Judaism, as it has been Holocaust and Israelism — asks that the religion, Judaism, or, as I prefer, the Torah, accomplish not the transformation of the Jews into Holy Israel but merely the transposition of the Jewish ethnic group from one mode of ethnicity to some other form of the same secular ethnicity. But the Torah — Judaism — defies the Jews' ethnicity. The Passover Seder without divine intervention celebrates not God's power to redeem but merely Israel's power to survive — and the meal becomes a secular banquet with a quaint ritual. And that is not religion. The Day of Atonement speaks of sin and atonement, humanity's contrition and God's mercy. Turned into an occasion for the gathering of the clans, the rite is ritualized and loses its power to transform and to enchant. Having sat in a Conservative synagogue in Tampa behind a couple that was engaged in caressing ordinarily appropriate in the bed room but not in a place of worship, I know that the widespread synagogue observance of the New Year signifies togetherness, but not a shared quest for God on the occasion of remembrance.

The broadly-based American Jewish conception, therefore, that if only we build programs of "continuity," we assure the future of the ethnic group represents a profound misunderstanding of the nature of religion. And that is because, in my view, two hundred years of militant secularism have left a huge proportion of the Jews completely uncomprehending concerning religion, religiosity, and the character of what the world calls "Judaism" and what is called, in its native category, "the Torah." The upshot is, what people do not believe, they cannot utilize. And that which they do believe to be truth stands beyond all secular utility. The retreat of Jewish secularism, the failure of ideologies resting on a this-worldly explanation of who the Jews are and why they should be what they are — these palpable events of the day do not open the way to a renewal of Judaism and a rebirth of Judaic religiosity, on the one side, and active piety, on the other. The alternative to secularism is not religion, it is nihilism.

To conclude, let me spell out why so secular a view of religion as the one that asks religion to carry out an essentially-this-worldly social task profoundly misunderstands religion. A religious group is formed and sustained by people whom God has marked, to whom God has been made manifest; a religion records what that group knows about God. Religions represent what happens when people believed that, in what happens, God speaks to them; meets them; sets forth what God wants them to do together. Those are to be sure convictions that can be manipulated for secular purposes, but they are not affirmations that can be fabricated for the occasion. All religious people know that fact to be self-evident; and no secular people understand that fact at all. Forming and sustaining a religious community in response to the encounter with, God is to be compared to dancing out music.

The matter is to be compared to the relationship of the dance to music. Martha Graham once said to me, "the dance is the physicalization of music." What she explained was, when she heard music, it would be in movement and gesture that she embodied what she heard. When in Chicago she saw for the first time the painting, the girl with the scarlet sash, she wanted immediately to dance the painting. And she knew just what she would do. Her limbs told her. Now, in the context of the religion, Judaism, which identifies God's revelation with words written down in a book, and in the context of the kindred religions that identify book-writing as a principal medium for conveying knowledge of God, Islam and Christianity, a book is the writing down of religion, that is to say, the encounter with God in time and in the present moment. Holy books in the view of those who made, valued, and later preserved them as authoritative and true, record and preserve what it means to know God — as much as the dance records and preserves what it means to embody music. The metaphor then compares "know" to "embody." Encounter with God is not philosophical, that is, the mere, factual knowledge that God exists, any more than the melody is the (mere) dance. Encounter with God is religious, that is, meeting with the living and very particular God who creates, commands, is concerned with Israel. But the knowledge of the encounter, recorded in words and in writing, makes possible our encounter afresh (so Judaism maintains concerning the Torah), just as the dance of the music makes possible the fresh re-presentation in physical ways of the melody.

True, the sages did not confuse map with territory, encounter through learning with the actuality of encounter itself, any more than Martha Graham conceived that the physicalization of music took the place of the music. The ballet would always begin with the notes of the orchestra (or the silent beat before the sound began), and the study of the Torah would always commence with the prior knowledge of God present in the Torah. The Torah is not God, the ballet is not the music. The encounter with God, for religion, the music itself, for the dance — these remain always other, but no longer, wholly other and inaccessible, and that is what Torah-learning promises for Judaism's knowledge of and encounter with God made manifest in the Torah, as much as it is what the ballet promises for the realization of music. These are, then, remarkable and noteworthy writings, not to be reduced to trivial dimensions of whether or not a particular ethnic group, in the perspective of history barely a day old, survives another day or not. Ahad HaAm stated the secular perspective, its profound incomprehension of what is at stake in the religion, Judaism, when he said, "More than Israel kept the Sabbath, the Sabbath kept Israel." From his perspective, he explained why the Sabbath matters. But that is not the perspective of God, who said, "I am the Lord your God who brought you out of the land of Egypt, out of the house of bondage: Honor the Sabbath day to keep it holy." If people keep the Sabbath so that the Jews will survive, they will not have kept the Sabbath, whether or not the Jews survive. And so for Judaism. The retreat of secularism marks not the advance of religiosity, only the demise of the old gods. To the God who is made manifest in the Torah that event is simply not relevant. And Christmas in the end abides in the creche, and not with Santa Claus.

XII

Can Jews Live in a Religious Society?

For two hundred years Jews have taken for granted that their welfare and even safety depend upon the religious neutrality of politics and the social order. They have identified threats to their security with heightened religious commitment among their neighbors. In the USA most Jews have favored a rigid interpretation of the First Amendment, and in Europe they identified with secular centrist and left-wing parties and opposed religious ones. That is because Jews took for granted Christians wished to deny them ordinary human rights as citizens and long-time residents of the countries of their birth. When the French Revolution declared war on all religion, but especially on Christianity, murdering Catholics, priests and nuns for their piety, Jews fastened their eyes on the Declaration of the Rights of Man, ignoring the selectivity governing who, in fact, would enjoy such rights, and, in the time of Napoleon, the rabbis of France abrogated vast areas of the law of Judaism in favor of state control of culture not only politics, conviction not only the social order. And that response, in the famous Sanhedrin of 1812, would stand for Jewish opinion, both religious and secular.

Now the long-term consensus in favor of the secularization of culture and religious indifference of politics accounts for the persistent politics of Jewry, favoring the left over the right, and also for the crisis that confronts Jews in the USA. That crisis has come about because the established conviction, secularization of politics and culture signals the wave of the future, has come under serious question and today constitutes an act of faith with little tangible evidence to sustain it. To understand the dramatic character of what has taken place in the last quarter-century in this country's political and cultural life, let me call to mind how things looked in the near-historical past, in the 1950s and 1960s. In the 1950s this country experienced what people regarded as a return to religion, with a great deal of church- and synagogue-building, on the one side, and a general affirmation, expressed by President Eisenhower, "It doesn't matter what you believe, as long as you believe something."

Then, a decade later, the mood shifted. The change found its voice in a wildly-popular book of the mid-1960s, a work of enormous influence, by the splendid theologian, Harvey Cox, called *The Secular City,* a principal statement of a still more influential theological movement that proclaimed "the death of God." Cox maintained that religion as an organized force had lost its bearings and no longer defined the norms of society. He argued that secularization of public life and culture defined the future, and he set forth a religious vision on the premise that, on the whole, religion had lost its central place in this country.

Alas for prophets! Even at that moment religious movements in this country were gathering strength and defining for themselves a political program, and, as we all know, now, some three decades later, most people concur, America sees itself as a fundamentally religious society. I need hardly go over the influence of the Moral Majority of the 1980s, of the Christian Right of our own day, the position in popular culture of important religious leaders, the vitality of churches of all kinds, and, as a matter of fact, the renewal, in the Jewish ethnic world, of a vivid Judaic religious life. In 1940 Orthodox Judaism scarcely possessed a voice; today various Orthodox Judaisms flourish, integrationist around Yeshiva University, segregationist around various yeshivot; Hasidic and mainstream; Zionist and anti-Zionist, and diversely classified in other ways as well. Fifty years ago Reform Judaism stressed morality and ethics to the near exclusion of all else. Today, Reform Judaism formulates a distinctively religious message, insisting that ethics without faith bears no promise of redemption. Conservative Judaism and its Reconstructionist offshoot focus intellectual energies in the search for what they call "spirituality," and the most influential thinker in that sector of Judaism is Abraham J. Heschel, the one name associated with Conservative Judaism to produce a serious and sustained account of the Judaic encounter with God.

When therefore we ask ourselves whether the Jews can live in a religious society, the question concerns not only how we shall accommodate the growing and powerful voice that various Christianities now possess, whether Catholic or Mormon, main-stream or Bible-believing. We have to wonder how that vast secular sector of the Jewish population of this country is going to cope with a militant Judaism, as much as a militant Christianity, and how the two-hundred year conviction that religion speaks out of the past and not into the future will face the unanticipated reality of the enormous power of religion to change lives and reform the social order. We taught ourselves how to live in a secular world and persuaded ourselves that our welfare and security require not a religiously-neutral but a rigidly-secular public policy. Those Jews, and they are very many, who regard "being Jewish" as an essentially ethnic identification, who do not practice any Judaism, or who resort to (a) Judaism only for formalities of the life-cycle, today contemplate a world that calls to mind dangerous days indeed.

1. We have to ask, first of all, whether the militantly secular Jews may not be right: Are we not better off in a secular than in a religious world? The

record of Christianity and Islam hardly allays fears. We need not look backward before our own day. In Eastern Europe today organized anti-Semitism nourishes itself in the Churches, particularly Russian and Rumanian Orthodox Christianity, the babushka-vote in Russian elections forming an implacable phalanx of reaction and hatred. In Islamic countries, diverse though they may prove in other ways, a single trait of loathing for Judaism governs everywhere. So were we citizens of Orthodox Russia or Muslim Iran, we should have sound reason to fear the renewal of religious fervor.

But we live in the USA, where Protestant, Catholic, and Orthodox Christianity defines matters differently. The profound response of Christianity to the Holocaust, leading to much soul-searching and sincere recognition of how Christianity, which did not produce the Holocaust — it was the work of the German National Socialist Workers Party, a secular group — proved complicit in the Holocaust; most Christians today identify in the heritage of anti-Judaism and anti-Semitism beginning with the Gospel of John sources of the Holocaust — and of the many holocausts before our own day conducted under pious Christian auspices. But the confronting the Holocaust, Christian theologians have taken the measure of their heritage and determined to reform it. From John XXIII to John Paul II, in the Catholic Church, with numerous important figures in the various Protestant communions as well, from Billy Graham to Pat Robertson in the Bible-believing Christian world, in one national church after another, whether Brazil, whether the Philippines, whether Poland, whether Britain, Christian Churches have said and done things unimaginable a generation ago.

So, it is clear, Christians of every persuasion and denomination have undertaken to show friendship to the Jews as a group, and most have furthermore undertaken heroic efforts to form a theory of how the covenant at Sinai that binds us to God endures, so that Judaism finds itself represented by many Christian groups as a valid religion, a way to God, and not merely a religion that died at Calvary, as they would say in times past. That is not to suggest Christians do not welcome converts from all sources, including the Jews, just as we welcome converts out of Christianity. It is to say, the teaching of contempt that endured for two thousand years has finally had to confront competition with another, authentically-Christian teaching about the Jews and Judaism. For Christianity we remain God's first love. For Christianity the Torah now presents a challenge, a way to God that has shown itself true and straight, at least for us. A generation ago we heard no such messages, but now, in Europe and the European diaspora in this hemisphere and elsewhere, we are learning to view Christianities as sources of friendship and sustenance. In that context, we have little to fear from a militant Christianity that finds in Judaism a rival but also an ally, that honors Jews who live by their faith, that atones and remembers and repents and seeks renewal. Aforetimes, when we heard the word "Christian," we took for granted that meant, "Christian, not Jewish," but in much (if by no means all!) of the Christian world, what Christians want us to hear is, "Christian, therefore friend to holy Israel."

2. If we need not face the future in a spirit of unease, still, ought we not prefer the passing age of militant secularism over the coming age of renascent Christianity? That "we" splits into two parts: should we Jews look back fondly on the passing of the secular age and the advent of a religious spirit? Should Judaism look forward with trepidation to an actively-religious situation? For we have to distinguish the Jews as an ethnic group, with a this-worldly life of its own, from Judaism as the body of the faithful who practice the religion. To take the Jews first, the answer is unambiguous. The secular age, beginning in various countries in the late eighteenth century and extending to our own time, has sorely tried the Jews. Without the restraints of Christianity, the West turned savage, and the Holocaust happened. Christian Europe produced an ambiguous record; for long centuries, Jews lived lives no less secure, no less satisfactory, than Christians — five hundred years in Poland, for example, and from early Roman times to the eleventh century in Germany, for another. True, entire territories closed their doors to Jews. True, massacres and deportations took place. True, measured over the long perspective, Jews in Christian Europe had good and substantial reason to greet with a sigh of relief the advent of an allegedly secular state. But, as it happened, the secular states continued the war against Judaism, but also turned against the Jews as well. Had Christianity determined to wipe out holy Israel, no Jews would have survived, but the Jews did survive. By contrast, Stalin's Russian Empire and Hitler's German Empire destroyed Judaism and murdered Jews, not in the name of Jesus Christ but in the name of the workers' paradise or the master race. So the case for the secular state proves, to say the least, ambiguous.

3. Now, when it comes to Judaism, the record is quite one-sided. Let me state matters very simply. The form of Judaism that predominated from ancient times to our own day, which is Rabbinic Judaism, answered just those questions that Christianity addressed to holy Israel, and answered them with such effect that the Jews, a secular group, affirmed themselves as Israel, a holy people. Christian and Muslim rule presented to Jews those very questions that Judaism answered: who are you? what relationship to you sustain with God? why do you persist? Judaism flourished in its classical forms in those times, and in those countries, in which Christianity defined the culture of the place, for Europe, and (until the rise of the State of Israel), the same is so for Islam.

Let me spell out what exactly I mean. Rabbinic Judaism took shape at the beginning of Western civilization, when the Roman Empire adopted Christianity. With Constantine Christianity became the definitive power in the politics of the West. Rabbinic Judaism began to face serious competition in the Western European countries and in the USA beginning in 1787, with the American Constitution (as we should see matters) or with the French Revolution (as Europeans might prefer). Then Christianity began its journey out of its dominant position in the center of the political arena. The Judaism that flourished in Christendom and in Islam addressed the questions of Judaic polity in a subordinated but tolerated status, that is, the polity that came into being in 312. That same Judaism passed away in 1787 (as we Americans would see it) or in 1789 (as Europeans would prefer), when a new and quite different set of questions impressed large numbers of Jews as urgent. Those questions concerned not a Judaic polity but the Jewish citizen, not the collectivity but the individual. Answers to these questions constituted the Judaisms aborning in modern times. The Judaism that had flourished throughout the history of the Christian West flourished in the Christian age. The reason, I maintain, is that when Christianity defined culture, the issues of Christianity defined what was relevant, and the urgent questions facing Jews took shape in those same issues. In fact, three powerful forces, all of them realized in wholly political forms, successively defined the questions Jews identified as urgent. These were Christianity, down into the nineteenth century, secularism, through the nineteenth and into the twentieth centuries, and the Holocaust, from the last third of the twentieth century.

Christianity defines the starting point, and, its demise, the death of that Judaism. Rabbinic Judaic system flourished through the history of the West as Christendom, took up the challenge of Christianity and therefore explained to Jews the context and meaning of Israel, political and supernatural alike. Christianity (and, in its time and place, Islam as well) took for granted the fundamental facticity of Israel's claim to form not only a distinct, but a distinctive and special nation in God's commonwealth. According special status to Israel, Christendom and Islam affirmed the biblical picture, though, of course, modifying it in light of what each deemed further chapters in the sacred history. True, Christianity would further maintain that the Church formed the new Israel, that along with the Hebrew Scriptures, a further set of holy books, the New Testament, contained the word of God. Along these same lines, Islam held that, beyond Moses, then Jesus, Muhammed formed the seal of prophecy, the Quran, God's last and perfect word. But both Christianity and Islam saw Israel, the Jewish people, within the same supernatural view of a world created and governed by one God, who had revealed himself to Israel (if also through Jesus Christ and Muhammed), a view contained within the Hebrew Scriptures revered, also, by Israel, the Jewish people.

For its part, a defeated and disappointed people, Israel in those same Scriptures read an account of itself that contradicted its present condition. The scriptural story of a contract between Israel and God, confirmed in the experience of exile and return from 586 B.C., with the destruction of the first Temple of Jerusalem, to 450 B.C., with the building of the second, pointed toward rules governing Israel's history that, for the moment, had not been kept. The advent of Christianity as the religion of the Roman empire made acute a long term chronic crisis in the divine economy, and that is why the Judaism that reached written expression at the end of the fourth century defined as its agenda the problems that it chose. The Judaism that took shape in the fourth century mediated between the expectation and the reality. It answered all of the questions then and, for the history of the Christian West, afterward pressing upon Israel, explaining its distinctive way of life in the here and now as a medium of sanctification and promising in response to acceptance of its subordinated political position and adherence to its way of life salvation in the end of days.

Challenging Israel to explain itself, Christendom and Islam therefore received from the Judaism of the dual Torah those answers that, for Israel, constituted self-evident truth: the way of life, the world view, formed by a concrete Israel, that in that time and place constituted a Judaism. Specifically, the urgent and inescapable question answered by the Judaism that first took shape in response to the rise of Christianity addressed the standing and status of Israel in a world in the charge of others than Israel. That Judaism had to explain the meaning of a history that produced the Christian Empire, Rome (and later on would yield the Islamic nation as well). Identifying, within its theory of Israel, Christendom and Islam with the family of Israel, that Judaism saw Rome as Esau, as against Jacob, and later on would identify Islam as Ishmael, as against Isaac. The Judaism of the dual Torah further answered that question — who is Israel, now in particular — by showing that Israel, living the holy way of life prescribed by the Torah as interpreted by Israel's sages, would humbly accept God's will now, and, in time, would receive that salvation that is coming to God's first love.

The defeated nation therefore learned from its political subordination the lesson of correct service to its true lord and master, God alone. The politics of the defeated and subordinated nation bore within itself confirmation of the supernatural standing of that same nation; nothing was what it seemed, everything pointed toward a deeper truth, beneath appearances. So long as Christianity, in its diverse forms, defined that intellectual and political structure that accorded to Israel, the Jewish people, a role of supernatural consequence, the Judaism that took up the challenge of Christianity retained its standing, among Jews, as a complete and ample reply to the urgent questions of the world. The world view of Judaism in its classic statement furthermore corresponded to the way of life lived by Jews in accord with that same statement, and both accounted for the condition of Israel, the Jewish people. The whole fit together and, moreover, proved coherent with the political context in which Israel endured.

A measure of the remarkable success of that Judaism is readily at hand. Two hundred years later, Islam swept across the Middle East and North Africa, by that point Christian for half a millennium. The Christian ocean evaporated, as vast once-Christian populations accepted Islam. But the small, but deep, pools of Judaism scarcely receded. That Judaic system that accounted for and made tolerable Judaic subordination in the here and now explained this new event. But Christianity that had triumphed by the sword of Constantine fell before the sword of Muhammed. And the same Judaic system, into the nineteenth century in Eastern Europe, and down to the middle of the twentieth century for the great Judaic communities in Muslim countries, flourished, which is to say, remained the self-evident answer to the urgent question.

Redefining the political civilization of the West, a vast process of secularization removed Christianity, first in the Protestant West, then in the Roman Catholic center and south, and finally in the Christian Orthodox (Greek, Russian) east, of Europe, from its established position as the definitive force. Through the nineteenth century important political movements, appealing to the nation-state and to man as the measure of all things, rather than to the kingdom of God and to heaven's will, set forth a new politics. That program of secularization raised a fresh set of questions also for Israel, the Jewish people. In the nature of things, these had nothing whatever to do with Israel's supernatural standing in God's plan for creation and the history of humanity. Posed by political changes — as much as the original questions had taken political form — the new set of urgent concerns engaged many Jews, at first particularly in Western European countries, later on in the Eastern European ones and in their extension in America, in a new set of inquiries. These inquiries produced a fresh program of self-evident answers, and those answers in the nineteenth century constituted a new set of Judaisms.

And this brings me to my answer to the question, Can Judaism live in a religious society? The answer that both ancient and contemporary history produces proves wholly affirmative. Judaism today flourishes in ways in which for two hundred years in the USA it did not flourish. We have a more intense and active synagogue life than we have known from the immigrant generation onward — for those who identify with the synagogue. We have a far more professional Jewish school system now than we have ever had before. The Orthodox yeshivot, Conservative and Reform seminaries, rabbinical associations, and other media of religious expression all flourish. A generation back, we had few day schools, the yeshivah-world languished, the Rabbinical schools struggled to fill their class rooms, and the synagogues, excluding certain Orthodox ones, bored people. Today Reform Jews sing out loud in services (or would like to), and Conservative Jews fill up the pews for Sabbath morning worship, and Orthodox Jews increase in numbers and in fervor. So, by this-worldly measures of other-worldly matters, Judaism flourishes as it has not in any Western country from the French Revolution onward. In my view, the general prosperity of religion, the plausibility of religious behavior, the acute relevance of religious belief — these spill over for us also into an age of rebirth and remarkable renewal. So Judaism can live in a religious society and the amazing growth of religious activity and conviction within that sector of American Jewry that practices Judaism attests to a beckoning future.

But, we all realize, the religious sector of American Jewry forms only part, and I think, the smaller part, of the Jewish population of this country and Canada. The secular sector, with its organizations and institutions, dictates the character of Jewry over all. That sector faces problems of sociology and politics. It is clear that secular Jewishness, in the form of the Judaism of Holocaust and Redemption, with stress on the tragedy in Europe and the rebuilding of the state of Israel, has lost all plausibility for the new generation. That is to say, as a medium for persuading Jews to be Jewish, to marry Jews and build Jewish families, the Judaism of Holocaust and Redemption has simply failed. Intermarriage rates tell us all we need to know. The stress on "continuity" lacks all content, and the attempt to exploit a great religion for essentially secular, ethnic purposes lacks conviction and must fail. Whether secular Jewry in the secular age derived strength from the secularization of culture I cannot say; I am inclined to think that it did, in the nineteenth century, under certain particular conditions. But today secular Jewry has used up its intellectual capital, the Judaism of blood and iron lacking the power to infuse personal life with meaning and community affairs with moral authority.

If the religious age that has come upon us offers slight comfort to militant secularism, therefore, Jews can live in a religious society. The reason is that Judaism will flourish as never before in the America that is aborning. Those Jews who practice Judaism — in any of its several cogent systems — will not only survive but thrive, because, after all, Judaism is the single most successful religion ever to come upon this earth. At the center of secular Jewishness, the philosopher, Ahad HaAm, opined, "More than Israel has kept the Sabbath, the Sabbath has kept Israel." He valued the Sabbath for its this worldly-uses. To him we may now reply, More than the Torah [that is, "Judaism"] has kept Israel, Israel has kept the Torah. And that has made all the difference — to God, at any rate.

XIII

Sorting out Jew-Haters

"The Jews" stand in people's mind for so many, and such strange, things that you can find Jew-haters in places where there are not many Jews around to hate — or even enough to attract much attention to begin with. Take for example that outlying fringe of the settled world, New Zealand. where I spent last summer, (winter in the southern hemisphere).

The closest spot on earth to the Antarctic, the South Island suffers a harsh winter, with cold gales sweeping up from the south; its scattered population, gathered in just a few towns and cities on the east coast, enjoys not only nature's grandeur, in the magnificent Southern Alps, the rain forests on the West Coast and the Tasman Sea, but also nature's earthquakes on a very regular basis, they breathe air as polluted as Denver's, and looking longingly to the warm sun to the north, endure a winter gloom to compete with Labrador's. And the people, with their impeccable manners, turned out coldly intolerant of difference, patronizing the Maori, scarcely pretending to tolerate Chinese and Indians and Jews (by the way, American accents don't fare all that well either).

And it is also the first venue in my long life where I encountered incidents some may class as anti-Semitism, often (three times in one month), and personally, and directly. As I'll explain, if not the real, thing, then, at least, what I found was gauche and stupid remarks about the Jews and Judaism untempered by courtesy or even a trace of embarrassment. And that led me to reflect on the varieties of species of the common genus, dislike of the unlike, Jewish subdivision. But, as always when it comes to the Jews, even Jew-hating gets complicated — because there are haters, and then, there are haters.

Since few Jews live in Christchurch — there is a synagogue with scarcely a hundred members, most of them secular and merely ethnic, many of them intermarried and unlikely to raise up another Jewish generation — nothing prepared me for my first encounter with a direct remark anent the fact that I am Jewish. That is something people take to form a part of me, but, like my nose or my left-handedness, not to require (or sustain) special comment. The initial incident left me puzzled and annoyed. It took place at the University of Canterbury, where I was a visiting professor for a couple of months (a wasted spell at a boring commuter college of no great distinction in most subjects). In the faculty lounge I was introduced to a colleague from one of the language departments.

My colleague: "This is Jack Neusner, visiting from America."

He (having seen announcements of my public lecture series, "Judaism after the Death of 'the Death of God'"): "Oh, you're the visiting Jew" (emphasis his)!

I: "What?"

He: "Oh, I mean, the *wandering* JEW."

Dumbfoundedly, I: "Don't you know people don't talk to each other that way any more?"

I wish I could have thought of something more devastating to say, but the experience of being told "oh, you're the Jew" proved so alien that I had not the wit to respond in kind. What was I supposed to say — "and you're the local Kiwi bigot, out of the museum of South Pacific curiosities"?

People later reassured me that the man is a Quaker and (therefore!) wouldn't hurt a flea, but also is the most gauche person they knew. Anyhow, it wasn't anti-Semitic, just dumb. I put it down to the isolation and provinciality of a professor in Podunk, the outer bound of civilization.. It was an odd fellow, nothing more — until Dunedin, further toward the polar ice cap still, settled by the Presbyterians when the Anglicans started Christchurch.

There, visiting friends, at a dinner party, I was seated — as co-baby-sitter, I found out, along with a young Canadian law professor at Otago University — next to a woman who clearly could not stop talking to save her life. She was a lawyer, paid to babble I reckon, and third generation in the law office founded by her family, Dunedin born and bred, speaking that nearly-unintelligible patois my Canterbury friend who is an English professor called "demotic Kiwi," meaning, English spoken with so bizarre an accent as (for American ears at least) to form a private, antipodean language, Presbyterian pidgin, really. Since on the other side sat a lawyer, she commenced to tell her "lawyer jokes," which rivalled in stupidity the old Polish jokes that mercifully have gone into oblivion.

Then, turning to me at her left, she announced, "Well, I have told my lawyer jokes. Now tell me your Jewish jokes," by which she clearly meant, ethnic jokes at Jews' expense. I said, as coldly as I could, "I don't know any and have never heard any, people don't tell me that kind of joke." Without a pause, she turned to her right and asked the young law professor, "Well, you tell me *your* Jewish jokes." I had the sense that he would not have minded dropping dead on the spot, but, between the two of us, we managed to steer her into the direction of a monologue on some — any — other subject. She favored us with one on the up-coming by-election right in Canterbury, where I was then living, turning a fascinating subject into a boring one in the process.

This too I wrote off as not anti-Semitism but just an example of how far we Americans have come in cleaning up our ethnic act. A woman such as this gives a bad name to feminism, which I favor, and a good name to political correctness, which I despise. But no, it was not anti-Semitism.

My third encounter was, and I think any reasonable person would concur. At Waikato University, in Hamilton, on the North Island. There, a professor told me, a student of his who in the context of a class discussion about religion identified her religion as Judaism had been told by another professor, *"No, Judaism is not religion — it's just a certain attitude toward money."*

When I heard that icy Kiwi judgment (I'd gotten hints of the same thing among students at Canterbury University), I began to reflect on the difficulty we find in distinguishing from one another the varieties of ethnic and religious bigotry that encircle us Jews and our religion: Jew-hatred, anti-Judaism, anti-Semitism, Jew-baiting, anti-Israelism or anti-Zionism, and the various other species of the common genus. I did not fully trust the judgment of my native-informant, who used the tale as evidence that New Zealand is an anti-Semitic country with a Fascist government, neither of which is true.

We lump all Jew-haters together and class them all as guilty of "anti-Semitism. But as I'll explain, that is misleading and obscures matters. It's like not knowing the difference between a headache and a brain tumor. Each should stand on its own terms. People call anti-Semitism anything from the casual ("Jewish jokes") and merely stupid ("wandering Jew, I presume") to the vicious ("attitude toward money") and dangerous. That is a mistake, since it obscures the facts and distorts them, making the trivial and the consequential into the same thing.

People may impute to Jews a set of qualities they do not like. That's Jew-hatred, common, for example, in the U.S. black world, less so, but still not rare, in the white world too. Class that as dislike of the unlike.

Faithful Christians for nearly twenty centuries have maintained that Judaism died at Calvary, meaning, Jesus Christ had replaced Judaism and Christianity had superseded it. That is anti-Judaism. Until Vatican II (for Catholicism) and its counterparts in Protestantism, that view prevailed universally. Class that as the quite familiar theological warfare — all against all in God's name.

People may say things they know will offend Jews, for example, ridiculing their ethnic traits or their religious practices. That's Jew-baiting. Some have thought Patrick Buchanan sometimes has gone out of his way to bait Jews, not just disagree on matters of public policy (Israel's "amen corner" in the U.S. Senate for instance); others suppose choice and colorful language was meant to accomplish a mere polemical goal. No one I know who knows him personally takes the former view. Class that as verbal bullying.

People who like Arabs and hate Jews may condemn the State of Israel in terms they do not use for any other country and impose a standard that no country can reasonably hope to attain. That's a form of anti-Zionism or anti-Israelism, and it too yields its own cruelly-expressive vocabulary, comparing Israelis to Nazis for instance. Class that as politics poisoned by bigotry.

None of these trivialities changes the world very much. None qualifies as anti-Semitism, because, by themselves or all together, none can have led to the Holocaust, a unique event in the history of humanity, as Cornell University Professor Steven T. Katz has recently argued in a landmark book on the subject.

Only anti-Semitism, which encompasses all of the above, so focused an entire civilization — Europe, east and west, north and south, as to make the Holocaust happen. But anti-Semitism is not the same thing as casual bigotry, mere dislike of the unlike, let alone theological animus or a particularly spiteful form of politics. Unlike the rest, anti-Semitism sets forth a world-view, a philosophy of life and culture and politics, like Communism or Socialism or Fascism or democracy or Christianity.

Anti-Semitism proclaims the doctrine that the Jews are a separate species within humanity, peculiarly wicked, responsible for the evil of the human condition. A political philosophy formulated in the world of late nineteenth century Germany and Austria, anti-Semitism formed the ideological foundation of political parties and served as the basis for the formulation of public policy. It provided an account of the human condition and how the Jews corrupt it. It offered a history of Western civilization and how the Jews pervert it. It formulated a theory of the future of the world and how the Jews propose to take it over. Anti-Semitism presented a philosophy, a theology, a politics, a metaphysic. People make sense of the world by appeal to anti-Semitism, and, in World War II, millions of Germans gave their lives willingly to fight for the realization of their country's belief in the anti-Semitic ideal of national life and culture.

An encompassing world view, anti-Semitism stands by itself, not to be confused with expressions of inter-group hostility (blacks' Jew-hatred for instance, as in Howard University's famous football chant, "Who killed Nat Turner? The Jews! the Jews! the Jews!"); inter-religious conflict over religious truth (the centuries-long struggle between Judaism and Christianity, as in "his blood be upon our heads and our children's"), simple dislike of the unlike in the setting of civil conflict ("the Senate's amen corner"), and even impatience spilling over into unreasonable irritation with one foreign country or another. All these are irritating, but trivial. Confusing with them that wholly other philosophy, theology, and metaphysics that constitute anti-Semitism trivializes anti-Semitism and imparts to matters of little consequence disproportionate importance.

When I was a visiting professor in Finland, some young men spent an estimated fifteen hours of hard labor, using heavy construction equipment, in destroying the hundreds of headstones of the Jewish cemetery of Åbo/Turku. When they were caught, the local Swedish-language paper interviewed me on whether I thought that that act of Jew-hatred showed Finland was an anti-Semitic country. I said no, not at all; Finland could never be compared to Poland, or Russia, or Austria, or Rumania, where vast sectors of the population express to polling agencies a variety of hair-raising anti-Semitic (not just anti-Judaic, not just anti-Jewish) opinions; I doubted that anti-Semitism in any organized form exists in Finland, the way it does in Russia and Germany today. Quite the opposite, I maintained. During Finland's continuation-war against the USSR as ally of Germany, from 1941 to 1944, Jewish Finns fought side by side with SS troops against the Bolsheviks. That hardly signifies an anti-Semitic country (though it makes one wonder about the Jewish Finns).

In response to the interview, an easily-provoked figure of the local Jewish community wrote an outraged letter to the same paper, accusing me of trying to "bagatellize" (the Swedish word, *bagatelisera,* has no known equivalent in English) the deep-rooted anti-Semitism expressed in the week's vandalism. I had, of course, done no such thing. But the fellow who wrote got to vent his anger and call his neighbors names.

And, in Finland, that's what set me to thinking about the need to sort things out and find the right words for the right things. For surely when we invoke the memory of Auschwitz in the context of a debate about Israeli foreign policy, or compare the work of a few vandals to the activities of the SS, or convert an ephemeral disagreement about religious truth into a renewed conflict in which Christians like Martin Luther demonize the Jews and Judaism, then we lose all perspective.

So, the next year, in New Zealand, I had to recognize the difference between a gauche Quaker professor or a provincial Dunedin lawyer, on the one side, and those dark and formidable forces, active in many countries and powerful in today's Russia and Austria and Croatia and in the Arab and part of the Moslem world even now, who would gladly continue and carry to its conclusion the work that Hitler started. When, from Japanese to Arabic, sales of the evil fabrication, *The Protocols of the Elders of Zion,* flourish as they do, we realize we had best know one Jew-hatred from another and take seriously what should be given weight — but then not invest energy in what can be set aside as inconsequential.

Still, much as I sympathize with his basic philosophy and accord with many of his views, I should have a very hard time voting for Pat Buchanan in 1996. But if I had to, I would.

XIV

WHEN *CHRONICLES* TALKS —

When *Chronicles* talks, people listen — at least in New Zealand. In the South Pacific last month I had my allotted fifteen minutes of total fame, all because of a a couple of paragraphs snatched by the Kiwi press out of a little piece of mine printed in these pages last month.

Then, readers will recall, *Chronicles* published my reflections — the preceding chapter — on the problem of sorting out the diverse forms of hostility to Jews and Judaism that the term "anti-Semitism" is supposed to encompass. To set the stage, I referred to three incidents last summer in New Zealand, which had set me to thinking about not what is, but what is *not,* appropriately labelled "anti-Semitism." In my piece — readers will notice — I didn't suggest New Zealand was a Fascist, anti-Semitic country — that was the judgment of a professor at Waikato University, whom I quoted and whose outrageous opinion I rejected. The pinpricks I did notice stood for something much less consequential. So I argued that these incidents did not strike me as anti-Semitic so much as gauche, provincial, and uncomprehending.

And, to make that point, I set into context my observations formed during my winter in a cold country, a place far off the beaten track, where little happens that matters to anybody anywhere else — that is, life in nowhere special, where all of us live, who are fortunate: in the heart of the human condition.

Since a reporter in Christchurch, at the *Press*, had taken an interest in my prior reflections on Canterbury University, where I had worked last summer, I sent him an advance copy of the article. He wrote an article about it, and poor O J Simpson lost his place as the USA news item on the New Zealand press, to be replaced by me. The *Christchurch Press* put the story on the Kiwi counterpart to the AP-A wire; it appeared all over the country. *The Press* even published an editorial of its own — a bit inane, but quite august in all.

But it did not end there — nor with more editorials elsewhere, follow-up stories, and columns and columns of mighty hot letters to the editor.

Radio New Zealand called from Wellington, for a half-hour live interview. When I returned their call, they interrupted their morning talk show to put me right on the air. They spent thirty minutes of expensive trans-Pacific phone time hectoring me on my observations, along the lines of, "Do you really think it's cold on the South Island in July?"

I: "Yes, very cold."

"Do you think you'll be invited back?"

"Not to Canterbury University."

"Would you go?"

"I'm busy next year and the year after, but try me in 1998."

Finally, at the climax of perfect fame, New Zealand TV asked me to come back to Auckland to take up the argument, appearing on their SIXTY MINUTES. "We know what other people say about you, now we want you to have your say." This is summer in New Zealand, so I would help on a slow news day.

When, thinking the matter somewhat disproportionate, I said I saw no point in pursuing the matter, having done several newspaper and radio interviews by phone, they immediately faxed back: "We will pay all expenses for a week's visit, to deal with you and your critics." (Evidently in their first invitation they'd imagined that I would pay my own way!) And, back home at the University of South Florida, my mail box and even my voice mail got crowded with letters, phone calls and even cassette tapes from unhappy Kiwi, some of whom actually signed what they wrote.

A distinguished religious studies professor at the University of Waikato explained the furore to me: "I was intrigued by recent media exposure you have received here. Frankly. I think your own perspectives are right on target — the locals just don't want to be told the harsh truth! New Zealand's worst prejudice is the prejudice that there is no prejudice here! In fact, there is, as you detected so incisively." My mail box had already told me that. I sent back to my reporter-colleague, Colin Espiner, at the *Press,* a sample of the letters that had come, as well as a tape; he could then judge for himself. But I'd not said the place was prejudiced, only a trifle provincial, as readers will remember.

In the storm I hoped to hear from Canterbury University some voices of reason and perhaps even contrary views, joined with solid evidence and compelling argument, against what I said. After all, if you want to know about the attitudes of a whole society, you turn not to episodic incidents and hearsay, but to surveys of public opinion, on the one side, and the evidence of systematic analysis thereof, on the other.

How, for instance, do Maori view New Zealand society — open or racist?

What about the locals of Indian or Chinese origin (letters from Indian and Chinese Kiwi confirmed my impression of a rather closed and uncomprehending society).

What came back may not qualify for a place on FIRING LINE, reasoned debate giving way to raw emotion, but mainly to blind, personal fury.

Here is David Novitz, Canterbury professor of philosophy, who is himself Jewish: "Professor Neusner's extreme sensitivity to his Jewishness made it impossible for people to speak to him for very long...Professor Neusner is an excellent scholar in his area of expertise, but that did not qualify him to comment on New Zealand society or the students at Canterbury." "Extreme sensitivity..." — that is to say, I'm "too Jewish." I reckon he's not.

Here is William Shepard, Canterbury lecturer in Religious Studies, who was in charge of my visit: "As the person who had the misfortune of having to host him in our department I can assure readers that their most negative conclusions about the character of this man and the value of his opinions will probably not be wide of the mark." Shepard is so gauche he can't even deliver a cutting insult.

Here is a man named Henry Tedder, describing himself as "a visiting retired college lecturer from Traverse City, Michigan:" "Professor Neusner is nuts. No one reads the magazine his article was published in except the writers and their students who are forced to read them. He reminds me of a jackass braying in the wilderness to his own confusion." So take that, *Chronicles* — right in the choppers!

Here is Norman Simms, Waikato University, who had been my guest for a year as visiting scholar when I taught at Brown University: "Neusner is prone to arrogance...he is known as a man who had never had an unpublished thought in his life." Quite how Simms knows what I haven't published I can't say. But he was the professor who told me he thinks New Zealand is an anti-Semitic country with a Fascist government, so perhaps when I said in these pages I thought that wasn't so, he took offense. But then, why he stays there I cannot say. But at any rate, here is one thought I'd not printed until this very morning: Norman Simms is an idiot.

Here is Professor Norton Moise, a visiting professor at Otago University in physics, who had already written to *Chronicles* and demanded "equal time" to reply to me. As reported in an article by John Gibb in the *Otago Daily Times,* Moise "was unhappy that the American publication had apparently seen fit to publish Prof Neusner's views without checking on the views of the many other American academics who had visited Christchurch and New Zealand. Prof Neusner's views were based on a very limited time in this country, could damage New Zealand's reputation abroad and potentially bring other visiting American academics into some disrepute in this country...Prof Moise was yesterday inquiring about the mail address of the American publication and planned to submit to it an article contradicting Prof Neusner's piece as well as sending a copy of the rebuttal to Prof Neusner."

Pow!! Zounds!! Everybody duck — he's sending an article bi'gosh— if he can find our address!!! And with a copy coming to me, whatever shall I do? Oh, oh.

Some may find a bit disappointing the intellectual quality of the replies to perfectly reasonable observations, expecting more than arguments that appeal to "extreme sensitivity," bad character, "arrogance," and so on and so forth. But don't wonder why it was mostly Jews (Shapiro, Novitz, Moise, and Simms) who volunteered to clobber the Jew — for self-hatred marks the hostile society. They prove my case.

And then there are the other outsiders, welcome only on the fringe of Kiwi society: the Americans, Shepard, Shapiro, Moise, Simms, who leaped to defend Kiwidom (Novitz is a South African refugee). But who can have predicted appeal to — of all things — good old American academic snobbery: "my university is better than yours, so shut up and sit down"? Leave it to our crowd to degrade already-despicable discourse. In some circles hereabouts it's not the power of your ideas that matters, nor what you have accomplished, but who pays your salary — an attitude as Yankee as apple pie, the Fourth of July, and racism: all against all.

It was an American teaching at Canterbury, a classicist named Harold Shapiro, who had earlier written to the *Press* and reassured people that University of South Florida students spend all their time on their surf boards (I reckon he's never seen Tampa Bay, where they build the causeways all of six inches above the water surface, to avoid the enormous waves, or perhaps he's confused the Gulf of Mexico with Big Sur.) Now here is the indignant Norton Moise, visiting-Jewish-American-physicist, delivering his knock-out punch, again in Mr. Gibb's report: "It was ironic that both Canterbury and Otago Universities enjoyed higher international standing than the University of South Florida in Tampa...Canterbury and Otago students were also of a high overall academic standard than students at the South Florida institution." Truth is, I asked my colleagues what international standing we at USF enjoy, and they didn't bother to reply — several were overseas, lecturing at foreign universities, just that very day.

To assess my response to Norton's snobby dismissal of little old USF, with its 36,000 students out on surf boards, the older readers of this magazine may be reminded of President Roosevelt's indignant objection that the Republicans had sunk to criticizing "my little dog Fala." Those guys really hit you where it hurts.

Thankfully, Norton doesn't know about my 90 pound yellow lab, Koby, what dreadful things he could say about him to defend his good name as a visiting American academic — "my dog doesn't piss on the rug the way your dog does, so you're wrong about lasers too"?

Oh well, now that the personal spleen has been ventilated by the Novitzes and the Shepards and the Moises and the Shapiros and the Simmses, perhaps it is time for a reasoned discussion about issues — if any survive for discussion.

Still, if you want to become famous in New Zealand, you can do worse than print an article in these pages, hoping that if Norton Moise finally locates the mailing address of *Chronicles,* he can turn up a stamp and send in his piece. If you're really lucky, out of *Chronicles* you too can get to turn down invitations to appear on SIXTY MINUTES in Auckland.

Next case.

South Florida Studies in the History of Judaism

South Florida Academic Commentary Series

South Florida-Rochester-Saint Louis Studies on Religion and the Social Order

South Florida International Studies in Formative Christianity and Judaism